Towards an Integrated Analytical Psychology

Towards an Integrated Analytical Psychology presents a comprehensive review of some of the salient philosophical, cultural, social, and clinical ingredients that have gone into contemporary visions of human personality development and psychotherapy and proposes a "unified field" theory of mental representation which puts psychoanalytic, analytic, and cognitive-behavioral perspectives in a mutually integrative framework.

The model proposed by Matthew Bennett, called Integrative Analytical Psychology, presents two major dimensions of personality development, and is integrative of Jungian and psychoanalytic perspectives, but places the Jungian concept of archetype as its core organizing principle. The six mental representations included within this model are: Archetype, Symbol, Object, Complex, Schema, and Self. This book strongly accents clinical application and more broadly considers the applied clinical implications of these mental representations to psychotherapy and clinical practice.

Towards an Integrated Analytical Psychology offers a novel model of understanding personality and will be of direct and immediate use for psychotherapists and students of psychotherapy, especially those from the psychoanalytic and analytic/Jungian tradition. It would also be of interest to social workers, marriage, and family therapists and psychiatrists.

Matthew Bennett, PsyD, is a licensed psychologist currently serving as a Department Chair and Full Professor in the Department of Counseling Psychology at Pacifica Graduate Institute in Santa Barbara, California. He lectures widely on personality development, personality disorders, and comparative models of psychotherapy.

Towards an Integrated Analytical Psychology

Return to Freedom and Dignity

Matthew Bennett

Routledge
Taylor & Francis Group

LONDON AND NEW YORK

Designed cover image: Phoenix Arise by Leigh J McCloskey

First published 2025
by Routledge
4 Park Square, Milton Park, Abingdon, Oxon OX14 4RN

and by Routledge
605 Third Avenue, New York, NY 10158

Routledge is an imprint of the Taylor & Francis Group, an informa business

British Library Cataloguing-in-Publication Data
A catalogue record for this book is available from the British Library

Library of Congress Cataloging-in-Publication Data
Names: Bennett, Matthew (Psychologist), author.
Title: Towards an integrated analytical psychology:
return to freedom and dignity / Matthew Bennett.
Description: Abingdon, Oxon; New York, NY: Routledge, 2025. |
Includes bibliographical references and index. |
Identifiers: LCCN 2024015597 (print) | LCCN 2024015598 (ebook) |
ISBN 9781032708713 (hardback) | ISBN 9781032708737 (paperback) |
ISBN 9781032708751 (ebook)
Subjects: LCSH: Personality development. | Psychotherapy.
Classification: LCC BF723.P4 B46 2025 (print) |
LCC BF723.P4 (ebook) | DDC 155.2/5—dc23/eng/20240412
LC record available at https://lccn.loc.gov/2024015597
LC ebook record available at https://lccn.loc.gov/2024015598

ISBN: 978-1-032-70871-3 (hbk)
ISBN: 978-1-032-70873-7 (pbk)
ISBN: 978-1-032-70875-1 (ebk)

DOI: 10.4324/9781032708751

Typeset in Times New Roman
by codeMantra

Contents

Acknowledgments

I am profoundly grateful for all the people, sentient beings, animals, natural forces, and other benevolent presences that moved me along toward writing and completing this book.

In particular, I would like to thank my high school teachers Laura Griffo, Georgia Geis, and Martin Cary for early encouragement and inspiration. I would also like to thank my graduate school professor John Dsurney, who oversaw the dissertation which would, in the fullness of time, become this book, and Anna and Dean Johnson, who introduced me to Jung and changed my life forever. I owe much love and gratitude to Ginny Robinson, who helped me to have a mother in the second half of life. I appreciate my supervisors along the way, especially Keith Harris and Christopher Ebbe.

I also wish to thank my students at Pacifica Graduate Institute, whose incessant question "When will your book come out?" helped me to finally make this happen. I also appreciate my students' interest and engagement with these ideas, which I feel that I have "field tested" in the classroom over the years. All of you are in this with me, and I'm proud of all of you. I deeply appreciate the fierce and noble Jemma Elliot, who supported the sabbatical I took in order to bring this book to fruition, which meant a lot of extra work for her, and otherwise helped me keep the faith.

The line drawing illustrations were provided by the very talented Sunnyadi, who has my thanks.

In terms of fellow writers: I am in particular debt to the inimitable Nancy McWilliams. Finding her book open on a library table to the chapter on Depressive Personalities during my second year of graduate school changed the fundamental direction of my life, not to mention my understanding of myself. Even longer ago, Edward Ormondroyd's children's book, *David and the Phoenix*, sets my foot upon this path at the very beginning. I'm so glad I finally got to meet you, Edward.

I owe particular appreciation and gratitude to Leigh McCloskey, a surpassing great soul, artist, and philosopher, whose masterwork The Heiroglyph of the Human Soul woke up so many archetypal ideas for me and helped me put them in a meaningful context. Strength and Honor, Leigh.

Foreword

The healing of the psyche and soul will have more to do with art (approach) than with science (facts). The empirical capacities of the human brain model the instrument, such as a piano, but cannot appreciate the piano's purpose until it is played. If the instrument is seen as a thing contained in itself it will be added to, analyzed, broken down, and put back together, eliciting a sense of achievement, but the instrument's real function will remain hidden. The instrument of the psyche can only be awakened and engaged by the individual. To know its function and purpose the instrument must be played, the keys to the psyche must be engaged, and one's unique relationship with archetypal and inner structures of imagination will begin to form inner relationships that psychologically liberate rather than enslave one's perception.

We do not abandon our humanity to find reality. This is why a return to freedom and dignity is an essential key to healing the many woes that beset the contemporary human heart and mind. Freedom and Dignity enables one to tell a better story of what being human means, and why it matters greatly that one do so. This is especially true of the stories one tells oneself about who and what one thinks oneself to be.

We must reclaim our human right to insist that the psyche, archetype, and art not be removed from psychology or that the essential dignity and freedom of the individual not be swept away by cynical reductionism or pharmaceutical panaceas. This is why, in alchemy, the revelation of the hidden nature and theater of the psyche and philosophical truth was always called "the Art," and the practitioner "the artist." This artistic approach to questions of consciousness, psyche, and personal experience is that of the polymath or Hermetic philosopher: philosophically, one must have the right setting, the right questions for the inquiry at hand and the appropriate archetypes, gods, and myths for discovering the hidden truths and implications behind the outer stories, symbols, and human experiences.

"I must create a system, or be enslaved by another man's. I will not reason and compare: my business is to create," writes William Blake (1815, Chapter 1, plate 10). These deeply resonant words find affinities within my own and Dr. Matthew Bennett's approach to mapping the psyche and the nature of its archetypal structure. Effective self-knowledge comes from direct engagement and symbolical bridging within oneself. In this spirit, Matthew Bennett and I have been working together to explore the inner theater of the human psyche and soul with art, archetype, and myth, seeking always to anchor the explorations in tangible and applicable ways. The purpose of this work is not to teach as much as to liberate perception by offering another lens, a deeper history.

A most significant leitmotif to this work has been the modeling and symbolical mapping of the psyche; this map has manifested as a circumplex model quartered into four archetypal quadrants, and the examination of unique self-structure and its growth through developmental stages and mythic symbols representing self-realization. The circumplex motif is based upon a circular, and ultimately a spiral model, allowing for integration as a contiguous process. This process ultimately hastens inner creative yearning for the assimilation of opposites, allowing for the possibility of a type of loving resolution that comprises the art and artistry of being human. This integrative approach amounts to the artistry of consciousness, more gnostic than scientific.

In my own philosophical and artistic evolution, the renaissance model of psyche and art emerged as an essential key to examining oneself and one's assumptions regarding perceived reality and its hidden or occulted side. Like everyone educated in the American culture, I was taught that the polymath and the renaissance models of mind and psyche were archaic notions, and impossible in this age because we know so much more now. We live in an age of specialization, artificial intelligence, designer drugs, ubiquitous media, and self-fascination inspired by our own "Spirit of the Age." The darker side of this culture shows up in shallow, self-absorbed beliefs and banalities, and thralldom to fantastical and the personal at the expense of mythic and archetypal thinking. The alternative is a much more remarkable ability of the individual to gain through personal effort true integration with the Spirit of the Depths. To do so, one must come full circle, must become the circle. As Ralph Waldo Emerson (1907) wrote, "Our life is an apprenticeship to the truth, that around every circle another can be drawn; that there is no end in nature, but every end is a beginning; that there is always another dawn risen on mid-noon, and under every deep a lower deep opens" (p. 260).

The last great English Hermetic philosopher, Robert Fludd (1575–1637) wrote, that, "To believe is to reflect, to know is to penetrate." His Hermetic Pythagorean model of the human psyche and soul too was circular like the Integrated Analytical Model (IAM) circumplex wheel, and based upon human and archetypal system wholeness, cosmic and mythic depth perception, symbolic structures, personal effort, and engaging one's inner quest to know directly the hidden realities behind the optics and chaos of this world and within oneself. The renaissance and its holistic models of the self and the imagination as key to unlocking the mysteries were also shared by Fludd's contemporary the great German Christian mystic, Jacob Boehme (1575–1624). Boehme's profound transpersonal revelations revealed a passionate universe reflected in human passions, drives, and divine energies, expressing every human being as a universe in miniature, a life atom, and that every human being is a living hieroglyph modeled after a divine archetypal imprint, a microcosm of the macrocosm as illustrated by Leonardo's "Vitruvian Man."

Jacob Boehme's (2007) fiery visions of humankind reveal a passionate and primal universe, not of abstract powers but of essential archetypal forces pulsing within and composing oneself, the world and cosmos. He viewed the human condition as consisting of seven principles, an octave which he called "The Clavis" or Keys. The first three keys reveal a great deal about the dichotomy of the collective human struggle. The first principle Boehme calls *Magnetical Hunger*, which is the overwhelming desire of consciousness to contract absolutely. Magnetical Hunger is woven within the second principle of *Motion* and the desire to expand absolutely. The first two principles make it impossible for either principle to contract or expand absolutely. From this perpetual tension of opposites or dynamism of resistance is generated the third principle of *Anguish*. To be human is to experience suffering, and from this desire that can never be satisfied in itself emerges the fourth principle of Love. Only Love, the fourth principle, which Boehme called *Shrack* (lightning), can illuminate the path and pathos of Anguish. Lightning is never fixed and no one knows where or when it shall strike. The sky is momentarily illuminated; one catches a glimpse of the horizon and as soon as it is seen it has vanished. This lightning is the act of divine Love in time, the great unifying principle, and power within the realm of manifestation that flashes but cannot remain fixed. Nothing that is of nature is fixed but is always in metamorphosis, and transformation always seeking its own greater expression. In this model, human existence is part of a divine alchemy, a living process of dissolution and recombining, the *solve et coagula* of the alchemists whose traditions revealed the human struggle as the Magnum Opus, the Great Work, and Human evolution as the implementation and perfecting of divine will within form and being.

Dr. Bennett's circumplex model celebrates this renaissance model of mind. I was first introduced to and attracted to Dr. Bennett's planning for the IAM in a manuscript he shared when we first met many years ago. I had recently published my original artwork and writings on the archetypes of the major arcana of the tarot in my book, Tarot ReVisioned (2003). Both works and models describe wheels within wheels of consciousness, coming full circle and coming home to the self, no longer through exclusion and critique, but inclusion, archetypal structure, and symbolical revelation.

It is essential to establish the context in the same way that the set for a play establishes the imaginative parameters and agreement field, allowing both the actors and the audience to suspend disbelief so each participant can both create and "behold the swelling scene," thus taking an imaginative adventure together that reveals the deeper story and meaning of the play itself. The context will be the silent actor, the setting that gives permission to frame the conversation and open inner doors of perception.

There are many models and theories regarding human consciousness which each shed light upon the psyche, like facets of a diamond mind, each illuminating a direction, a priori assumptions, and insights regarding approach, theory, and application into the human condition. Dr. Bennett's circumplex model reveals the significance of that diamond mind, not unlike a book that reflects in itself the story and purpose of the greater library in which it is situated. In other words, this book seeks to reassert what C.G. Jung insisted upon, that the psyche should not be lost to psychological theory and mere intellectual practices or clinical reductionism and literalism.

Dr. Bennett offers us an inspired and potentially healing model and approach to mapping and navigating a theory of mind. He offers brilliant insights into inner mythic and archetypal structures and their symbolic meanings. His approach honors the important works of other deep thinkers and explorers of human consciousness and clinical psychology, weaving them together with contemplative critical insights rather than rejection of their alternative systems, approaches, and assertions. Dr. Bennett deeply examines other psychological models and symbolical frameworks for both their strengths and shortcomings. Most importantly, his IAM circumplex model establishes a bold and brilliant path toward psychological wholeness and a rediscovering of human self-worth: a return to personal freedom and dignity, and telling a better story of what being human means and why the way we model the psyche and what is included or rejected matters so greatly. Here's to a return to freedom and dignity and honoring the most difficult art of all, being human.

Leigh J McCloskey
Author, Artist, Actor, Philosopher
Malibu, California
December 2023

Introduction

This book is the work of years, a descendant of my doctoral dissertation, a love note to the psychotherapy clients I have been privileged to work with, a treasure map resulting from years of teaching and learning from my graduate students, and also a personal account of my work as a psychologist and psychotherapist. The resulting work is an attempt to integrate two deeply meaningful influences in my life: Jungian theory, which lured me into studying Psychology in the first place, with its cosmic mysteries, and psychoanalytic theory, with its anguished and remorseless kind of emotional honesty. It has felt to me, over the years, that the the Jungian myth reminds me that there are other worlds than these, beyond the veil, and that the psychoanalytic myth has urged me to stay here, in my body, in the mud and the blood, and the ineffable sadness that can never be fully quenched. Jungian theory promised transcendence, and psychoanalytic theory asked me to sink back into my animal body, in its neediness, its ambivalence, its tragic incompleteness.

These two love interests of mine, I have discovered, have made me feel like an orphaned child, or like the child of divorce. My two loves don't get along with each other, and reject each other. But I've always loved them both, and I've always felt the pull of the primordial symmetry (more on that idea later on) promised by their integration. If the Jungian story promises ultimate completion and wholeness, the psychoanalytic story helps explain how we never seem to quite get there. Psychoanalytic traditions have tended to focus on the tendency of the psyche to defend against painful emotional realities leading to an elaborate conceptualization of ego psychology and offers articulate descriptors of the ways in which humans prefer comforting fictions to unnerving realities: regression, projective identification, introjection, dissociation, and so on. Jungian traditions tend rather to focus on the archetypal nature of those emotional realities, which emanate from the foundational core of psyche and soul. In other words, Jungian models focus more on raw internal psychological experience, and psychoanalytic models focus more on the ways in which the psyche defends against some of those experiences. Taken together, what these two voices describe is psyche as creative force, struggling to emerge in a way that integrates internal essence with local circumstance.

The Jungian narrative, as we will discover in this book, challenges our current cultural and philosophical assumptions in a way that invites incredulity from those

DOI: 10.4324/9781032708751-1

whose perspectives are more embedded in our post-modern mindset. Ideas like "archetype" and "collective unconscious" feel even more absurd in the context of reductive materialism than "penis envy" or the "oedipus complex." Freud wrote as an agent of the Enlightenment period, using (relatively) clear language and scientific sensibilities. Jung was a romantic and more of a mystic, and his conceptualization of the unconscious was deeper and richer than Freud's. Freud's intellectual legacy led most directly to an institutionalization of psychoanalysis based in a medical model; Jung's perspective has been far more warmly received in metaphysical and New Age contexts than in clinical psychology. Both perspectives have long ceased to be directly influential to the mainstream practice of clinical psychology, because they are both predicated on aspects of human experience that are impossible to prove or measure. Jonathan Shedler (2010) notes that this prejudice is reinforced through the very ways in which psychology gets taught to students:

> Undergraduate textbooks too often equate psychoanalytic or psychodynamic therapies with some of the more outlandish and inaccessible speculations made by Sigmund Freud roughly a century ago, rarely presenting mainstream psychodynamic concepts as understood and practiced today. Such presentations, along with caricatured depictions in the popular media, have contributed to widespread misunderstanding of psychodynamic treatment.

(p. 98)

Beyond Freedom and Dignity

In 1971, American psychologist B.F. Skinner (2002) published *Beyond Freedom and Dignity*, a manifesto for a behaviorally based vision of human civilization. In this work, Skinner criticizes the very idea of both freedom and dignity on the basis that they are mental states that cannot be observed or quantified. But more than this, Skinner argues that both freedom and dignity are ultimately illusory, and that human behavior is a function of contingencies of reinforcement: environment is everything, and human beings are blank slates to be inscribed by learning and association.

To be fair, Skinner's radical behaviorism has lost much of its currency in contemporary psychology; the more evolved model of cognitive behavioral theory at least allows us to acknowledge the existence of thoughts, in addition to behaviors. Yet the foundational assumptions of radical behaviorism remain persistent, because they are products of the spirit of the age. Within a few hundred miles of each other and around the same time, Francis Bacon and René Descartes delivered a double-whammy on behalf of what would become our model of scientific inquiry: Bacon outlawed teleology (and by extension the idea of destiny) from the sciences in *Novum Organum* (see Robertson, 1894), and Descartes offered up his famous dualism, which partitioned the non-material and non-spatial reality of mind from the the world of matter. Dualism, as it turned out, was all the Western world needed to commit fully to its favorite side of the dualistic coin: science would be all about the empirical study of observable phenomena. In 400 years, then, we progressed from acknowledging that the world of mind and matter are separate to conclude that there is only matter.

Jung (2005) rather had opinions on this development:

> The modern preference for physical grounds of explanation leads, as already remarked, to a "psychology without the psyche" — I mean, to the view that the psyche is nothing but a product of biochemical processes. As for a modern, scientific psychology which starts from the mind as such, there simply is none. No one today would venture to found a scientific psychology upon the postulate of an independent psyche that is not determined by the body. The idea of spirit in and for itself, of a self-contained world-system of the spirit that is the only adequate postulate for the belief in autonomous, individual souls, is extremely unpopular with us, to say the least... If we keep this in mind, we can perhaps summon up the courage to consider the possibility of a "psychology with the psyche" — that is, of a field of study based on the assumption of an autonomous psyche. We need not be alarmed at the unpopularity of such an undertaking, for to postulate mind is no more fantastic than to postulate matter.
>
> (p. 184)

Psychology without the psyche is fair descriptor for where we have arrived; Jung's observations are even more remorselessly true now than they were when he wrote those words in 1933. Except now we call it *evidence-based practice*, which is a phrase that goes even further in disappearing the idea of an autonomous psyche, hiding its extermination behind a facade of an empirical imperative. In its haste to become a science, psychology has decided that anything which cannot be measured under laboratory conditions either doesn't exist or doesn't matter. This is how we lose freedom and dignity.

As we shall see in some of the ensuing chapters, the cognitive sciences have inched away from radical behaviorism and the purity of the social learning theory upon which behaviorism was based, and instead is moving towards models that come closer to resemble the drive theory of early psychoanalysis: the human brain isn't just learning, it is also an organizing and ordering force—a hypothesis-generating device. I will elaborate those conclusions a bit more: the human mind is not just a passive subject of operant conditioning; it is a creative force.

A Map of Canada

I have developed a passing interest in road maps of Canada. The road maps I've seen only cover the southern fourth or so of the country; they leave uncharted the vast, thinly populated northern reaches. For example, a road map of Ontario will typically only cover the lower third or so of that province, leaving the rest a sort of *terra incognita*, which reminds me of the old medieval maps, bordered by treacherous and monster-riddled unknown waters.

I first became interested in the phenomenon because of my many airplane flights to Europe. The flight routes the airlines usually used crossed into Canada either in Ontario or Newfoundland, and then arced over Labrador and out over the ocean. If the weather was right, I could plainly see small, isolated towns connected by narrow roads and power lines. *Someone* was living up there! I became interested in these outlying areas and began to seek them out on maps, because my mind is drawn by liminal places. So far I have been unable to find a good road map of Canada, which covers those empty northern areas. I found this to be true even for road maps of specific provinces: generally only the southern portions of the provinces were mapped in detail.

I take the Canadian road map phenomenon as a symbol of a larger issue. Collectively, we ignore (leave unmapped) a vast area of hum an experience simply because few people live there. This sort of omission makes a kind of sense on a utilitarian level. Probably it bothers very few Canadian citizens that road maps of their province leave out the frozen wastes of the north, where few people have reason to go. Furthermore, I am certain that the peoples of medieval Europe experienced the same level of comfort with the maps of their day, although we study those maps today with amusement because of the many areas of the world that are left blank or simply illustrated with sea-monsters.

When I was a student at the University of Glasgow in Scotland, I was enamored of the Ordnance Survey maps of the British Isles. The Ordnance Survey maps, in case you have never seen them, carve up the British Isles into neat grids, and each grid is mapped in detail. The maps include roads, streets, and highways as well as geographical contour lines, areas of forest, ancient ruins, power pylon lines, and other significant man-made and naturally occurring landmarks. No area of the British Isles, however unpopulated and remote, is omitted. I like the fact that these maps cover wild and unpopulated places without prejudice. These maps bring a sort of empirical fidelity to the landscape, whether focus is a teeming downtown block in London or a remote vale with an abandoned crofter's hut in the Outer Hebrides.

For those of us who are mapping human psychology, is it not important to map out human experience as fully as possible, to observe all that can be observed, regardless of the type of data, and to record as much of that experience as possible, even those areas that are epistemologically remote? Is it any less legitimate for psychology to study unconscious motivations, defensive styles, and even archetypal experience than to study neuroanatomy, operant conditioning, or the behavior of rats in mazes? Any model of human psychology, to be robust and useful, must involve some attempt at describing aspects of human experience that cannot be measured under laboratory conditions. Irwin Hoffman (2009) critiques what he calls "the privileging of systematic quantitative research and of neuroscience" (p. 1045) over more abstracted concerns like culture, personal values, and relational dynamics. Hoffman writes that this privilege accorded to systematic empirical research (i.e. "science") differentiates not just the researcher from the clinician but a theoretical fault line between constructivism and objectivism to be found in many models of human behavior, including those that may be described as psychoanalytic:

The critical or "dialectical" constructivism that I have been encouraging replaces a diagnostic, knowing, prescriptive psychoanalytic attitude with one that requires responsible, creative, improvised, and collaborative efforts on the parts of the participants to make something of the ambiguous, context-dependent reality that evolves in the course of their interaction.

(p. 1044)

We will, by the by, revisit the idea of constructivism later in this book as we investigate it as a potential frame for understanding mental representation in a way that is parallel to psychodynamic sensibilities.

The determination that contemporary psychology has shown to become and remain "scientific" has done violence to its own principles, goals, and methodologies. The underlying (and for the most part, unspoken) value system reinforced by "scientific" psychology and by extension of its so-called "evidence based practices" is that if any aspect of human experience cannot be measured under laboratory conditions, then it either doesn't exist or doesn't matter enough to be studied or addressed. An even deeper implication of this point of view is avoidance of ambiguity and uncertainty, and the commitment to "being sure" in the way that a physician might confirm the presence of a cancer through a biopsy. In the realm of psychological research, this value system delimits the areas of inquiry that will be funded; in the realm of clinical practice, it restricts what kinds of interventions are designed and what questions raised with patients, and therefore by extension which values and realities are reinforced in psychotherapy and which ones are neglected.

Narrowly reductive approaches to scientific inquiry also have critical implications for social justice. Remorseless flat-land materialism, which denies the intrinsic existence (let alone value) of freedom and dignity, undermines human and humane values that maintain the sociogenic fabric of human civilization. Hansen et al. (2023) critiques modern psychiatry's biologism from a feminist perspective, arguing that psychiatric treatment cannot ignore very real social forces that don't show up among the lab values. Frantz Fanon (2018), an inspiration for this article, compellingly locates a profound wounding, disintegration, and healing that has been left unaddressed by scientific and clinical paradigms that ignore psychological and social spaces, as well as the effects of time:

Our thinking is scarcely able to liberate itself from the anatomo-clinical. We think in terms of organs and focal lesions when we ought to be thinking in terms of functions and disintegration. Our medical view is spatial, where it ought to become more and more temporal.

(p. 215)

Why is it more desirable to be certain? Why is ambiguity a liability? Why do we endeavor to make a sterile laboratory of the buzzing, refracted, troubled riot that is human experience? Why must we resist the imaginal, the creative, the instinctive, the intuitive function?

Scientific inquiry represents the well-lighted room in our collective house, but it is the musty, dusty, and dark reaches of the neglected basement levels that will hold the promise of humanity, for the very reason that few people are looking there. "It's God's nature to come on in the bottom of the ninth," writes Stephen King (1999, p. 185), a master myth teller who has dedicated a career looking into the interstitial spaces of reality. What we need most comes from the direction of the unexpected; it will not be where we focus our attention. Clinical psychology, and especially academic psychology, should heed the 13th-century monk Mumon Ekai, who admonishes: "If he hesitates even a moment, he is just a person that watches from a narrow window for a speedy horseman to pass by and misses everything in a wink" (Reps & Senzaki, 1998, p. 1). Contemporary Western psychology (especially in the United States) follows a sort of evidence-based model of science, which provides us with a particularly narrow window.

Consider the regimen of coursework undertaken by the typical student in an American graduate school offering a doctorate in psychology. There are courses on the empirical method, scientific inquiry and statistical analysis, courses in theory of personality and therapy, courses on theories of learning, behavior, and development, courses on treatment models for various populations, courses of testing, assessment, and interviewing, and so on. What's missing from this array of academic subjects? The whole northern half of the province is missing. By limiting itself to a survey of empirically based meta-analyses of the gross tendencies of human behavior (at the macro-level amenable to scientific research), modern applied and academic Psychology avoids the metaphysical and ignores the phenomenological. In essence, Psychology does not dare to (or care to) map out the northern reaches of Canada. And why not? Why, because there are no (or few) roads and towns in the area that would make the effort worthwhile. And why are there no roads or towns? Because no one cares to move into that area. And why don't people move there? Because the area is desolate, unknown, uncharted. And so the reasons loop in upon themselves and become circular. We don't think about certain things because people don't think about such things. I have heard the sinister term *managed consciousness*[1] to describe this state of affairs, this deep wagon-rut of feeling and thinking that leads ever to sameness and discourages both free-thinking and the new directions it makes possible.

The wagon ruts of managed consciousness will, I hope, remind you, the reader, by the end of my tale, of the chains of mental representation that comprise human consciousness. The psychological tragedy of human life is that mental representations become our only realities, because we forget that we are all artists who are trying to tell a story. Mental representations, from the most unconscious selfobject to the most erudite of philosophical systems, are an attempt to tell a story. The particular genius of psychodynamic perspectives on the human mind, of both the Jungian and psychoanalytic strains, is to remind us that our capacity for curiosity and the imaginal represents human psychological experience at its highest art form. Curiosity, and a capacity for the imaginal, helps us to remain open to that which has not been mentalized, that which has been left out of the story.

The Integrated Analytical Model

T.S. Eliot (1975) in *The Music of Poetry,* writes: "Runes and charms are very practical formulae designed to produce definite results, such as getting a cow out of a bog" (p. 22). In clinical psychology, we are trying to pull cows out of bogs, not storm the gates of Heaven. Yet paradoxically, we know that our patients yearn for Heaven in some form or another…and this yearning, this expectation of meaning, is a human kinship that we all share. Jung was distressed at what appeared to be at the time (and is even more so now) an over-emphasis on the current phase of philosophical understanding of what constitutes science, resulting in a form of psychology that attempts to reduce psychic functioning to either behavior or to biology.[2] The reasons for Jung's objection were that he believed it necessary for psychology to study aspects of human experience that do not lend themselves to the methods of reductive materialism. Jung (2005), therefore, freely admits in *Modern Man in Search of a Soul* that his psychology will, therefore, not be a modern psychology because there are aspects of his model that cannot be recognized using our current philosophical, psychological, and sociological frames.

Biologist Edward O. Wilson (1999), writing in his book *Consilience: The Unity of Knowledge,* writes "The love of complexity without reductionism makes art; the love of complexity with reductionism makes science" (p. 59). How can psychology, the study of human experience, do anything other than both? Anything so important to human experience must by definition also be important for psychology. The study of psychology ought to include study of the products of the psyche; that is, the things people write, say, do, and even paint and dream. Psychology cannot afford to ignore the very products of the human mind, no matter how imaginal. If freedom and dignity are important to the human experience, then Psychology must concern itself with those things, scientific or not.

Speaking of freedom, you will notice that I have taken some liberties with the scholarly tone of this project; my writing style shifts from expository precision to impressionistic artistry (and even in places, stream-of-consciousness) as I move up and down the harmonic progression of representation. I do so because each level of human consciousness has its own language, and because I think that we come to grief when we force the empirical language of science upon the outer mysteries of human experience. Similarly, my references will range from literary to empirical sources, from J.R.R. Tolkien, Stephen King, and Pat Conroy to Allan Schore, Harry Guntrip, and Nancy McWilliams. In the immortal words of Willy Wonka (Stuart, 1971): "Little surprises around every corner, but nothing dangerous."

It is in this spirit that I offer my tale, the tale of the Integrated Analytical Model.[3] It represents my attempts to reunite my divorced parents, Jungian and psychoanalytic theory, at least in terms of a model of mental representations, and have some fun deconstructing behaviorism along the way. I call it a "tale" because that's what it is: a narrative structure that does what the model suggests is the function of the human mind: to tell a story. Through the interplay of empirical hypothesis testing (successive fractal levels of mental representations) and the imaginal (freewheeling and experimental applications of archetypal energies like paint on a canvas), enabled by the human capacity to become and remain curious, we become capable of telling *better* stories. The human mind does not just *assess* reality, it *creates* reality.

I hope you enjoy this particular story, and learn something from it, as I have.

Matthew D Bennett
Santa Barbara, California
December 2024

Notes

1 As far as I can tell, credit for naming this sinister-sounding concept goes to science fiction writer Bruce Sterling (1990), particularly in his short story "The Spook."
2 For those of you wondering "Well what else could psychology be based on?", this book is for you.
3 My colleague Leigh McCloskey, an inveterate discoverer of acronyms, could not help but notice how the initials spell out I AM. Who am I to argue with that particular example of synchronicity?

References

Fanon, F. (2018). *Alienation and freedom*. Bloomsbury Academic.
Hansen, H., Gutierrez, K.J., & Garcia, S. (2023). Rethinking psychiatry: Solutions for a sociogenic crisis. *Daedalus, 152*(4): 75–91.
Hoffman, I. Z. (2009). Double thinking our way to "scientific" legitimacy: The desiccation of human experience. *Journal of the American Psychoanalytic Association, 57*(5): 1043–1069.
Jung, C. G. (2005). *Modern man in search of a soul*. Routledge.
King, S. (1999). *The girl who loved Tom Gordon*. Scribner.
Reps, P., & Senzaki, N. (1998). *Zen flesh, Zen bones*. Tuttle Publishing.
Robertson, G. C. (1894). Bacon's Novum organum. In G. C. Robertson & A. Bain, T. Whittaker (Eds.), *Philosophical remains of George Croom Robertson, with a memoir* (pp. 368–372). Williams and Norgate.
Shedler, J. (2010). The efficacy of psychodynamic psychotherapy. *American Psychologist, 65*(2), 98–109.
Skinner, B. F. (2002). *Beyond freedom and dignity*. Hackett Publishing.
Sterling, B. (1990). *Crystal Express*. Ace Books.
Stuart, M. (Director). (1971). Willy Wonka & the Chocolate Factory (Film). Paramount Pictures.
Eliot, T.S. (1975). *Selected prose* (F. Kermode, Ed.). Faber and Faber.
Wilson, E.O. (1999). *Consilience: The unity of knowledge*. Vintage Books.

Chapter 1

Models of Mental Representation

Let heaven and men and devils, let them all, all, all, cry shame against me, yet I'll speak.

-William Shakespeare
Othello

This book, and the model of personality that it describes, represents a story of mental representation. The idea that internal representations "stand for" different aspects of reality[1] is a very old one (at least as far back as Aristotle) and generally assumes that we humans do not perceive reality directly; rather, we perceive our representations of reality. When we get angry, we are ultimately getting angry at an internal representation, and I'm afraid that when we fall in love, we fall in love with an internal representation…the lucky recipient of our love is a real, autonomous, and integral being, our internal representation of that autonomous and integral being is not the same. This basic idea serves as an organizing principle for most, if not effectively all, models of psychotherapy. The diversity in theoretical perspective comes in how these mental representations get encoded, what they're called, and how they interact with the psyche (if there is a psyche) and with the external world. It could be argued that early psychoanalytic theory was almost entirely about mental representations interacting with each other; it took decades of clinical and research innovation for psychoanalysis to become more interested in the actual relationships that inspire and shape mental representations. In contemporary intersubjective theory of psychoanalysis, the general understanding is that mental representations are co-created within a relational field: this is the so-called "therapeutic third," which describes a third interpersonal reality spawned by the intersection of therapist and client.

Radical behaviorism had little use for mental representations; human behavior was said to be shaped by contingent reinforcement through a social learning framework. It took the evolution of behaviorism into cognitive-behaviorism, which opened up a foundational research basis in cognitive science. Later in this book, especially in Chapters 8 and 9, we will explore some of the promising theories about so-called Complex Adaptive Systems and the interesting implications brought to bear by elements of complexity theory.

DOI: 10.4324/9781032708751-2

In this book, I will propose a model of mental representation, which attempts to syncopate Jungian and psychoanalytic perspectives on mental representations, with some additional integration with cognitive theory and especially constructivism. The Integrated Analytical Model has at least two dimensions; I say "at least," because I'm sure the ultimate model is a sphere rather than a circle, which would require a third dimension, but the psycho-geometry then becomes quite complex and I have chosen to settle for simplicity now. The vertical dimension that describes successive levels of mentalization, starting with the "fundamental frequency" of archetype and increasing in complexity, dissociability, and access to consciousness across a gradation of quantum leaps in representation. The horizontal dimension describes thematic organization of mental representation, which as I argue in Chapter 11 takes the place of a circumplex model. As we shall see in Chapter 11 and later, the interaction of vertical representational "vectors" with circumplex "axes" generates a spiral progression of mental representation with its origin point in archetypal reality and its outer aspect representing the complexity of the individual human self in interpersonal space.

We have quite a bit of ground to cover before we arrive upon the Spiral Path; however, let us begin with one of the earliest and most influential perspectives on mental representation of the 20th century, that of Jean Piaget.

Nature vs. Nurture: Piaget's Environmentalism in Context

Jean Piaget (1962), along with his moralist counterpart Lawrence Kohlberg, set out to describe mental representations within a general epistemological framework; that is to say that he undertook a scientific conceptualization of the mental representation as building block for psychological functioning. Flanagan (1991) opines that what Piaget (and Kohlberg) had in mind was to "chart their way between the Scylla of naïve empiricism and the Charybdis of extreme nativism and arrive at some empirically and philosophically safe port" (p. 119). In this sense, Piaget sought to navigate between the hard behaviorists and their vision of the mind as *tabula rasa* on one hand and the nativists who saw human nature as determined by some form of primordial reality on the other hand. By "primordial reality" we mean psychoanalytic assumptions about the biological basis of drives and the Jungian perspective that archetypes function similarly to instincts: both perspectives suggest *a priori* architectural models of the personality that claim that human beings are born with *psychological stuff* inside of them.

As we have acknowledged, Piaget's attempts to reconcile empiricism and nativism has a long historical context in philosophy. One illustrative example is the philosophical difference between the followers of Kant (2003), with their promotion of the absolute (for example, from a perspective of ethics, the Kantian perspective is that some actions are inherently good or evil), and the utilitarian perspective of Mill (which suggests that good and evil are relative, and that the difference derives from the ultimate outcome). As we shall see, Jung was profoundly influenced by Kantian philosophy, from which he seems to have drawn a perspective emphasizing intrinsic essence rather than Mills' idea that mental life is driven by deterministic and causal laws. It could be argued that Piaget and Aaron Beck were not even the first cognitive psychologists...Hume anticipated their models when he enumerated the three structural principles of the mind called "laws of association": resemblance, contiguity, and cause-and-effect (see Selby-Bigge, 1975). Hume's prescription resembles modern attempts on the part of cognitive psychologists to identify the orthogonal organizing principles of human thought. Such discrete organizing principles even have their place in the form of "strange attractors" described in the context of chaos theory, as we shall see in Chapter 8.

However, Piaget appears to have attempted one of the earliest formulations within modern psychology to reconcile nativist and empiricist approaches in the creation of the nascent field of cognitive-developmental constructivism. But to what extent did he, or his like-minded colleagues, succeed? Piaget sought to circumnavigate the "excesses" of pure behaviorism by elaborating on the *complexity* of learned behaviors. He achieved this end by postulating the unfolding development of developmental capacities that result not just in *new* experiences but in *qualitatively different* experiences. That is to say, far from being the inert "storehouse of ideas" derived from experience as John Locke originally hypothesized, the mind is equipped to impose some kind of order on new experience, sorting them in a new way...by means of mental representations. Piaget counters nativism by highlighting the sensitivity of the developing mind to environmental conditions and to its apparent development of completely novel cognitive strategies for interacting with the environment. Flanagan (1991) summarized the argument this way:

> The thinking of an intelligent eighteen-year-old differs from the thinking of an intelligent one-year-old not only in content - for example, in thinking about sex, music and geometry as opposes to blocks, the sandbox, and the mother's breast- but in form as well. The eighteen-year old is able to represent things to herself linguistically, to rotate geometrical figures mentally, to deploy deductive proof procedures, to make reliable inductive references, and to utilize unconsciously and unerringly the principles of conservation and transivity...
>
> (p. 122)

This elegant observation about qualitative and quantitative shifts along a trajectory of increasing complexity is taken up by constructivism and by contemporary models of cognitive psychology informed by chaos theory. Neimeyer (1993) defines the perspective this way: "At the core of constructivist theory is a view of human beings as active agents who, individually and collectively, co-constitute the meaning of their experiential world" (p. 222).

A nativist response to this constructivist perspective is articulated by Fodor (in Flanagan, 1991): "it is never possible to learn a richer logic on the basis of a weaker logic, if what you mean by learning is hypothesis formation and confirmation" (p. 138). Put another way, it does not appear likely that the mind would be able to make up quantum-leap advancements in spatial perception out of whole cloth, without the ingredients for such an advancement already being present in some fashion in the construction of the developing brain. This counter-argument suggests that the precursors...the initial conditions, or starting states (I will later refer to this as *primordial symmetry* starting in Chapter 8) to more complex and refined cognitive processes suggested by Piaget are somehow "already there" in a potential or nascent state, ready to be accessed in the right way by a developing mind expanding in complexity. The existence of such "already there" elements has been called *preformation*. In supporting preformation, Fodor, of course, champions the nativist cause along with his colleague Noam Chomsky. Chomsky's debate with Piaget on the nature and origin of psychological functions (such as speech) is one of the better-known arenas of contention within this area and reflects the epistemological importance of the question (see Chomsky, 2000). Chomsky, Fodor, and the nativists respond to the associationist by repeating the classical formula: *ex nihil nihil fit*, nothing comes of nothing.

Jung's perspective on the so-called archetypal seems to come down solidly on the side of nativism and preformation, with its emphasis on innate forms of representation. Jung (2014) emphasized that it was the very inheritance of archetypal forms that defines the human species as what it is:

> No biologist would ever dream of assuming that each individual acquires his general mode of behavior afresh each time....it is more probable that man is born with a specifically human mode of behavior and not with that of a hippopotamus or with none at all. Integral to his characteristic behavior is his psychic phenomenology, which differs from that of a bird or a quadruped.
>
> (p. 227)

The question becomes: are there mental representations that are neither learned nor constructed by the individual organism? Flanagan (1991) offers a bird's eye view of the situation by means of three elements to the representational system that may be influential to varying degrees: (1) innate representational capacity present at birth, (2) an equilibration mechanism that acts as a mediator between the innate representations and the environment, and (3) the environment itself (the outside world of people, animals, things, etc.). Flanagan specifies that the various points of view represented in the developmental versus nativist approach may be satisfied by elaborating or emphasizing one or the other elements of this proposed system. All that remains is to delineate a characterization of innate representations and equilibration mechanisms that are sufficiently compatible with both ends of the nature/nurture debate, or, more specifically for our purposes, between the psychodynamic and cognitive models of clinical psychology.

In this book, I will propose that the Integrated Analytical Model fills in the blanks of Flanagan's three elements this way:

1 Innate representational capacity at birth is represented by biological drive in the psychoanalytic model and by archetypal and symbolic fields in the Jungian model.

2 The equilibrium mechanism is a trajectory of nested mental representations ranging from primordial, unconscious, and ineffable to conscious, measurable, and objective. We shall describe this trajectory of mental representations, which I call *harmonics* after music theory, in a number of different ways, borrowing from the existing literature in Jungian, psychoanalytic (including self psychology, Lacanian theory, and intersubjective theory in particular), cognitive behavioral, and constructivist literatures, including perspectives offered by chaos theory.

3 The environment as a source of learning is well represented by social learning theory and the increasingly sophisticated conceptualization of cognitive and neurocognitive models. For the purposes of this book, I will focus less on the third element, except to note its implications in intersubjective psychoanalysis and in attachment theory.

The Circumplex Model: Linking Inner with Outer

Integrated Analytical Psychology suggests that the personality develops as a means of negotiating inner content with outer circumstances, not simply through the taming of primitive impulses or the sharpening of reality testing but by an expansive process of becoming and manifesting: an activation of potential structures and levels along a gradient of complexity and deterministic chaos (see Chapter 8). The ultimate telos of our proposed trajectory of mental representation is to reconcile all (or as much as possible) of native potential with all (or as much as possible) of the external cues and feedback derived from the vicissitudes of human experience. Put more simply, the "task" of the personality is to bring what is internal out, in some safe and reliable way, and to bring what is external in, in some safe and reliable way, in such a way as results in a stable system. Even more simply, the personality must somehow reconcile its own nature with the demands of the environment. The organizational principles of this adaptive process will include complex adaptive systems of mental representation, which are motivated by affect states (emotion) and which function to generate "hypotheses" about how to most effectively interface with the external world. This process of hypothesis generation, as we shall see, is intrinsically a creative process that results in *emergence* of adaptive processes originally inspired by a primordial symmetry, the breaking of which serves as an imperative for psychological growth through cognitive and affective innovation.

In developmental terms, the evolving personality takes note of experiences within itself, which may be understood as instincts, feelings, desires, dreams, forebodings, intuitions, fears, and other "internal" events suggested by the primordial symmetry. Increasingly as the childhood psyche approaches adulthood, it becomes concerned with making some sort of settled peace with the world in which it finds itself: a world of roles, responsibilities, policies and procedures, traditions and precedents, expectations, and a set of rules contained within the matrix of consensual reality. In other words, the first task of life is to survive childhood! Typically, there comes a time in life in which a more or less conscious process begins in which the individual gradually relinquishes focus on the former (the inner world of ideas, thoughts, and instincts) and concentrates increasingly on the demands of the latter (roles and responsibilities). This process, which I am not cynical enough to call "growing up," may reflect a barely conscious transition— a seemingly seamless boundary between childhood fancy and adult responsibility. The transition may come invisibly and insidiously, it may happen all at once, either as part of a traumatic event which precipitously destroys the promise and innocence of the childhood world, as a dramatic change in responsibilities or lifestyle circumstances (such as a descent into poverty, a teenage pregnancy, or a sudden transition into a demanding adult career). The transition may involve a protracted period of mourning for the Lost World, which may take the shape of refusing to grow up, clinging to fading youth and beauty, or simply a melancholy withdrawal into a depressive state. Many of these more unfortunate forms of transition from "inner to outer" result in a poor adjustment to adult life, and clinical experience teaches us that it is around these transition zones that mental illness often manifests itself. However, it also sometimes happens that the transition to adulthood is successfully negotiated, and internal potentialities are maintained and nurtured even as the individual negotiates the demands of a complex adult world.

The vertical and horizontal aspects of the Integrated Analytical Model result in a circumplex model, which is meant to serve as a speculative map of mental representations at different levels (representing a developmental sequence of complexity) and angles (representing synergistic themes). This model is intended to clarify and illustrate the abstract ideas and suppositions that go into this and other models, serving especially as a conceptual scheme to integrate psychoanalytic and Jungian models of mental representation, and is also intended to provide a source of speculative hypotheses and predictive power. As is the case with all models of the personality, it represents not physical objects "located" somewhere in material space, or even specific regions or functions of the brain, but a useful means of organizing ideas, which effectively explains observed phenomenon and predicts some aspects of human behavior and experience.

Holons and Harmonics

The vertical model consists of a series of levels of progressively complex mental representation, originating with archetypal source and progressing to the level of "self," as it would be described in the Self Psychology of psychoanalytic literature. I will describe six of these levels, devoting a chapter to each. I do not believe there are concretely six levels of mental representation; this number is arbitrary, and we could just as well divide the continuum into 9, or 12, or 28 levels. The six I have chosen to describe were chosen because they represent well-documented phenomena in the various literatures of Jungian, psychoanalytic, and cognitive/constructivist theory. The levels represent a continuum, but nevertheless likely show quantum leaps of complexity, which have important clinical implications, which we shall discuss throughout Chapters 2–10. We will eventually characterize this trajectory of mental representations as following principles of *deterministic chaos*, meaning a critical mass of linear associations and transformations passes a phenomenological event horizon and results in qualitatively different and unpredictable outcomes (a process we will come to call *emergence*). This deterministic chaos reminds me of the mathematical principle of *nonlinear systems* (see Scott, 2007), which describes properties of a system in which the output does not map onto input in a linear (and therefore predictable) way. Nonlinearity prevents the kind of assumptions and approximations that make for easier computations and modeling. Nonlinear systems are more than the sums of their wholes; they cannot effectively be reduced to component parts. Following the time-honored tradition of all the natural sciences, we will attempt to cope with these complexities by approximating the nonlinear mathematics of personality with simpler models, while at the same time acknowledging that the resulting models will remain inadequate. To lay the groundwork for the rest of the model, I will invoke some phrases borrowed from other disciplines, including mathematics and music theory.

The trajectory of mental representations described in this book represents a *holarchy*, which is a system comprised of *holons* (Koestler, 1967). Holons, as described by Koestler, are simultaneously wholes and parts of wholes. Holons comprise self-regulating, open systems that show both autonomous properties of wholes and dependent properties of parts. A holon contains the seeds of the totality of all the "higher level" forms that evolve from it and are orthogonal in themselves. Within the context of the IAM model, I will call these holographic layers *harmonics* to borrow a word from music theory which suggests orthogonal themes that build upon each other. In the language of acoustics, a harmonic is a whole-integer multiple of a *fundamental frequency*. In the case of music, the fundamental frequency (denoted f_o) is a particular note generated by, say, plucking the open D-string of a guitar. The harmonics of a particular musical note describe multiples of the frequency of that note, such that the second harmonic represents twice the frequency of the fundamental frequency (the first harmonic), and the third harmonic represents a value three times the frequency of the fundamental, etc. As I will describe below, the archetypes are, in this model, the "fundamental frequency" of the psyche, and in that sense represent the most irreducible and orthogonal building blocks of meaning-making and mental representation that constitutes the personality. The other harmonics represent multiples of the fundamental frequency in the sense that the psychological content represented in those layers of the personality reflect variations on the theme of the earlier, more primitive and dynamic content. Symbols are harmonics of archetype in the sense that symbols are *multiples of the fundamental frequency of archetype*.[2] Each harmonic level of mental representation is therefore a variation on a theme, which has roots in archetype, which we shall describe as the primordial symmetry references earlier in this chapter. The literature on music theory is replete with methodologies designed for isolating f_o, called fundamental frequency estimation (see Doval & Rodet, 1993). Fundamental frequency estimation is an exquisitely relevant metaphor for psychology: psychotherapy amounts to fundamental frequency estimation of the client. The therapist practices pattern recognition as she gently and systematically traverses the various harmonic representations unfolding in the therapeutic alliance.

All these higher level multiples, the most conscious of the harmonics, are essentially made up of the building blocks of archetypal experience. At the center of everything (psychologically speaking) is the archetypal holon or harmonic. Archetypal experience represents the bedrock level of human nature, the "raw material" of humanity, and the center of gravity for the development of the personality. The archetypal harmonic is a single point—the center of the sphere. The point is a useful geometric model because it suggests indivisibility; I have taken the position in my own analysis that archetypes are the ultimate irreducible orthogonal units of "psyche." As the center of the sphere, this point represents the infinite possibility of directions that may develop from here. Archetypal experience that becomes "constellated" through life experience: some strong affect becomes associated with an archetypal idea (or more accurately, a symbol which contains the archetypal content, for only symbols can be directly apprehended even by the unconscious mind). In this way, a symbol becomes "turned on" or activated and imbued with emotional energy. From this point on, the symbol and its associated emotional energy loom large in the psyche, either in its direct effects or through the psyche's efforts to compensate for it. Therefore, the developing mind becomes aware of the Prodigal Child, or the Misfit, or the Conquering Hero, the Good Son, or the Terrible Mother, or the Long Suffering Daughter, and this symbol casts a shadow upon the rest of the personality. The resulting symbols-*cum*-affect (which, as I have suggested, are ultimately organized around a symbol as their center of gravity) result in the formation of objects when they become associated with important persons, objects, of the self. By this time, the resulting mental representations are ripe for targeting by defensive operations, as we have discussed previously. At this point, the mental representations may be projected, repressed, compensated for, or used as a foundation for the resulting self or selves that make up the recognizable personality.

Representational Vectors

As we shall discuss in Chapter 10, constellated and complexified archetypal content plus external experience plus the energy of affect sets off developmental "pathways" of increasingly rarified mental representations. Following certain mathematical traditions, I will call these pathways *vectors*, implying a quantity characterized by both magnitude and direction. Archetypal content that becomes constellated through primary experience initiates a vector, which radiates outward from the archetypal harmonic on into the higher level harmonics. Similarly, an external experience (such as, for example, a job promotion or demotion) can initiate a vector into which may radiate inward, triggering activation of content in the deeper holons "below." Representational vectors can even affect each other directly, as happens when one deeply held belief contravenes a powerful transport of desire.

Vectors proceed from a start point (the origin) to an end point (the destination). In psychological terms, the representational vector's origin is a stimulus and the destination is a goal (later on we will address the issue of teleologies and goal-drivenness). Hearkening back to our discussion of artificial intelligence languages, a goal is a predetermined state of high value that is considered desirable by the individual.

Seen in this way, the personality itself can be seen as the total set of its vectors, which observed in detail appears chaotic and disorganized, but from a holistic perspective, can be seen as containing certain dominant currents resulting from a lot of vectors, which tend to point in the same direction. A depressive personality, as defined from without, is characterized by a predominance of vectors that suggest over-valuation of the inherent destructiveness of the self, and resulting assumption of responsibility for failures and losses (introjection).

Starting with Chapter 11, we will turn from the Vertical Model of Integrated Analytical Psychology to the Horizontal Model, which will reshape our harmonic levels into concentric circles that comprise a circumplex model of personality functioning. But for now, let us take a brief tour of the harmonic progression of mental representation across a range of theoretical perspectives...beginning with the primordial symmetry of archetype.

Notes

1 This perspective has been variously called the Representational Theory of Mind, Representationalism, and Indirect Realism.
2 Some systems of nomenclature do not consider the fundamental frequency a harmonic at all, and this question has interesting implications for us.

References

Chomsky. N. (2000). *New horizons in the study of language and mind.* Cambridge University Press.

Doval, B., & Rodet, X. (1993). Fundamental frequency estimation and tracking using maximum likelihood harmonic matching and HMMs. *International Conference on Acoustics, Speech and Signal Processing, 1,* 221–224.

Flanagan, O. J. (1991). *The science of the mind* (2nd ed.) Bradford Books.

Jung, C. G. (2014). *The structure and dynamics of the psyche* (R. F. C. Hull, Trans.). Princeton University Press.

Kant, I. (2003). *Critique of pure reason* (M. Weigelt, Trans.). Penguin Classics.

Koestler, A. (1967). *The ghost in the machine.* Hutchinson.

Neimeyer, R. A. (1993). An appraisal of constructivist psychotherapies. *Journal of Consulting and Clinical Psychology, 61*(2), 221–234.

Piaget, J. (1962). P*lay, Dreams and imitation in childhood.* Norton.

Scott, A. C. (2007). *The nonlinear universe: Chaos, emergence, life.* Springer.

Selby-Bigge, L. A. (1975). *A treatise of human nature.* Clarendon Press.

Part 1

The Vertical Model

Chapter 2

The First Harmonic

Archetype

And once you are awake, you shall remain awake eternally.

-Friedrich Nietzsche
Thus Spoke Zarathustra

What shall we say of archetype? Of all of Jung's psychological, metaphysical, and psychoid contraptions, the idea of archetype has proved the most controversial, and remains a matter of contention and consternation even among Jungians. Perhaps I should say "especially among Jungians," because research and clinical psychology have largely ignored the topic.

Jung was quite aware of what he was doing to us with the archetypes, and did it anyway...a testament to the importance of this concept to his greater cosmology. Jung was quite aware of the ways that the "spirit of the times," the *zeitgeist*, exerts a tidal influence on what we can think about, and how we think about it, and that the spirit of the times would not like all this archetype business. This zeitgeist, Jung writes in *Modern man in search of a soul* (2005), is "an inclination, an emotional tendency that works upon weaker minds, through the unconscious, with an overwhelming force of suggestion that carries them along with it" (p. 175). Jung goes on to say:

Just as formerly the assumption was unquestionable that everything that exists takes its rise from the creative will of a God who is spirit, so the nineteenth century discovered the equally unquestionable truth that everything arises from material causes. Today the psyche does not build itself a body, but on the contrary, matter, by chemical action, produces the psyche. This reversal of outlook would be ludicrous if it were not one of the outstanding features of the spirit of the age. It is the popular way of thinking, and therefore it is decent, reasonable, scientific and normal. Mind must be thought to be an epiphenomenon of matter. The same conclusion is reached even if we say not "mind" but "psyche", and in place of matter speak of brain, hormones, instincts or drives. To grant the substantiality of the soul or psyche is repugnant to the spirit of the age, for to do so would be heresy.

(pp. 175–176)

DOI: 10.4324/9781032708751-4

One way to understand the history of science was that the ancient sensibilities that valued symmetrical divine order (resulting in, for example, the *Unus Mundus*) was bifurcated by the emergence of Cartesian dualism: the separation of the spirit world from the world of matter. Descartes did not necessarily privilege matter over spirit; he merely differentiated them and proposed an empirical system of thought, which would follow the rules of matter. However, in a broad sense, René Descartes gave the Western World tacit permission to deny the world of spirit, as Jung articulated above. The post-modern world view, therefore, is by the standards of the entire grand sweep of human cultural history, remorselessly deconstructive (or critical) and skeptical, and it cannot abide metanarratives, foundationalism, or essentialism. For this reason, Jung's idea of archetype has been enthusiastically embraced by spiritually minded laypersons but firmly unincluded from the literature of research and clinical psychology. We can't have archetypes in psychology for the same reasons we can't have freedom or dignity ... they are illusions that have no basis in empirical research, or at least are not subject to falsifiability, and beyond the scope of the randomized controlled trial (RCT), which is the current standard of scientific inquiry.

Archetypes, Metaphysics, and the Philosophy of Science

Let us acknowledge that what we call "science" in this age, which was very different from what it was 300 years ago and will be very different in another 300 years, is strongly influenced by logical positivism, broadly and essentially represented by the philosophy of Rudolf Carnap. Carnap's (1937) ideal of scientific inquiry was a sort of transparent representation of knowledge, the principles of which are systemically distorted by both language (which poorly represents knowledge because it is idiomatic and imprecise) and metaphysics (which may amount to depictions of what we want to be true rather than what is verifiably true). Carnap did not attempt to deny that metaphysical realities are phenomenologically important to human perception and experience, only that metaphysical experience can only function at the individual level and should not be confused for scientific inquiry, which is a rigorous, falsifiable, and systematic attempt to discern objectively true phenomena that are *objectively true for everyone*. Carnap acknowledged that artists investigate metaphysical experience, and that this is the rightful provenance of art to do so, but that art and metaphysics do not amount to actual knowledge. One of the important outcomes of this sort of logical positivism was therefore a distinction between so-called "analytic" truths versus "synthetic" truths: analytic truths (which can be described as *a priori* knowledge) are elementally true in a way that is independent of experience, and synthetic truths are relative to perception and experience. Logical positivism, as described by Carnap, therefore relies on good old Cartesian dualism. As we shall see later on in this book, contemporary Jungian perspectives confront Jung's own tendency to apparently violate Carnap's principles, in that he mixes metaphysical claims into what he otherwise claims is an empirical model of psychology.

Carnap's perspective, as well as logical positivism itself, has by many accounts "softened" into a perspective that is often called "naturalism" and represented by Willard van Orman Quine. Quine (1951) rejects the dichotomy between analytic and synthetic truth in the name of *holism*, which critiques reliance on single observations or statements of truth and instead affirms systems of knowledge, which derive their truth from their totality. This perspective acknowledges that virtually *all* truths are relative to experience, perception, and language. This perspective, instead of just critiquing synthetic perspectives for failing to be analytic, deprives empirically derived knowledge of special status. As Quine (1951) himself puts it, "no statement is immune to revision" (p. 43). Quine's shift from Carnap's logical positivism reflects a parallel shift in the philosophy of science since the 1960s or so, which moves away from strict logical positivism more towards environmentalism. This shift is evident with the rise of uncertainty and the principle of probability in many sciences, and in psychology in particular with the evolution of strict behaviorism into first cognitive-behaviorism and then constructivism, which we will continue to explore in this book.

Quine's perspective, then, put the metaphysical back on the map, as it were. For the same can be said of metaphysical propositions as for the propositions of empirical science: our best theory at the current time represents the best we can do in describing a phenomenon, and that's as close as we are ever likely to get, notwithstanding the evolution in our views along with our methods for establishing those views. The more mature scientific perspective on Jungian archetypes should therefore be that we are responsible for operationalizing the concept the best we can and do not have to discard such propositions because they fall on the wrong side of the empirical line.

Jung on Archetypes

For purposes of the Integrated Analytical Model, we will take the archetype as the most basic layer of the psyche, likely (according to Jung and consistent with contemporary speculation) inherited with the physiognomic organization of the brain itself (see Knox, 2003). By definition unconscious, archetypes are beyond the everyday experience of the conscious "self"; speaking more technically, they lie beyond the influence of the ego. We are no more aware of the archetypal foundation of consciousness than we are of the action of the individual neurons making up the nervous system. Like the unpronounceable name of God in Hebrew tradition (YHWH or G-d), the archetypes cannot be directly apprehended but only experienced through their effects, much as astronomers have postulated the existence of Black Holes not because any have been observed (which would be an impossibility), but because they may be inferred from their effects on surrounding space. As the raw material, primal "stuff" of the unconscious, archetypes cannot be readily defined or categorized. Instead, they may be conceptualized as "fields" of possibility and probability, which describe the parameters of human experience. Jung argues that it is archetypal experience that defines the very essence of humanity, because the archetypes contain within their fields of effect the full range of human experience dating from the beginning of our evolutionary tree.

Jung was not alone in looking under the veil and into the interstitial space of primordial forms. Abraham Maslow (1968) affirmed the necessity for such a primordial form if we are to describe the phenomenological world, as is the charge of the discipline of psychology:

> This development toward the concept of a healthy unconscious and of a healthy irrationality, sharpens our awareness of the limitations of purely abstract thinking, of verbal thinking and of analytic thinking. If our hope is to describe the world fully, a place is necessary for preverbal, ineffable, metaphorical, primary process, concrete-experience, intuitive and esthetic types of cognition, for there are certain aspects of reality which can be cognized in no other way.
>
> (p. 208)

Wilfred Bion (1970) similarly addresses a priori reality in what he calls "O":

> Psychoanalytical events cannot be stated directly … any more than can those of other scientific research. I shall use the sign O to denote that which is the ultimate reality, absolute truth, godhead, the infinite, the thing-in-itself. O does not fall in the domain of knowledge or learning save incidentally; it can be 'become', but it cannot be 'known'. It is darkness and formlessness but it enters the domain K when it has evolved to a point where it can be known, through knowledge gained by experience, and formulated in terms derived from sensuous experience; its existence is conjectured phenomenologically.
>
> (p. 26)

In *On the Nature of the Psyche* Jung (1969) stated that archetypes are themselves unrepresentable, but that they may be visualized as images and ideas. This difference between the "archetype-as-such" and image of the archetype raises questions about comparative levels of mental representations, especially within Jungian theory in terms of differentiating archetype from symbol or complex. I will make the case in this book that those three constructs represent orthogonally (and holarchically) different levels of harmonic representation, occupying the first, second, and fourth harmonic, respectively. Jung himself clearly considered archetypal experience as occupying a continuum linking a spiritual realm (see below) to the instinctive world:

> Psychic processes therefore behave like a scale along which consciousness 'slides'. At one moment it finds itself in the vicinity of instinct, and falls under its influence; at another, it slides along to the other end where spirit dominates and even assimilates the instinctual processes most opposed to it.
>
> (para. 408)

Additionally, it is clear in other contexts that Jung considered the domain of archetype and complex to occupy a somewhat oppositional and dynamic relationship to the conscious attitude of the egoic self, further reinforcing the idea of a continuum of mental representations.

Jung (2014) further specified that archetypes have a "specific charge" manifesting as affects. He writes:

> Affect produces a partial *abaissement du niveau mental*[1], for although it raises a particular content to a supernormal degree of luminosity, it does so by withdrawing so much energy from other possible contents of the unconscious that they become darkened and eventually unconscious... We regularly find that unexpected or otherwise inhibited unconscious contents break through and find expression in the affect. Such contents are very often of an inferior or primitive nature and thus betray their archetypal origin.
>
> (p. 437)

The affect that invests archetypal experience is important in a theoretical sense because it suggests something important about the way in which affect serves as a motivator for mental representation in complex systems, as we shall explore in Chapter 8, and that mental representations further "downstream" the trajectory of harmonic representation will result at the fourth harmonic in what Jung described as complexes. Regarding the relationship between affect and representation, Jung (2014) writes "Every affect tends to become an autonomous complex, to break away from the hierarchy of the unconscious and, if possible, to drag the ego after it" (p. 330). This process seems to parallel the phenomenon of splitting as conceptualized within the object-relations tradition: because it is a developmentally difficult task to maintain strong ambivalent or contradictory emotions about a single person, human psychology tends to split representations of other people up into good and bad parts. Indeed, in the Integrated Analytical Model, the complex harmonic is situated "right next door" to the object harmonic, suggesting that they are functionally similar levels of representation. Jung further lends credence to the idea of an hierarchy of mental representations in this citation.

Perhaps most inconveniently of all, Jung contextualized archetype in terms of the *numinous*, a term derived from Rudolf Otto's (1958) use of the word in *The Idea of the Holy*, which seems to have had an impact on Jung. Jung (1969) writes that "the archetypes have, when they appear, a distinctly numinous character which can only be described as 'spiritual', if 'magical' is too strong a word. Consequently, this phenomenon is of the utmost significance for the psychology of religion" (para. 405). And in *Symbols for Transformation*, Jung puts it even more explicitly: "The archetypes are the numinous, structural elements of the psyche and possess a certain autonomy and specific energy, which enables them to attract, out of the conscious mind, those contents that are best suited to themselves" (para. 344). After the fashion of Rudolf Otto, Jung was taken by the arresting and awe-inspiring experiential field of archetypal experience, like St. Paul blown off his horse in Caravaggio's (1600) painting, *Conversion on the Way to Damascus*. Otto coins the term *mysterium tremendum et fascinans,* a reaction of shuddering and also fascination. If it is Jung's sense that consciousness slides, then it seems to slide between the conscious attitude of the waking mind, which represents the settled status quo of the personality and its defenses on one hand, and the unspeakable *otherness* of numinous archetypal experience on the other.

James Hillman's (1975) model of archetypal psychology depicts archetype differently than does Jung…as fluid and imaginal facets of immediate experience rather than holding a primordial symmetry, but Hillman strongly advocates the return of soul that cannot be reduced to biology, the body, or material presence:

> By "soul" I mean the imaginative possibility in our natures, the experiencing through reflective speculation, dream, image and fantasy—that mode which recognizes all realities as primarily symbolic or metaphorical,…that unknown component, which makes meaning possible, turns events into experiences, is communicated in love, has religious concern.
>
> (p. xvi)

We can already readily see how the idea of archetype will not play well with psychology defined as a research science. However, the archetypal hypothesis is not an obscure irrelevancy within analytical theory, but rather a central and crucial concept that provides the context for analytical conceptualization of psychological health and mental illness. The archetype represents Jung's trapdoor in the basement floor of analytical psychology, a portal that if opened would let all kinds of unscientific things into the house. The idea of archetype suggests something altogether numinous and certainly stands apart from other models of mental representation in the sense that it is by definition beyond the scope of direct empirical inquiry. "Are archetypes necessary?" asks June Singer (1994). She answers her own question this way: "Perhaps the research psychologist will be the last to know. But the great playwrights and artists have always known, and the poet has asked the right questions." Perhaps so. To contemplate archetypes requires a kind of leap of faith.

Jungians and Post-Jungians on the Subject of Archetype

There has been, to say the least, a wide variety of efforts to operationalize the idea of archetypes within the discipline of Jungian and post-Jungian analysis. Roughly speaking, one of the major controversies has to do with disagreements about what represents the "archetype-as-such" and what constitutes an image or epiphenomenon of archetype. George Hogenson (2004) notes an example of this difference in definition between the perspective of Anthony Stevens (2003), who suggests a model of archetype as an expression of a genetically defined need, which is itself the product of evolutionary processes, and James Hillman, who identifies archetype as a function of human imagination and perception.

Joseph Cambray (2009) articulates the contemporary perspective of *emergence* in archetypal theory and also as it relates to Jung's concept of synchronicity. We shall explore the concept of emergence further in Chapters 7 and 8, especially, and explore some intriguing parallels with constructivism and chaos theory. Cambray's depiction of emergence is certainly consistent with parallel theoretical models derived from cognitive theory, placing archetype in the perspective of a fractal and holarchic whole:

> By moving to a field model Jung's view of the archetypes of the collective unconscious can be reformulated. Each archetype can be seen as a node embedded within the larger context of a polycentric whole, with sets of links or connections weaving the archetypes into a network that, as I have suggested elsewhere, has scale-free properties.
>
> (p. 43)

Other conceptualizations of archetype have taken the perspective of describing archetype as an endogenous structure of the brain itself, such as in the work of Anthony Stevens (2003) and Jean Knox (2003). Jean Knox's perspective casts archetype as an image schema, which are embodied, prelinguistic representations of spatiotemporal relationships. It is Knox's perspective that image schema mediate attachment in complex ways because of the fashion by which relational experiences become encoded.

In general, Jungian and post-Jungian perspectives have become increasingly critical of the Cartesian and Kantian assumptions that characterize Jung's ideas and especially his foundationalism. One such vector of critique comes from so-called cultural complex models, which we will explore further in Chapter 5. These perspectives in particular challenge Jung's normalization of the *unus mundus*, which is a shared universal field of understanding enabling the idea of a collective unconscious. Many of these critiques come down to a rejection of the *a priori*, the essentialism which is central to Jung's conceptualization of the self.

Hogenson (2004) undertakes a review of the various contemporary takes on archetype and comes to this conclusion:

> It appears to me that the course that will have to be taken will be a return to the beginning of Jung's theorizing about the archetype... we remain in need of an account of the nature and workings of the symbol that is congruent with the theory of archetypes that Jung spent his lifetime trying to work out.
>
> (p. 52)

A little later, Hogenson concludes:

> A theory of archetypes must give rise to a visible theory of symbolization that satisfies the demands of the clinical setting, in which the amplification of a symbol is able to transform the psyche and the behavior of the analysand, and give an account of the range of phenomena that Jung tried to pull together under the rubric of the archetypes of the collective unconscious.
>
> (p. 53)

Archetype: The Integrated Analytical Perspective

Where do we go from here, given all the riotous complexities sparked by Jung's central mystery?

Conceptualizations of archetype in the emergentist tradition (such as described by Cambray), and the essentially brain-based, cognitive, or constructivist perspectives (such as those offered by Stevens and Knox) represent alternative levels of mental representation, which I would describe as "downstream" from the archetypal harmonic, and from the perspective of the Integrated Analytical Model are actually describing other harmonics such as the complex, schema, or self level. We will consider those later, higher-order harmonics in their respective chapters ahead.

Consistent with Hogenson's call for a return to Jung's original conceptualization of the archetype, I will invoke now some of Jung's original observations, which we discussed previously in this chapter. In particular, I notice that some of the more contemporary perspectives on Jung's archetype have in particular lost contact with his characterization that archetypes are *unrepresentable,* and that they have a *numinous* quality.

Jung's conviction that archetypes are unrepresentable, of course, is asking for all kinds of trouble with post-modern assumptions about reality. Our current spirit of the times does not like a priori arguments, partly out of the deeply philosophical perspective of skepticism that encourages dissent and relativism, and bristles at anything deemed foundational or "universal." The social justice perspective, strongly represented in cultural complex theory (see Brewster, 2019), challenges "universal" assumptions about reality systems that are culturally relative. Certainly the historical flirtation of scientific philosophy with logical positivism, as described earlier in this chapter, further marginalizes any attempt at including anything unrepresentable in a scientific paradigm.

For all these reasons, an unrepresentable, a priori primordial reality becomes a hard pill to swallow. And yet the historical and biological reality of primordial states is undeniable even in a historical sense. No one denies that adult human beings grow out of the union of haploid gametes. No one denies that the estimated 8.7 million species of plants and animals evolved from a single primordial ancestor. No one denies that all of this, gametes and species of planets and animals, not to mention rocks and stars and asteroids and all the 92 naturally occurring elements, all somehow came from whatever pre-existed the Big Bang, and that all this physical and energetic complexity came from a primordial source, which must have been neither, transitioning perhaps through a Grand Unification Epoch (see Mohapatra, 2010) that existed in the seconds after the Big Bang, comprised of a primordial soup of elementary particles. Whatever existed before the Big Bang is certainly unrepresentable as well, at least for now. Why is it that we can accept the primordial origins of life on earth and the universe itself, but not primordial origins in human psychological experience? By the same token, why do so many people sneer at the idea of archetype, who then go on to accept such concepts as love, or freedom, or dignity, as central to their own experience and motivation? We all believe in archetypes, whether we are comfortable with that belief or not, whether we admit it or not. The great irony of the debate over archetypes is that phenomenologically speaking, archetypes aren't controversial at all.

Even by the standards of Quinean model of scientific philosophy described above, I would argue that we have "permission" to speculate about the nature of unrepresentable archetypes in the absence of full understanding of their natures. We meet the standard of scientific inquiry, in its current more forgiving form, by making our best efforts at devising the best theories we can. And as I have argued, the jurisdiction of psychology cannot afford to leave out phenomenologically critical aspects of human experience, no matter how unrepresentable they may be.

My favorite epistemological framework for archetypes is the Zen tradition, a school of Mahayana Buddhism influenced by Taoist Philosophy. The Zen tradition expresses itself the colorful language of koans, which are stories, questions, or dialogs intended to first generate insight and then "Great Doubt" (see Boshan, 2016), which refers to a kind of willingness to question reality: in fact, it is similar to curiosity. The underlying value of this Great Doubt is the capacity to question self structure, to cure "word drunkenness" (Reps & Senzaki, 1998), and avoid categorical thinking or absoluteness. Consider this example of a dialogic koan:

Joshu asked Nansen:	"What is the path?"
Nansen said:	"Everyday life is the path."
Joshu asked:	"Can it be studied?"
Nansen said:	"If you try to study, you will be far away from it."
Joshu asked:	"If I do not study, how can I know it is the path?"
Nansen said:	"The path does not belong to the perception world, neither does it belong to the nonperception world. Cognition is a delusion and noncognition is senseless. If you want to reach the true path beyond doubt, place yourself in the same freedom as sky. You name it neither good nor not-good." At these words Joshu was enlightened. (pp. 133–134)

The language of Zen koans leads us to integrate trust and doubt in ways that we will revisit later in this book when we consider contemporary perspectives on cognitive processing, which depict the mind as a kind of hypothesis-generating machine. Zen suggests that both the hypothesis and the negation of the hypothesis are valuable.

A central concept in the narrative of many koans is the word *mu* (Japanese 無), which defies easy translation, but is often given as the answer to a koan. Broadly speaking, *mu* suggests that there is no answer, or that a question is fundamentally inappropriate or cannot be answered. Zen Master Mumon Ekai (in Reps & Senzaki, 1998) speaks to the importance of the concept of *mu* as a kind of disciplined contemplation:

To realize Zen one has to pass through the barrier of the patriarchs. Enlightenment always comes after the road of thinking is blocked. If you do not pass the barrier of the patriarchs or if your thinking road is not blocked, whatever you think, whatever you do, is like a tangling ghost. You may ask: What is a barrier of a patriarch? This one word, Mu, is it. This is the barrier of Zen... If you want to pass this barrier, you must work through every bone in your body, through every pore of your skin, filled with this question: What is Mu? and carry it day and night. Do not believe it is the common negative symbol meaning nothing. It is not nothingness, the opposite of existence. If you really want to pass this barrier, you should feel like drinking a hot iron ball that you can neither swallow nor spit out.

(p. 115)

Robert Pirsig (1981) puts it this way:

Mu means "no thing"...it points outside the process of dualistic discrimination. Mu simply says, "No class; not one, not zero, not yes, not no." It states that the context of the question is such that a yes or no answer is in error and should not be given. "Unask the question" is what it says. Mu becomes appropriate when the context of the question becomes too small for the truth of the answer.

(p. 329)

I have taken this bit of a detour into Zen Buddhism because this disciplined way of reflecting upon reality represents one of the better ways to approach the concept of archetype. Archetype does not belong to the perception world, and it does not belong to the nonperception world. The question of defining archetype has become too small for the truth of the answer. Archetype represents a nondual and yet fully human experience of reality, which has no location or manifestation in either thought or language. To begin to communicate the contours of the unrepresentable archetype, we must back out of formal representational categorization, and our contemporary models of science, which are all too dichotomous, focused, and *local* to contain the phenomenon. Archetypes are probability fields of experience only perceptible to an instrument as complex as the human mind and are not located "in the brain" at all but probably reflect the very structure of reality itself. Archetype is not technically a level of mentalization at all, but a precursor to mentalization, closer to physics than biology. It is my hope that we hold a space for the mystery that they represent, and consistent with the Quinean model of the philosophy of science, settle for the fact that the best we can do at present is an array of metaphors, and that we resist the temptation to make a *thing* of them. I am highly aware that this perspective is unfashionably *sui generis*, but here we are.

Finally, I will briefly address Jung's perspective that archetypes carry a *numinous* quality. I notice with regret that contemporary Jungian models seem to have all but given up on the numinosum in their haste to make a cognitive schema of archetype. Jung's fidelity to Rudolf Otto's concept of "the holy" or the numinous, not from a primary religious perspective but as a psychological experience, was profoundly valuable. One of the critical implications of Jung's sensibilities about the numinous is that this quality underlines the original *participative* and transformational quality of religious experience rather than a belief system, which is what religion has become by modern standards. Similar to the concepts of freedom and dignity, religious experience, and resulting religious doctrine is one of the most powerfully motivating forces in human behavior, at both the individual and collective level. No "science of human behavior" can afford to ignore humanity's enduring participation in the numinous. Furthermore, I would argue that the archetype is the very source of the numinous, and for this reason authentic experiential reactions to approaching the archetypal harmonic carry charges of awe, wonder, reverence, and even overwhelm or horror.

Susan Rowland (2016) sums up both the numinous and the creative qualities of archetype:

> Archetypes are story-generating, deathless, and endlessly creating via their images. They are gods seeking to live out their particular genre of stories, known, of course, as myths. In Jungian psychology, myth has a specific function as the narrative form of the archetype, or a god prominent at any particular moment of individuation. Put another way, myths fashion relations between consciousness and the archetypal collective unconscious. Myths are not what the ego chooses, but rather how the individuating psyche generates a story of being in a dialogue between the ego of consciousness and the greater divine powers of archetypes. For the individual person, myths are the stories of our fate.
>
> (p. 9)

To extend the musical metaphor behind the term harmonic, I will conclude by observing that the archetypal harmonic is the fundamental frequency of the harmonic progression of mental representation, the f_0 as we discussed in Chapter 1. The archetypal harmonic, itself unrepresentable, serves as a creative and generative probability field, which constitutes the primordial symmetry of the psyche that is broken and reformed through psychological experience. The rest of the following several chapters will describe outcomes of variations on the archetypal theme.

Note

1 A term used by Janet, generally translated as "lowering of the mental threshold." It was Jung's impression that during states of low energy due to fatigue, depression, or discouragement, the "tone" of the conscious mind was lowered. This state of affairs creates a differential gradient between the unconscious and the unconscious such that unconscious content flows into the consciousness. Freud had similar ideas about libido, after the fashion of a closed hydraulic system.

References

Bion W. R. (1970). *Attention and interpretation.* Tavistock Publications.

Boshan (2016). *Great doubt: Practicing Zen in the world* (J. Shore, Trans.). Wisdom Books.

Brewster, F. (2019). *The racial complex: A Jungian perspective on culture and race.* Routledge.

Cambray, J. (2009). *Nature and psyche in an interconnected universe.* Texas A&M University Press.

Caravaggio, (1600). *The conversion of Saint Paul [oil painting on cypress wood].* Rome, Italy.

Carnap, R. (1937). *Logical syntax of language.* Routledge.

Hillman, J. (1975). *Re-visioning psychology.* Harper & Row.

Hogenson, G. B. (2004). Archetypes: Emergence and the psyche's deep structure. In J. Cambray & L. Carter (Eds.), *Analytical psychology: Contemporary perspectives in Jungian analysis* (pp. 32–55). Routledge.

Jung, C. G. (1969). *On the nature of the psyche* (G. Adler & H. Read, Eds., & R. Winston, Trans.). Princeton University Press.

Jung, C. G. (2005). *Modern man in search of a soul.* Routledge.

Jung, C. G. (2014). *The structure and dynamics of the psyche* (R.F.C. Hull, Trans.). Princeton University Press.

Knox, J. (2003). *Archetype, attachment, analysis.* Routledge.

Maslow, A. H. (1968). *Toward a psychology of being* (2nd ed.). D. Van Nostrand.

Mohapatra, R. N. (2010). *Unification and supersymmetry: the frontiers of Quark-Lepton physics.* Springer.

Otto, R. (1958). *The idea of the holy* (J.W. Harvey, Trans.). Oxford University Press.

Pirsig, R. (1981). *Zen and art of motorcycle maintenance.* Bantam Books.

Quine, W. V. O. (1951). Two Dogmas of empiricism. *Philosophical Review, 60*(1): 20–43.

Reps, P., & Senzaki, N. (1998). *Zen flesh, Zen nones.* Tuttle Publishing.

Rowland, S. (2016). *Remembering dionysus.* Routledge.

Singer, J. (1994). *Boundaries of the soul.* Anchor Books.

Stevens, A. (2003). *Archetype revisited: An updated natural history of the self.* Inner City Books.

Chapter 3

The Second Harmonic
Symbol

It seems to leave the darkness rather blacker than before.

-Arthur Conan Doyle
The Hound of the Baskervilles

The second harmonic of mental representation is the symbolic representation. In crossing the demarcation line from the archetypal to the symbolic, we also cross a boundary from the transpersonal realm to the level of individual consciousness. In the various Jungian traditions, symbol is generally held to represent a container of archetypal force or the manifestation of archetype into the personal consciousness in a way that can be represented metaphorically. In a sense, symbols are the means by which archetypal content becomes operationalized within the psyche, and therefore symbols represent a kind of antechamber to the spiritual and transpersonal realm (or an antechamber into the personal psyche of the individual, depending which direction we travel). The Jungian context contrasts with the psychoanalytic sensibility that the symbolic is usually taken to represent figurative representations of a drives or conflicts, as we will discuss below. One of the important implications of this difference in perspective is that the Jungian model suggests that symbolic manifestations reflect the native and ineffable content of archetypal energies rather than "projected images" of external referents or emotional conflicts. Jung (1993) used religion to make this point, contrasting the deadening effects of "external objects of worship" from the internal symbolic world, which represents the path into individuation:

In an outward form of religion where all the emphasis is placed on the superficial figure (that is, where we are dealing with a more or less complete projection) the archetype is identical with externalized ideas but remains unconscious as a psychic factor. When an unconscious content is replaced by a projected image to that extent, it is cut off from all participation in an influence on the conscious mind. Hence it largely forfeits its own life, because it is prevented from exerting a formative influence on the consciousness which is natural to it; what is more, it remains in its original form — unchanged, for nothing changes in the unconscious.
(p. 11)

DOI: 10.4324/9781032708751-5

Also, significantly, Jung (1938) makes the point that "anything a man postulates as being a greater totality than himself can become a symbol of the Self" (para. 233), which reinforces the point that there is a qualitative difference between the Symbolic Harmonic and the Object Harmonic: the symbolic harmonic belongs to the transpersonal realm that transcends the individual psyche and therefore relates more to mythic figures, numinous experiences, and spiritual revelation than early, infantile, or primitive individual mental states. In Chapter 12, we shall explore the Christ mythos as central to Jung's perspective on the Symbolic.

Jung's perspective also suggests that symbolic representation enables unconscious content to "participate in an influence" on the conscious attitude. This perspective highlights another key feature of symbolic function from the Jungian point of view as well as an applied methodology critical to Jungian psychotherapy: optimal psychological development is a teleological process that includes integration of deeply unconscious content with the conscious attitude of the waking mind. Psychotherapeutic process, therefore, invites exploration and amplification of symbolic content as a means of inviting individuation:

> The history of religion in its widest sense (including therefore mythology, folklore, and primitive psychology) is a treasure-house of archetypal forms from which the doctor can draw helpful parallels and enlightening comparisons for the purpose of calming and clarifying a consciousness that is all at sea. It is absolutely necessary to supply these fantastic images that rise up so strange and threatening before the mind's eye with a sort of context so as to make them more intelligible.
>
> (p. 33)

It is clear from Jung's words that he considered religion a critical source of symbolic content. The Jungian emphasis on religious function differentiates it from psychoanalytic sensibilities, which beyond relating to Freud's atheism and his depiction of religion as a wish-fulfilling illusion, reflects the psychoanalytic tendency to frame religious, mystical, or spiritual (and by extension, symbolic) experience as outcomes of cultural or personal defensive processes. In fact, there is something in the intrinsic culture of classical Jungian analysis that specifically privileges symbolic approaches over "clinical" interpretations:

> Those who were analyzed by Jung, and many others who have followed the Zurich model, are most comfortable using the symbolic method not only for our patients but for ourselves, in our efforts as self-analysis. It is implemented by the use of amplification of dream or fantasy contents in order to draw upon the archetypal source of all inner imagery. In contrast, there is an alternative method, which has always existed in Jungian analysis or psychotherapy as a sort of reaction-formation to the symbolic method. It is a purely clinical method of dealing directly with the patient's personal problems.
>
> (Henderson, 1985, pp. 16–17)

This passage points to one of the more more profound disagreements between the Jungian and psychoanalytic sensibilities, specifically regarding the symbolic function. This disjunction is primarily the result of the proximity to mystical and metaphysical associations with the symbolic function. As we shall see, the two movements have sorted themselves very differently when it comes to the first and second harmonic levels in particular. As Michael Eigen (1998) puts it, just before stepping across this line he draws in the theoretical sand in his introduction to *The Psychoanalytic Mystic*

> Psychoanalysis and mysticism appear to be mutually exclusive. Analysis sticks pins in mystical bubbles. It traces in mysticism outlines of infantile ego states and early feelings clustering around mother-father images. It hopes to free humanity from mysticism by promoting the evolution of analytic consciousness.
>
> (p. 11)

Here we have it, then, Jungians accusing psychoanalysts of "reaction formation" when they attend patients' personal problems and psychoanalysts dismissing the mystical as "infantile ego states." Small wonder we have ended up where we have: two rich cultural traditions which each undertook to take seriously the internal psychological life of human beings barely able to speak to each other, to the impoverishment of both.

As a result of the current state of affairs, it is fair to say that Jungian partisan forces have effectively occupied the First and Second Harmonics, although a few hardy psychoanalytic scouts have encroached upon the Second Harmonic, and now have effective fire control over some of its outlying transportation corridors.

Because of the Jungian consensus that the realm of the symbolic represents a "carrier signal" for archetypal meaning, a significant percentage of classical Jungian scholarship is given over to analysis of symbols across a broad range of cultural and historical contexts. Marie-Louise von Franz (1996) exemplifies Jungian conceptualizations of the symbolic through her extensive scholarship of fairy tales, emphasizing their function as an elaboration not of individual neurosis but rather reflections of archetypal themes associated with the collective unconscious. Similarly, Edinger (1999) exemplifies a focus within the Jungian tradition on symbolic content of dreams and alchemical processes. Von Franz and Edinger, in particular, have exemplified a characteristic feature of the classical Jungian approach to the symbolic, which often feels closer to anthropological studies than clinical or psychotherapeutic narratives.

Jungian narratives generally depict symbolic reality in teleological and transpersonal terms and treat symbols most importantly as metaphors for the self to be approached through a kind of controlled regression (regression in the service of the ego, or in the service of the Self). The hermeneutical process of amplification is central to Jungian psychotherapy and involves exploration of metaphorical unconscious content as a means of approaching their archetypal origins. In this sense, significantly, the Jungian praxis approaches symbolic representation as a means of articulating, and therefore gaining meaningful access, to archetypal content, presumably providing a helpful context in which image provides a context enabling psychological change. Henderson (1985) articulated the controlled regression inherent in psychotherapeutic access to the symbolic harmonic as well as its ultimate status as a kind of self-representation:

> I find that what happens during deep regression is a fresh encounter of the ego with its dimly remembered 'primal' Self-image, following which the ego separates itself from that primal image in collaboration with the analyst. The patient is thus able to be aware of the process by which separation occurs, and of how it inevitably leads to reunion with original parent figures, as a healing experience.
>
> (p. 16)

It is worth noting that the Jungian conceptualization of symbolic representation therefore leads to an intersubjective working style with the psychotherapist, since the therapist participates richly in the amplification of symbol. This intersubjective quality invokes the Lacanian perspective that the symbolic order belongs to the dialectic of the Other (see below).

June Singer (1994) described the teleological function of symbolic representation within the Jungian tradition: "The symbol attracts and therefore leads individuals on the way of becoming what they are capable of becoming. That goal is wholeness, which is integration of the parts of the personality into a functioning totality" (p. 392).

Contemporary Jungian perspectives appear inclined to deconstruct classical Jungian perspectives on symbolic representation alongside the critique of archetype (see Chapter 2), and for similar reasons: because of Jung's foundationalism and his more metaphysical assumptions, but perhaps most particularly because of what critics call his model of an isolated mind comprised on innate structures, which differs from the more culturally relative and multipolar, intersubjective contemporary way of parsing human experience. In fact, I would argue that what Jung named the "spirit of the times" has shifted away from any kind of monolithic or unitary depictions of human experience, and towards more sociological and political perspectives. The *Unus Mundus* is no longer fashionable.

Bruno Bettelheim (2010) wrote extensively on the power and function of the symbolic representations common in fairy tales. His perspective is ultimately psychoanalytic by extraction, but resembles in its focus on fairy tales the corpus of classical Jungian writers interested in the symbolic function. Bettelheim supposed that children use fairy tales as a medium for dealing with unconscious content rather than confronting the unconscious content directly

> [The child] can achieve this understanding, and with it the ability to cope, not through rational comprehension of the nature and content of the unconscious, but by becoming familiar with it through spinning out daydreams - ruminating, rearranging, and fantasizing about suitable story elements in response to unconscious pressures.
>
> (p. 7)

Bettelheim supposes the childhood occupations of daydreaming, and play are de-signed not only to make sense of the outer but the inner world as well, responding to unconscious forces as the developing ego encounters them: the emphasis on unconscious pressures is consistent with the vestiges of drive-theory perspectives in psychoanalytic depictions of symbolic functioning.

Wilfred Bion represents an intriguing interface between the Jungian and psy-choanalytic perspective on symbolic representation. As we discussed in Chapter 1, Bion's theory of the unknowable "O" approaches the nuomenal mysteries of archetype. Partly as a result of concern about increasing determinism in psychoa-nalysis, Bion sought to restore a kind of "uncertainty principle" to psychoanalytic theory which not only stopped short of mysticism but also focused on emotional truth, which may not map on to other kinds of truth. Grotstein therefore interprets in Bion's work a "truth drive" which is both emotional and relational. According to Grotstein (2004), this truth drive involves identifying with, and even becoming, an object as a means of truly perceiving it

> The analyst, rather than being distant or neutral, must become the analysand's unacceptable (as yet) emotional truth about his/her ultimate reality (the symp-tom of the moment) by unconsciously resonating with the analysand's anxiety from within his/her own unconscious and then transcending it.
>
> (p. 1084)

Elsewhere, Grotstein continues:

> The analyst, like the mother in reverie with her infant, has the task of helping the analysand realize and accept the ongoing truths of his/her emotional life. These truths include all the impacting elements of raw circumstance, including emotions and the surging drives. When we stop to think about it, the procedure of psychoanalysis has as one of its major aims the elucidation of the analysand's emotional truths. That is the goal of every interpretation. Bion's impression that the infant projects its fear of dying into its mother could just as well be restated that it projects its ontological terror into her as a consequence of its relentlessly surging vitality (entelechy), its surging 'truth' about the pain of being alive, which may be felt to evolve more forcefully than the infant can momentarily encompass—all in the face of being constantly confronted on the outside with centripetally directed objects and opportunity stimuli to which it must be ever ready to accommodate and assimilate.
>
> (p. 1092)

From Grotstein's take we transition from the Jungian perception of symbol-as-fairy-tale to the psychoanalytic emphasis that symbolic experience represents "one's own personal, emotional truth in the maw of raw experience" (p. 1094). I take these contributions by Bion and Grotstein to depict dynamics of the Sym-bolic Harmonic because they represent, at the most primordial level possible, the very imaginal boundaries of selfhood where they share a border with the ultimate and unknowable mysteries that prevail at the level of Archetypal Harmonic. It is characteristic of the psychoanalytic, rather than Jungian, sensibility that symbolic content would be depicted ultimately as comprised of affective and relational forces: suckling breasts, fantasies of rescue, murderous rage, and atavistic urges to merge with loved objects rather than alchemical diagrams, sun discs, and draconic monsters.

Along with Bion, Lacan (2002) is another psychoanalytic theorist who makes a foray into the Second Harmonic. In particular, and especially when compared with most other psychoanalytic theorists, Lacan attempted to enshrine the symbolic harmonic as an organizing principle for psychoanalytic theory. What Lacan terms *The Symbolic* is the origin of his so-called *signifiers*, the linguistic units through which human reality is constructed, and is therefore the "determining order of the subject" (Lacan, 1998, p. 279). From the Lacanian point of view, the symbolic is that which can be symbolized; anything which is too ineffable to be signified in this way therefore belongs to the realm of the real, which belongs in the Integrated Analytical Model to the archetypal harmonic (see Chapter 2).

From the perspective of Integrated Analytical Model, the Symbolic Harmonic represents the most fundamental, protean, and unconscious level of mental representation that can be said to belong to the perceptual world of the individual rather than the foundational otherworldliness of archetype. As we have discussed in this chapter, the Symbolic Harmonic represents close proximity to the realm of the archetypal, represents the interface between the archetypal and the individual psyche and therefore is also the level at which transformative mystical and spiritual experiences are organized, creating a tension between the Jungian and psychoanalytic perspectives. The boundary between the First and Second Harmonic therefore represents Kant's (2003) Noumenal and Phenomenal realms. The Noumenal represents an absolute that cannot be experienced directly and can only be described in a negative, metaphorical, or speculative sense; the Phenomenal represents the world of relative experience. The impermeability of Kant's boundary is a matter of current philosophical debate; Gabriel and Žižek (2009) soften the boundary within the context of German Idealism, arguing for self-reflexivity that carries its own meaning and represents a kind of "conscious mythology" (Gogröf-Voorhees, 2012). Jung (2014) himself seems to have struggled with the issue of whether or not the noumenal world of archetype can be experienced directly, as evidenced by his glancing exploration of the so-called "psychoid," a concept that has been controversial with contemporary post-Jungian analysts (see Brooks, 2011). Whether the boundary between the First and Second Harmonic is therefore absolute, or whether it represents a semi-permeable membrane as Jung and the German Idealists suggest, is a matter for continued debate. I am personally satisfied to acknowledge the problem as a legitimate paradox: it appears that archetype and symbol represent orthogonally different levels of reality (as per Kant), but at the same time it appears that there is a "psychoid gradient," which makes a sort of gray zone transition between the Archetypal and Symbolic Harmonics.

Finally, there are important gendered considerations underlying our cultural and psychological approaches to the symbolic realm, especially as they relate to religious and symbolic function as an interface with the spiritual or metaphysical realm. In *The Creation of the Patriarchy*, Gerda Lerner (1987) makes the point that patriarchal forces have resulted in a kind of gender appropriation of the symbolic function in response to male resistance to existential issues of loss and decay: "Man (male) has found a way of dealing with this existential dilemma by assigning symbol-making power to himself and life-death-nature finiteness to woman" (p. 200). Lerner goes on to articulate the cultural result, that "Only males could mediate between God and humans," as evidenced by all-male priesthoods and hundreds of other examples of the gender-stratified division of symbolic function in cultural and social contexts. Merlin Stone (1978) similarly makes the point that historically, male-dominant cultures have historically suppressed and even destroyed cultures that cultivated goddess worship and symbols of the sacred feminine. We will explore this historical revisionism of the feminine power especially in the myth of Lilith (see Chapters 12 and 15). The tides have turned somewhat in certain cultural perspectives in the Western world; there has been a resurgence of interest in goddess worship and the sacred feminine, especially among the psychologically minded and especially among those who find depth psychology to be compelling. At the same time, as the symbolic and religious function have been increasingly devalued, and a sure sign of Western culture devaluing an idea or function is to associate it with the feminine. The Jungian willingness to reconceptualize and attend upon the symbolic function is often contextualized (especially in Jungian and depth psychological circles themselves) as a return to the sacred feminine. By the same token, it seems to me that psychoanalytic resistance to mysticism recapitulates an unconscious cultural tendency to relegate the symbolic function to the feminine and therefore to dismiss it.

The realm of the symbolic, then, represents a critical energetic interface between the individual personality and the transpersonal world of archetypal potential. Therefore, the Symbolic Harmonic is the first level of mental representation at which "psychopathology" becomes possible, in the sense that a discontinuity at this level (see Chapter 10) impairs the capacity for abstract representation, a critical function of the personality. Failure to mentalize at the symbolic harmonic results in either psychotic organization, in which the Second Harmonic fails to metabolize and make sense of protean archetypal material, or a kind of neurotic impoverishment in which discontinuities at higher level harmonics result in loss of effective access between the waking mind and its archetypal origins. In the former case, psychotically organized personalities remain overwhelmed and invaded by primal symbolic forces without the transmuting holding environment of higher order psychological context. Jung (1993) described this outcome when "the contents of the personal unconscious (i.e., the shadow) are indistinguishably merged with the archetypal contents of the collective unconscious and drag the latter with them when the shadow is brought into consciousness" (p. 32). In the latter case, individuals who are more "psychologically adjusted" in the sense that they have established a reliable egoic identity in the world may reveal an inner impoverishment suggesting over-identification with the world (Jung's "superficial figures" and "externalized ideas") at the expense of their own inner life and vibrancy, which has its source at the archetypal level.

In terms of psychotherapeutic process, then, the Symbolic Harmonic takes on profoundly different aspects depending on the individual's trajectory through psychological space. For a psychotically organized personality, the Symbolic Harmonic represents an opportunity for the psychotherapist to provide necessary context for the stygian monstrosities that haunt the edges of psychotic experience, helpfully providing space for them while acknowledging their fearsome aspect in an empathic manner. For neurotically organized personalities, the Symbolic Harmonic represents an opportunity to regress in the service of the ego, to reconnect with the life-giving psychic valences of archetypal reality through saga, story, myth, and bedtime story.

References

Bettelheim, B. (2010). *The uses of enchantment: The meaning and importance of Fairy Tales.* Vintage.

Brooks, R. M. (2011). Un-thought out metaphysics in analytical psychology: A critique of Jung's epistemological basis for psychic reality. *Journal of Analytical Psychology, 56*(4): 492–513.

Edinger, E. F. (1999). *Anatomy of the psyche: Alchemical symbolism in psychotherapy.* Open Court.

Eigen, M. (1998). *The psychoanalytic mystic.* Free Association Books.

Gabriel, M., & Žižek, S. (2009). *Mythology, madness and laughter subjectivity in German idealism.* Continuum International.

Gogröf-Voorhees, A. (2012). Mythology, madness and laughter subjectivity in German idealism - A review. *German Studies Review, 35*(1): 155–156.

Grotstein, J. S. (2004). The seventh servant: The implications of a truth drive in Bion's theory of 'O'. *International Journal of Psycho-Analysis, 85*(5): 1081–1101.

Henderson, J. L. (1985). Reflections on the history and practice of Jungian analysis. In M. Stein (Ed.), *Jungian analysis* (pp. 3–26). Shambhala.

Jung, C. G. (1938). *Psychology and religion.* Yale University Press.

Jung, C. G. (1993). *Psychology and alchemy* (R. F. C. Hull, Trans.). Princeton University Press.

Jung, C. G. (2014). *Spirit in man, art, and literature* (R. F. C. Hull, Trans.). Princeton University Press.

Kant, I. (2003). *Critique of pure reason* (M. Weigelt, Trans.). Penguin Classics.

Lacan, J. (1998). The field of the other. In J.A. Miller (Ed.), *Four fundamental concepts of psychoanalysis* (A. Sheridan, Trans.). W.W. Norton.

Lacan, J. (2002). The function and field of speech and language in psychoanalysis. In *Écrits: A selection* (B. Fink, Trans., pp. 31–106). W. W. Norton (Original work published 1953).

Lerner, G. (1987). *The creation of patriarchy* (Women and History; V. 1). Oxford University Press.

Singer, J. (1994). *Boundaries of the soul.* Anchor Books.

Stone, M. (1978). *When god was a woman.* Mariner Books.

Von Franz, M. L. (1996). *The interpretation of fairy tales.* Shambhala.

Chapter 4

The Third Harmonic
Object

But the stars that marked our starting fall away. We must go deeper into greater pain, for it is not permitted that we stay.

- Dante Alighieri
Inferno

Gaining altitude now, we ascend the developmental trajectory and gain the third level of mental representation: the Object Harmonic. Object representations are a theoretical construct shared among traditional psychoanalytic, Jungian, and object relations perspectives. Lucid definitions of the term "object" are hard to come by in any of the three traditions, and I find that most sources bypass explaining them and instead focus on how they function.

"Objects" have been generally described along a continuum as internal representations of another person or thing (a more "thingy" interpretation of the object) to simply the arbitrary focal point of the drives and desires of an individual psyche. Freud's original conceptualization of the word "object" certainly belonged in the latter camp: his first mention of the term was as as a "sexual object," meaning the destination of sexual instinct. Lest we become entirely too romantic about the nature of objects as targets of sexual instinct, Freud (1915) clarified that the object:

> is what is most variable about an instinct and is not originally connected with it, but becomes assigned to it only in consequence of being peculiarly fitted to make satisfaction possible . . . It may be changed any number of times in the course of the vicissitudes which the instinct undergoes during its existence.
>
> (pp. 122–123)

If an object is "peculiarly fitted to make satisfaction possible," then the original Freudian conceptualization of the object reduces the object to cipher; it does not have its own identity or shape. Although later in the same piece, Freud does name the mother's breast as an early target for the sexual instinct (experienced as receiving nourishment from the breast); this elaboration proved to be ephemeral, and it is generally assumed that Freud conceptualized the object as merely an arbitrary

DOI: 10.4324/9781032708751-6

focal point of drives, without its own identity or inherent characteristics. From this early point of view, the object is nothing more than a creation of drives (Greenberg & Mitchell, 1983, p. 42).

Another interesting trail to follow in the psychoanalytic literature about unconscious mental life is the concept of *phantasy*, which we will presently relate to the realm of internal objects. Ogden (2011) reviews Susan Isaacs's (1952) work on phantasy as a primal generator of meaning-making in unconscious life: "The infant's earliest unconscious phantasies draw on the primitively organized mental state of the infant, on the mature psychological life of the mother, and on the interplay between the two" (pp. 928–929). This depiction is a far cry from Freud's reductive take on object representations as the outcomes of biological drives, in that Isaac's portrayal of infantile phantasy suggests a co-creative process with the mother, which eventually takes on a life of its own and generates meaning. However, Isaac's depiction of phantasy does retain the Freudian assumption that mental representation at the level of phantasy does spring from tactile and physical sensation in interacting with the mother:

> The hungry or longing or distressed infant feels actual sensations in his mouth or his limbs or his viscera, which mean to him that certain things are being done to him or that he is doing such and such as he wishes, or fears. He feels as if he were doing so and so – e.g. touching or sucking or biting the breast which is actually out of reach.
>
> (Ogden, 2011, p. 932)

Ogden makes the point that Isaac's proposed scenario involves the infant registering the sensations of physical interaction with a mother and then going on to interpret or make sense of those interactions (which is the "phantasy"). In other words,

> In order for unconscious phantasy to hold meaning of the sort that Isaacs is describing, it must mean something to someone who is an interpreting subject capable of differentiating between symbol and symbolized, between internal and external reality, between thought and what is being thought about.
>
> (p. 933)

Ogden (and Isaac) are describing a kind of symbolic function, and name it as such. In a sense, Ogden's conclusions about connecting internal and external reality from infantile sensory experience suggest something similar to Jung's psychoid function, raising the possibility of crossing over the Kantian boundary between the noumenal and phenomenal and level of mental representation belonging to the Symbolic Harmonic. However, if we adopt the perspective (following the Jungian style) that the Symbolic Harmonic represents a manifestation of the noumenal (archetypal) in the personal psyche's phenomenal realm, then the psychoanalytic concept of phantasy does not quite fit there. If phantasy, consistent with early psychoanalytic theory in general, is traced back to discrete sensory experiences of events in the world (e.g., with a mother or her breast), then by the Kantian (and Jungian) definition, it involves not a movement from the noumenal to the phenomenal but from one level of the phenomenal to another level of the phenomenal. That is to say, phantasy, as advertised here, involves a quantum leap from sensory experience of interpersonal interactions to an internal working model of that interpersonal interaction within the psyche of the person experiencing it. The implications that phantasy rises from personal sensory experience rather than personal amplification of noumenal or archetypal experience, and that it emerges in a relational context, leads me to argue that this level of mental representation is an early Object Harmonic phenomenon rather than a Symbolic Harmonic phenomenon.

Fairbairn (1943, in Ogden, 2011) reacted in a roughly similar way to the concept of phantasy, reframing the concept in terms of what would be a central organizing principle in object relations theory: the idea of an autonomously functioning object:

> I cannot refrain from voicing the opinion that the explanatory concept of 'phantasy' has now been rendered obsolete by the concepts of 'psychical reality' and 'internal objects', which the work of Mrs Klein and her followers has done so much to develop; and in my opinion the time is now ripe for us to replace the concept of 'phantasy' by a concept of 'inner reality' peopled by the ego and its internal objects. These internal objects should be regarded as having an organized structure, an identity of their own, an endopsychic existence, and an activity [a capacity for thinking and feeling] as real within the inner world as those of any objects in the outer world.
>
> (p. 938)

With these words, Fairbairn brings us well and truly into the third harmonic and the domain of object representations, as defined by object relations theory. An important distinction of this transition from the second to the third harmonic is the relational quality of the former: the Object Harmonic represents the earliest and most fundamental level of mental representation that may be related to personal experiences with people, places, animals, ideas, and things that exist outside the self rather than experience with some nativistic, transpersonal, biologically coded, noumenal, metaphysical, or archetypally based symbolic experience, which transcends individual experience. The reader may note that within the strict confines of the psychoanalytic world view, there is no effective difference between the Symbolic and Object Harmonics; their differentiation for the most part depends on indulging in Jungian thinking.

Fairbairn's take on internal objects must be understood in terms of the functioning of the ego, or rather, egos. From this early perspective, internal objects have their origins in split-off parts of the ego following upon relational experiences with (frustrating) objects.

In Guntrip (1969), we see the shift in the psychoanalytic conceptualizations of object representations approaching their eventual fullness: "It is the object that is the real goal of the libidinal drive. We seek people, not pleasures. Impulses are not psychic entities but reactions of an ego to objects" (p. 21). This emphasis from seeking pleasures to seeking persons finalizes Fairbairn's pivot from emphasis on phantasy and indicates that we are now well and truly located in the third harmonic. Guntrip continues to elaborate in his appealingly humanistic way:

> What is meant by a world of internal objects may be put in this way: in some sense we retain all our experience in life and 'carry things in our minds'. If we did not, we would lose all continuity with our past, would only be able to live from moment to moment like butterflies alighting and flitting away, and no relationships or experiences could have any permanent values for us. Thus, in some sense everything is mentally internalized, retained and inwardly possessed; that is our only defense against complete discontinuity in living, a distressing example of which we see in the man who loses his memory, and is consciously uprooted.

> (p. 21)

I must say that through his comparison to butterflies alighting and flitting away, Guntrip has made a lack of objects sound quite pleasant (is he suggesting that lack of objects could make me pretty?). But Guntrip goes on to delineate the different ways in which good objects and bad objects are held within the psyche, and this brings us to a critical feature of the Object Harmonic...that at this level of mental representation, the protean and undifferentiated unconscious content associated with archetypal and symbolic levels of mentalization start to be organized in "good" and "bad":

> Good objects are, in the first place, mentally internalized and retained only as memories. They are enjoyed at the time; the experience is satisfying and leaves no problems, it promotes good ego-development, and can later on be looked back to and reflected on with pleasure. In the case of a continuing good object relationship of major importance as with a parent or marriage partner, we have a combination of memories of the happy past and confidence in the continuing possession of the good object in an externally real sense in the present and future. There is no reason here for setting up internalized objects. Objects are only internalized in a more radical way when the relationship turns into a bad-object situation through, say, the object changing or dying. When someone we need and love ceases to love us, or behaves in such a way that we interpret it as cessation of love, or disappears, dies, i.e. deserts us, that person becomes, in an emotional, libidinal sense, a bad object... Then the lost object, now become a bad object, is mentally internalized in a much more vital and fundamental sense than memory. In the language of Bion, bad experiences cannot be digested and absorbed; they are retained as foreign objects which the psyche seeks to project.

> (pp. 21–22)

The "good versus bad" distinction emerges as a distinctive feature of the ways mental representations get coded at the Object level, in a way which was not true in the previous Symbolic Harmonic. This duality is famously articulated through Melanie Klein's (1932) conceptualization of the good breast and bad breast, representing competing experiences of the mother as either nourishing and protective or punishing and abandoning, respectively. To be sure, the fairy tales related by von Franz, Bettelheim, and Joseph Campbell are populated with both heroic and villainous figures; however, at the level of the Archetypal and Symbolic Harmonics, darkness and light remains abstract concepts, which are intrinsic qualities of, and belong to, the narrative fabric of the mythic world. The villains of Tolkien's mythos, such as Sauron or Shelob, are figures of supernatural evil and chthonic horror rather than personal experiences of the observer's own personality. They are experienced as seasons, or conditions of the human experience, rather than *something that happened to us*. Let us pause for a moment to behold Shelob in Tolkien's (1986) singular style:

> There agelong she had dwelt, an evil thing in spider-form, even such as once of old had lived in the Land of the Elves in the West that is now under the Sea, such as Beren fought in the Mountains of Terror in Doriath, and so came to Lothien upon the green sward amid the hemlocks in the moonlight long ago. How Shelob came there, flying from ruin, no tale tells, for out of the Dark Years few tales have come. But still she was there, who was there before Sauron, and before the first stone of Barad-dur; and she served none but herself, drinking the blood of Elves and Men, bloated and grown fat with endless brooding on her feasts, weaving webs of shadow; for all living things were her food, and her vomit darkness. Far and wide her lesser broods, bastards of the miserable mates, her own offspring, that she slew, spread from glen to glen, from the Ephel Duath to the eastern hills, to Dol Guldur and the fastnesses of Mirkwood. But none could rival her, Shelob the Great, last child of Ungoliant to trouble the unhappy world.
>
> (p. 755)

Here, friends and neighbors, we have a true Symbol rather than an Object: a mythic figure of archetypal evil whose eldritch and otherworldly qualities disqualify her as an actual interpersonal experience in the waking world.[1] Shelob is not just "bad" or "dark" but is consummately *evil* in a way that would not, and could not, manifest directly in the everyday world of the material plane of existence. If the Integrated Analytical Model could be said to have a cosmology, that cosmology would suggest that there is a difference between "evil" and "bad" or "dark." Symbols are evil; objects are bad. Guntrip's bad objects belong to the former realm, as phenomena of the Object Harmonic, while Shelob remains a denizen of the Symbolic Harmonic.

Psychological evolution from the Symbolic Harmonic to the Object Harmonic has complex and profound implications for personality development, as we shall explore more in Chapters 9 and 10. The kinds of "mythic fairy tale" level contents of the Symbolic Harmonic represent the kinds of unconscious content that rise to the surface in prominent ways in individuals who are psychotically organized (that is to say, if the contents of the Symbolic Harmonic are never refined, metabolized, or contextualized in a relational way at the Object Harmonic (which happens in attachment, as we shall discuss below). The raw psychic content (that is to say, the thought content, ideation, and perception) that prevails in a psychotically organized personality, therefore, remains mythic and chthonic: their concern is not that they have been abandoned, disappointed, or betrayed, or any such actual transactional interpersonal experience in the real world of objects and the humans they represent; their concern is that they are literally being stalked by Shelob through the shadowed boles of Mirkwood. This distinction between Symbolic and Object Harmonic resonates immediately in the heart of the psychotherapist: is it easier for us to dismiss (or a least, remain comfortably unconcerned at the personal level) about the possibility of being hunted down by Shelob, while the anxieties associated with object representations are more likely to penetrate the defenses of a more securely organized psyche. To put it another way: if my psychotically organized patient tells me that they're being tracked by an alien brain implant, which controls their thoughts, it is relatively easy for me to respond with empathic protective advocacy, and then to go home that evening and never give another thought about alien implants. However, if my patient tells me that they feel I have been acting seductively with them, that will unnerve me, and I will worry about things like professional liability, my vulnerability to ethical complaints, and the sufficiency of my progress notes that evening. From the point of view of a "well-integrated" so-called neurotically organized personality, it is easy to let the symbolic stay symbolic, but object-level representations have a more disturbingly plausible resonance.

A final characteristic of object representations, as published and described by object relations theory, is the developmental scaffolding inherent in the progression from so-called part-objects to whole objects. This scaffolding is generally understood to start with affective responses to basic interactions with objects themselves, to affect connected to the object itself, which represents the transition from being gratified by the breast to loving the mother who has the breast. This transition marks a shift from part-object relations in which an object represents a particular function to whole object relations in which rich and dynamic relationships among peers become possible, thanks to an eventual recognition of the person behind the object. Thus, the dénouement of object relations development leads to the gateway of actual interpersonal attachment, which transcends gratification of desires through object functions. From there, object representations become possible with a broader range of potential recipients of attachment, including abstract concepts (like loyalty to a cause, or love of country).

With the work of John Bowlby (1958) and Mary Ainsworth (1969), object relations theory gradually tilted into attachment theory *per se*. Ainsworth in particular specifically rejected the early psychoanalytic narratives that chalked interpersonal relatedness up to need gratification, pointing to bountiful research evidence that attachment happens independently of the provision of oral supplies, such as Harlow and Zimmermann's (1959) iconic work with rhesus monkeys, which suggested that infant-mother attachment is much more than feeding. Ainsworth (1969) goes so far as to equate attachment with love and to critique social learning perspectives, which would reduce attachment (or love) to chains of reinforced behaviors, asserting instead that intrinsic structures that are biologically coded into individuals represent organizing principles of attachment:

> Throughout both the phylogenetic and the ontogenetic accounts of development, a cardinal biological principle is that development takes place through transformations of structures already present, rather than through a process of accretion or replacement, and that these transformations take place through continuous organism-environment interaction. To me, therefore, the emphasis placed by the social learning theorists upon environmental control seems excessive, and their relative neglect of intra-organismic states and structural organizations seems a fault.
>
> (p. 41)

Object relations, therefore, has remained a consistent foundational theme in psychoanalytic models ranging from drive theory to contemporary perspectives on attachment, and an important through-line of this foundational theme remains the presence of object representations as dynamic organizers of interpersonal experience.

The Object Harmonic is therefore the crucible of attachment representing the level of mental representation at which affective responses to relational and interpersonal experiences are invested into internalized working models of actual sentient beings who exist outside the self, in the form of other people. Therefore, as we shall explore in Chapter 10, disturbances or trauma that impair or subvert the process of attachment early in life will show up at this level, disrupting the natural progression towards object wholeness and complex, reality-based representations of other people. The Integrated Analytical Model would predict that the emergence of reliable and functional mental representations at the Object Level is the most important outcome of attachment. The psychic scaffolding up out of the Symbolic Harmonic into the Object Harmonic and beyond, therefore, also marks the tipping point from clinical presentations dominated by annihilation anxiety to presentations marked primarily by abandonment anxiety (see Chapter 10), and by extension, from psychotic organizations to borderline states.

Note

1 Or so it is to be hoped....

References

Ainsworth, M. D. S. (1969). Object relations, dependency, and attachment: A theoretical review of the infact-mother relationships. *Child Development, 40*: 969–1025.

Bowlby, J. (1958). The nature of the child's tie to his mother. *International Journal of Psycho-Analysis, 39*: 350–373.

Freud, S. (1915). Instincts and their vicissitudes. In J. Strachey (Ed.), *The standard edition of the complete psychological works of Sigmund Freud* (pp. 109–140). The Hogarth Press.

Greenberg, J. R., & Mitchell, S. A. (1983). *Object relations in psychoanalytic theory.* Harvard University Press.

Guntrip, H. (1969). *Schizoid phenomena, object-relations and the self.* International Universities Press.

Harlow, H. F., & Zimmermann, R. R. (1959). Affectional responses in the infant monkey. *Science, 130*: 421–432.

Isaacs, S. (1952). The nature and function of phantasy. In J. Riviere (Ed.), *Developments in psychoanalysis* (pp. 62–121). Hogarth Press.

Klein, M. (1932). *The psycho-analysis of children.* Hogarth Press.

Ogden, T. H. (2011). Reading Susan Isaacs: Toward a radically revised theory of thinking. *International Journal of Psychoanalysis, 92*(4): 925–942.

Tolkien, J. R. R. (1986). *The two towers.* George Allen & Unwin.

Chapter 5

The Fourth Harmonic

Complex

[…]for hope is always born at the same time as love…

—Miguel de Cervantes
Don Quixote de la Mancha

Ascending into the fourth harmonic, the domain of the complex necessitates that we zigzag back into Jungian theory. Jungian theory generally defines the complex as an emotionally charged group of ideas or images, organized around an archetypal theme and functioning autonomously within the psyche. In this sense, a complex is a constellation of activated mental representations that orbit an affective center of gravity like planets orbiting a star. Jung himself (2014b) characterized the complex as "the image of a certain psychic situation which is strongly accentuated emotionally and is, moreover, incompatible with the habitual attitude of consciousness" (p. 100) and as "objects of inner experience" (p. 97). Jung assumed that the etiology of complexes lies in some powerful affective experience which resulted in the splitting of some aspect of the psyche, and his understanding of the concept was strongly influenced by his experience with word association tests. He attached such importance to the concept that he claimed that complexes, and not dreams as Freud had said, represent the royal road to the unconscious. Freud also developed a comparable conceptualization of the complex (as did Bleuler before him), but cast them as inevitably pathological, while Jung saw the complexes as necessary to the healthy functioning of the personality and not necessarily pathological. In fact, Jung (2014a) seems to have regarded complexes as creative wellsprings inspiring works of art.

It is an interesting footnote of the history of psychodynamic psychology that Freud's singular foray into the world of complexes (or archetypes, for that matter) was one of his most enduring models: the Oedipus Complex, which remains one of the most powerful and influential organizing principles within psychoanalytic theory. In fact, Jung considered the Oedipus Complex to contain a sort of archetype, and for Jung, this seems to have been one of the first, if not *the* first, archetypes that Jung discussed in his sprawling body of work. Furthermore, Jung (1987) criticized Freud for acknowledging only the archetype of the Oedipus Complex and stopping

DOI: 10.4324/9781032708751-7

there: "[The Oedipus Complex] is what I call an archetype. It was the first arche-type Freud discovered, the first and only one. He thought this was the archetype. Of course, there are many such archetypes" (p. 289). While Freud became scornful over Jung's idea of archetypes and didn't make much use of the term "complex" after the Oedipus Complex, Jung made this level of mental representation a centerpiece of his model.

For our purposes of taxonomizing the various levels of mental representation, it appears significant that Jung (2014b) regarded the complexes as "splinter psy-ches," and associated them with traumatic experiences:

> The aetiology of their origin is frequently as so-called trauma, an emotional shock or some such thing, that splits off a bit of the psyche. Certainly one of the commonest causes is a moral conflict, which ultimately derives from the ap-parent impossibility of affirming the whole of one's nature. This impossibility presupposes a direct split, no matter whether the conscious mind is aware of it or not. As a rule there is a marked unconsciousness of any complexes, and this naturally guarantees them all the more freedom of action. In such cases their powers of assimilation become especially pronounced, since unconsciousness helps the complex to assimilate even the ego, the result being a momentary and unconscious alteration of personality known as identification with the complex.
>
> (p. 98)

Interestingly, Jung defined the "ego" as itself a complex; just another fragment of the personality that has for developmental-historic reasons assumed some kind of administrative power over the other complexes. Jung delineated three essen-tial characteristics of the complex: (1) inner coherence, (2) autonomy, and (3) dissociability.

In describing the complexes as having *inner coherence*, Jung draws attention to the complementarity of the complex's "central image" and its corresponding affective valence. The complex, Jung claims, appears to stand for something; it ap-pears to have purpose. Indeed, the intentions of the complex usually seem to lie at cross-purposes to that of the ego-complex and the conscious mind. For this reason, Jung compared them to the "gremlins" of European folklore (and now American cinematic folklore), who sneak their way into the inner workings of the mind in order to wreak havoc there.

Jung (2014b) colorfully describes the *autonomy* of the complexes in the follow-ing passage:

> Complexes behave like Descartes' devils and seem to delight in playing impish tricks. The slip just the wrong word into one's mouth, they make one forget the name of the person one is about to introduce, they cause a tickle in the throat just when the softest passage is being played on the piano at a concert, they make the tiptoeing latecomer trip over a chair with a resounding crash.
>
> (p. 97)

These metaphorical paraphrases are all by way of describing a rather intractable "splinter psyche" which ends up generally in opposition to the properly socialized conscious attitudes. Jacobi (1974) describes the complexes in a similar "anthropogenic" fashion:

> Some rest peacefully, embedded in the general fabric of the unconscious, and scarcely make themselves noticed; others behave as real disturbers of the psychic economy; still others have already made their way into consciousness, but resist its influence and remain more or less a law unto themselves.
>
> (p. 10)

Jung himself credited Pierre Janet with describing the *dissociability* of the complexes and believed that complexes were analogous to split-off, "fragmentary" personalities. This quality of dissociability lends the complexes a sort of alien, or ego-dystonic, feel, which prompts the mind to react with "apotropaic" thinking: the personality seeks to assimilate the inner disturbance by denying its independence. In describing the apotropaic tendencies of the mind, Jung (2014b) states "Consciousness behaves like some one who hears a suspicious noise in the attic and thereupon dashes down into the cellar in order to assure himself that no burglar has broken in…in reality, he has simply not dared to go up into the attic" (para. 206). The underlying motive for this kind of intrapsychic behavior, Jung claims, is to make anything unpleasant as unreal as possible: the essence of dissociation, or ultimately, cognitive distortion.

   Jolande Jacobi (1974) arguably moved somewhat beyond Jung's original conceptualizations in further defining and exploring the anatomy of the complex itself. The complex, she argues, is composed of a cluster of memories organized around a particular feeling tone, rather like the spiral arms of a galaxy organized around a nucleus. She defines this feeling tone as the "nuclear element" of the complex which serves as a sort of vehicle of meaning. According to the properties of internal coherence discussed above, particular memories and associations have been drawn to the affective nucleus of the complex; these associations are derived partly from personal disposition and partly from experiences *conditioned by the environment.* I emphasize this latter characteristic because it presages the usefulness of the complex construct in relating Jung's archetypal psychology to cognitive schema theory. Comparisons between complexes and cognitive schema, however, are immediately apparent and will be explored further in Chapter 6.

Cultural Complexes

It appears that Joseph Henderson of the CG Jung Institute of San Francisco was one of the first Jungian scholars to propose elaborating the complex into the level of cultural consciousness, suggesting that complexes act as organizing principles at the level of cultural consciousness in a similar way that they do within an individual psyche. Singer and Kimbles (2004) picked up the theme decades later, on the leading edge of what has become a rich dialog on the subject. Singer and Kaplinsky (2010) note that the Jungian community was culturally resistant to the idea of cultural consciousness and cultural complexes for some time, and that as often seems to happen, a collective willingness to critique entrenched and unspoken narratives paved the way for this new direction:

> Perhaps the willingness of a younger generation of Jungians over the last decade and a half to address more openly the highly charged issues surrounding Jung's attitude to Jews has freed up a considerable store of bound-up energy from a Jungian cultural complex. Now we can once again, more openly, explore the implication of Jung's psychology in relation to the group or collective psyche.
>
> (p. 23)

In recapitulating the foundational work of Thomas Singer and Samuel Kimbles on the cultural complex, Carmen Lívia G. Parise and Guilherme Scandiucci (2022) write:

> Such complexes would emerge from the cultural unconscious, a layer that is in relationship, simultaneously, with both the archetypal layer and with the personal layer of the psyche, and also with the shared external world. They are formed through repetitive and historical group experiences that are rooted in the cultural unconscious and take the collective psyche of the group or the individual or collective psyche of the individual autonomously, and may even use quite irrational forces in the name of their logic.
>
> (p. 60)

Such narratives open up lines of inquiry about the differential experiences of people of color and other populations that have been marginalized as "other" by unspoken underground rules of whiteness, the dominant cultural theme in the West of the world. In this sense, the study of cultural complexes from a Jungian and post-Jungian point of view resembles the methods and focus of critical theory, a sociological perspective that reveals and critiques power structures, describing and challenging hidden assumptions that perpetuate oppressive systems designed to protect some groups at the expense of others, maintaining a power structure, especially along lines of gender, race, and other categories of human difference. James Hillman (1986) provided vivid commentary on the cultural complexes of American culture in particular, stating that *innocence* is "*the* theme of the American psyche," which Hillman defined in terms of "not knowing life's darkness and not wanting to know, either" (p. 133). Similarly, Fanny Brewster (2019) explores the cultural complex underlying blackness and whiteness, elaborating on the shadow aspects of whiteness such as white privilege and white fury which exert profound cultural hegemony, generated and reinforced through multigenerational trauma.

Singer and Kaplinsky (2010) outline several characteristics of the complex, at the individual and cultural levels:

1. They express themselves in powerful moods and repetitive behaviors. Highly charged emotional or affective reactivity is their calling card. 2. They resist our most heroic efforts to make them conscious and remain, for the most part, unconscious. 3. They accumulate experiences that validate their point of view and create a store-house of self-affirming ancestral memories. 4. Personal and cultural complexes function in an involuntary, autonomous fashion and tend to affirm a simplistic point of view that replaces everyday ambiguity and uncertainty with fixed, often self-righteous, attitudes to the world. 5. In addition, personal and cultural complexes both have archetypal cores; that is, they express typically human attitudes and are rooted in primordial ideas about what is meaningful, making them very hard to resist, reflect upon, and discriminate.

(p. 30)

The Location of Complexes in the Harmonic Trajectory

So far, we have ranged freely among three related models of mental representation: the archetype, the symbol, the object, and the complex. We have seen that different people mean different things by these terms at different times, but we have also started to see the glimmerings of a broader pattern: gossamer, abstract, difficult to glimpse, but arresting and persistent in its understated suggestiveness. We begin to see a relationship among a series of hypothetical unconscious organizing principles, ranging from the most inchoate and dynamic (the archetype) to the more organized and "visible" in its effects on conscious life (the complex), with intermediate organizing principles (symbol and object) which seems to represent a transitional step between one and the other. We are gradually building up to a peculiar "trajectory" for psychological themes, ranging from the crucible of their creation within the world of archetypes and evolving into more complex and differentiated themes.

I have placed the Complex Harmonic in the fourth position, between the Object Harmonic and the Schema Harmonic, because complexes appear to occupy a kind of theoretical middle ground between those two other levels of mental representation; furthermore, the complex seems to occupy a dynamic range that leads from one to the other.

In the first place, the Jungian idea of the complex, insofar as it represents a level of mental representation organized around a strong affective valence, and comprises a range of heterogenous associations and components (associations with people, ideas, memories, sensations, etc.), might seem to represent the epiphenomenon of constellated object representations organized around a common emotional theme that holds them together thematically. That is to say, if the archetype and its symbolic representations can be metaphorized as stars, then object representations are planets orbiting that star in a solar system, and complexes are galaxies made up of many solar systems, each astronomical level a fractal representation of the other with their own centers of gravity. The complex therefore emerges as a dynamic system made up of object representations linked by affective themes.

At the same time, complexes seem to occupy a level of psychological mentalization which although resistant to conscious awareness, are more readily perceived in their aggregate effects upon behavior (whether it is the behavior of an individual or a culture), suggesting that complexes represent a relatively "higher" level of mentalization which is relatively closer to conscious awareness and representation.

Furthermore, the Jungian consensus that complexes represent psychic shards of consciousness that have been split off by conflict or trauma suggests that they are "located" closer to the level of direct influence on human motivation and behavior, providing further evidence for their position as higher-order mental representations than the object or symbol level. The Jungian consensus is that complexes manifest in behavior in more direct, observable ways than we would assume of object representations, which as we discussed in Chapter 4 represent very primal levels of psychological organization. In fact, as mentioned above, Jung used measurable human behavior in response to word association tests to gauge the presence of complexes by extended reaction times (measured in fifths of a second).

Jung's depiction of complexes as "splinter personalities" or "partial personalities" similarly suggests that complexes represent superordinate, composite mental representations that can readily be identified as primary storylines, themes, and organizing principles, which make up the larger personality. The fact that a wide range of voices within Jungian psychotherapy have articulated ways in which complexes readily show up at the cultural level similarly suggests that complexes are a quantum level removed from the kinds of mental representation that emerge from discrete, somatic units of attachment experience at the object harmonic.

References

Brewster, F. (2019). *The racial complex: A Jungian perspective on culture and race.* Routledge.

Hillman, J. (1986). Notes on white supremacy: Essaying an archetypal account of historical events. *Spring Journal, 46*, 29–58.

Jacobi, J. (1974). *Complex/Archetype/Symbol in the psychology of C.G. Jung.* Princeton University Press.

Jung, C. G. (1987). The Houston films. In G. McGuire & R. F. C. Hull (Eds.), *C.G. Jung Speaking* (pp. 276–352). Princeton University Press.

Jung, C. G. (2014a). *Spirit in man, art, and literature* (R. F. C. Hull, Trans.). Princeton University Press.

Jung, C. G. (2014b). *The structure and dynamics of the psyche* (R. F. C. Hull, Trans.). Princeton University Press.

Parise, C. L. G., & Scandiucci, G. (2022). From the narcissistic pact of whiteness to co-responsibility: A look at the racial cultural complex. *Junguiana, 40*(3): 53–66.

Singer, T., & Kaplinsky, C. (2010). Cultural complexes in analysis. In M. Stein (Ed.), *Jungian psychoanalysis: Working in the spirit of C.G. Jung* (pp. 22–37). Open Court.

Singer, T., & Kimbles, S. (2004). *The cultural complex: Contemporary Jungian perspectives on psyche and society.* Routledge.

Chapter 6

The Fifth Harmonic

Schema

Anxiety is the dizziness of Freedom.

—Soren Kierkegaard, *The Concept of Anxiety*

We are close now, close to breaking the surface of the water, from our origin in the depths. Approaching the strata of the fifth harmonic, we encounter levels of mental representation that are more directly observable and testable, and which are dialectically closer to the realm of consciously motivated behavior. As we do so, we enter territory more comfortable and familiar to mainstream, so-called "evidence-based" treatment models which thrive on factors of human motivation and behavior that can reliably be quantified and measured, such as cognitive-behavioral psychotherapy (CBT). CBT has long been the darling of American psychology in particular, and especially in research psychology and applied psychology in the public sector.

Cognitive-behavioral psychology and other "evidence-based" models readily lend themselves to manualized approaches to clinical intervention, which provide specific algorithmic treatment recommendations which theoretically inform the clinician about what's going to be effective with a given client. Because higher-order levels of mental representation, such as the so-called schemas as operationalized in cognitive-behavioral models, are more readily measurable in the context of randomized controlled trials, the kinds of psychotherapeutic models that get funded and replicated by research psychology, in public mental health systems, and at state universities tend to focus on those levels. In other words, the psychological research scientist tends to ignore the levels of mental representation below the fifth harmonic.

Historically, CBT grew out of the unapologetically reductionist worldview of applied behavior analysis, which applies operant conditioning and learning theory to empirical behavior change. Behavior modification perspectives were expanded and elaborated over time by cognitive therapy perspectives, which went "deeper" than behavior analysis in focusing on changing systems of cognition and perception that manifest as behavior. The hard line of Skinnerian behaviorism was thus tempered somewhat through the influence of cognitive theorists, probably beginning

DOI: 10.4324/9781032708751-8

with Aaron Beck. Beck himself (Beck & Weishaar, 1995) describes cognitive psychology as:

> A collaborative process of empirical investigation, reality testing, and problem solving between therapist and patient. The patient's maladaptive interpretations and conclusions are treated as testable hypotheses. Behavioral experiments and verbal procedures are used to examine alternative interpretations and to generate contradictory evidence that supports a more adaptive beliefs and leads to therapeutic change.
>
> (p. 229)

From this point of view, the therapist tries to expose the patient's faulty belief systems and correct them using "contradictory evidence," something like a lawyer in a courtroom. Cognitive-behavioral therapy is pre-eminently about perception, ideation, and thinking; it assumes that people employ *systematic bias in processing information*. For example, depressed persons interpret reality in ways that foster a negative view of self, the world, and the future (Beck et al., 1987). Panic attacks result from catastrophic misinterpretation of certain somatic experiences like breathlessness (Clark, 1986). In other words, CBT assumes that distortions in ideation, perception, and mediation are often faulty and can be corrected.

The family of CBT-based models share some common perspectives, which set them apart from the psychodynamic models we have discussed so far (Thase et al., 2023): they depict psychotherapy as intrinsically about psychoeducation (rather than an attachment experience), they limit their scope of inquiry to psychological constructs which can be effectively measured (rather than indulging in rationalism or metaphysics), they are typically manualized (rather than open-ended and nondirective experiences of co-created reverie), and they view themselves as products of empirical research (rather than elaborations of certain philosophical, humanistic, or rationalist perspectives). A core feature of psychotherapy from a CBT perspective is characterized by the "downward arrow technique" (Burns, 1990), a systematic method of uncovering core beliefs that generate perception and therefore behavior.

Mental Representations in the Cognitive-Behavioral Paradigm: The Schemas

Traditionally, cognitive theory has articulated three "levels" of cognitive phenomena: *automatic thoughts*, *cognitive distortions*, and *schemas* (occasionally named in the literature as "schemata").

Automatic thoughts represent a "higher order" level of cognition that can be consciously identified fairly readily, and their mediation of several personality variables has been empirically demonstrated (see Kopala-Sibley & Santor, 2009). They represent immediate, spontaneous cognitive leaps that suggest a tendency to interpret reality in particular ways. In this sense, automatic thoughts can be taken as epiphenomena of the more deeply rooted schemas. Cognitive theory assumes that schemas have activation thresholds that trigger automatic thoughts; these activation thresholds may be particularly low in individuals identified with mental illness. Commonly cited examples of automatic thoughts are the readiness with which depressed persons interpret events in such a way as to interpret situations as hopeless or themselves as helpless, whereas people with prominent anxiety tend to evidence automatic thoughts concerned with dangers and threats.

Cognitive distortions constitute the epistemological interface between automatic thoughts and the cognitive schemas that underlie them. Consistent with the information-processing model so central to cognitive theory, cognitive distortions were defined by Robins and Hayes (1995) this way:

> Cognitive distortions are links between dysfunctional schemata and automatic thoughts. When new information or memories are cognitively processed, the information often is distorted or biased to fit a relevant schema. The result of this biased appraisal may then become accessible to consciousness in the form of automatic thoughts or images.
>
> (p. 43)

The earliest conceptualizations of schemas as mental representations come from Pierre Janet (see van der Kolk & van der Hart, 1989), who depicted "fixed ideas" as moderated by memory processes that acted as mental organizing systems, setting us up for our coming conversations in this book about complexes and cognitive schemas that represent "neighboring" representational harmonics. From Janet's point of view, when schemas function smoothly and optimally, they would incorporate new information into existing cognitive structures resulting in mental order and organization. In a manner which quite resembles the Kleinian concept of phantasy discussed in Chapter 4, Janet's model suggested that "by combining cognition, conation, and emotion with action, psychological automatisms represent rudimentary elements of consciousness that are both psychologically and biologically encoded" (van der Kolk & van der Hart, 1989, p. 1531). An important outcome of Janet's early thoughts was one of the first applied conceptualizations of trauma: so-called "subconscious fixed ideas" represented memories of traumatic events that continue to organize memory, affect, and somatic experience in ways that elude conscious experience and are therefore resistant to modification or adaptation. One of the outcomes of trauma, therefore, will be a kind of attachment to an unconsciously encoded mentalization of the traumatic event at the expense of new ways of experiencing reality. This line of thinking resembles Freudian and object relations-based perspectives about attachment to bad objects.

Piaget (1962) articulated a similar model of psychological response to trauma through his notions of accommodation and assimilation, theorizing that psychic trauma involves unusual events with a strong affective valence that cannot be readily assimilated into the existing schema structures. Therefore, trauma results when events and circumstances collide with deeply held assumptions and worldviews. Piaget further investigated some of the psychological functions that parallel information processing later ascribed to the schemas.

If we understand automatic thoughts as the surface-level ideational phenomenon, and cognitive distortions as the mid-level processing biases which generate them, then the cognitive schemas represent the generative engines of the entire system. Aaron Beck (1967) defined a schema as "a structure for screening, coding, and evaluating the stimuli that impinge upon an organism... On the basis of the matrix of schemas, the individual is able to orient himself in relation to time and space and to categorize and interpret experiences in a meaningful way" (p. 419). Within cognitive-behavioral theory, schemas are assumed to be "working models" comprised of thematically related belief systems, which are assembled during the course of life experience. Some specific models underline early formative experience in the formation of schemas, but the practice of cognitive-oriented psychotherapy depends on the presumption that they may be modified at any time during life (otherwise cognitive therapy wouldn't work). The schema owes its integrity to the processing biases which they generate, which help to ensure that in the midst of everyday interpersonal experience, data that most closely fits the schema will be "encoded" most quickly and efficiently.

Jeff Young et al. (2003) added to this paradigm a model of "deeper" cognitive representation, which may be considered a "fourth" level, termed *early maladaptive schemas*. Young defines these "deep" schemas as pervasive themes regarding oneself and one's relationship with others, which are developed during childhood and elaborated across the lifespan, and which are dysfunctional to a significant degree. According to Young's formulation, early schemas develop in the midst of painful experiences with parents, siblings, and peers during childhood and develop as children attempt to make sense of their experiences and avoid further pain. Young's conceptions of the early maladaptive schemas have received empirical support. Schmidt et al. (1995) identified orthogonal factors corresponding to early maladaptive schemas (EMS), which are supposed to rest "at the core of the individual's self concept" but which "[prevent] realistic processing of schema-inconsistent information" (p. 296).

The research on schema-focused clinical intervention has developed to the point that there is a robust literature describing psychotherapeutic treatment of personality disorder from this perspective (Jacob & Arntz, 2013), including evidence of efficacy with severe personality disorder (Bernstein et al., 2023). This apparent clinical utility in conceptualizing personality disorder is enriched by the expending library of *schema modes* that are being described in the context of this model, including blended modes that represent overlapping categories of this level of mental representation. For example, Simpson and Smith (2020) describe a so-called "Helpless Surrenderer" mode, which "can manifest with different 'flavors,' e.g., aggrieved, passive-aggressive, histrionic (theatrical, 'flouncy'), sullen ('teenager'), entitled, hopeless, negative, or complaining, under a façade of deference or submissiveness" (p. 47).

The present state of cognitive schema theory has thus arrived at a sort of layered, hierarchical model, with four main "tiers" of cognitive functioning:

1 Automatic thoughts
2 Underlying assumptions
3 Cognitive schemas
4 Early maladaptive schemas

The four tiers represent cognitive elaboration of increasing complexity and per-
vasiveness, ranging from particular thought associations which could be easily
identified by an alert observer to deeply ingrained, personality-like traits that are
only observable in the context of long-term behavior patterns, especially within the
context of interpersonal relationships. Taken together, these four levels of representation likely represent various strata of the schema harmonic, phasing at some point
into the complex harmonic just below.

The Constructivists

Young seems to suggest that his early maladaptive schemas are somehow more
"orthogonal" than the traditional conceptualization of the schema. Yet in another
sense, the entire enterprise of plunging the depths for "deeper and deeper" schemas
appears to merely push the associationist envelope, as it continues to leave unan-
swered the question of any inherent structure (if any) upon which the intricate su-
perstructure of cognitive schemas may be erected. CBT theory presumes the *tabula
rasa* and assumes that people are born as essentially blank slates ready to be filled
up with learned associations. Guidano (1995) assesses the situation as follows:

> While allowing for the description, analysis, and modification of isolated be-
> liefs, internal dialogues, and distortions of thought, [the cognitive-behavioral
> approach] left unsolved the most basic problem for the foundation of an applied
> cognitive psychology, namely, the development and organization of human
> knowledge…In the face of such problems, it seems unreasonable to continue
> attempts to extend the range of applicability of the associationist-behaviorist
> paradigm.
>
> (p. 89)

Enter the constructivists, who comprise a sort of "post-modern" movement within
the cognitive school. Growing out of the literatures of evolutionary epistemology,
constructivism seeks to shift focus away from the traditional analysis of beliefs
and perceptions and back to the individual's own activity as the basic mediator of
experience. I say "back" here because it seems as if this development may represent a rapprochement with more dynamic, including analytical, approaches: the
constructivists presume that individual organisms actively explore their environments and organize experience around pro-active, creative, and, significantly, tacit
expectations, hypotheses, and theories. The term *constructivism* itself implies
"form-giving," which in turn suggests that the individual becomes the architect of
her experiences and the world models she bases on them; this conceptualization

significantly differs from the passive receptacle described by the traditional associationist paradigm. Constructivism may represent an attempt to fulfill Piaget's incomplete attempts to divine underlying mechanisms for the categorization of experience. Mahoney, Miller, and Arciero (1995) outline three essential features of the constructivist approach: the proactive nature of the cognitive process, nuclear morphogenic structure, and self-organizing development.

Constructive theory invokes the proactive nature of the cognitive process in arguing that the individual constructs reality not merely on the basis of data supplied by the five senses, but "*in formare*, that which is formed from within" (Mahoney et al. 1995, p. 105). Mahoney et al. (1995) go on to note that radical constructivism goes so far as to assume that "all experienced order is self-generated and organismically recursive" (p. 105). Describing all experienced order as "self-generated" and "recursive" may be a stretch in the context of cognitive-behavioral paradigm, but approaches the central assumptions of Jung's analytical theory of archetypes. Clearly then, what makes for radicalism in one model would qualify for old-school traditionalism in another! Once again, the constructivists seem to be "circling back" toward nativism, which is far from a radical new, maverick hypothesis but rather the long-standing other side of the equation long since neglected by traditional associationists in the cognitive-behavioral school.

Another very significant aspect of the proposed proactive nature of cognitive processes challenges the associationist tradition of objectivism: cognitive-behaviorist theory presumes that there must be an objective veracity to interpersonal reality against which the various schemas may be assessed in order to determine their relative degree of "reality distortion." This assumption underlying CBT has historically tied its philosophy of psychotherapy to the idea of *consensual reality*, which becomes enshrined as the ultimate standard for perception and behavior. Constructivism, in high post-modernist style, argues that since there is no "objective reality," it doesn't make sense to talk about "distortions" of reality. There are no cognitive distortions, just more or less viable hypotheses.

A primary theme emerging from the cognitive implications of constructivism is the theme of cognitive control: the capacity to effectively manage cognitive processing, anticipate outcomes, access memory, and regulate thoughts and behavior "in accordance with internally represented behavioral goals" (Braver, 2012, p. 106). Recent research has suggested that underlying mechanisms of cognitive control include both proactive and reactive cognitive control, which reflects the capacity to invoke and sustain goal-specific information in order to cope with a cognitive challenge, and the capacity to invoke transient cognitive control in response to a cognitive challenge that has already occurred. These two mechanisms both seem to recruit different areas of the prefrontal cortex and seem to contribute to optimal organization of attention, perception, and behavior.

Mahoney (1995) describes a second constructivist principle called "nuclear morphogenic structure" (also called "core ordering processes" elsewhere in the related literature) reflecting hierarchies of neural networks that mediate information processing systems. This construct implies a central core of processes which are protected from undue change from without, and which in turn limit the flexibility of the peripheral assumptions associated with them. This theoretical construct bears uncanny resemblance to the "complexes" described by both Freud and Jung, although they are perhaps closer to Jung's conceptualization since the constructivists assume that such nuclear structures are essential to the ideological survival of the individual. Indeed, Mahoney acknowledged increasing convergence toward psychoanalytic thinking with ill-concealed distaste:

> Because the mere mention of the term unconscious may evoke associations with psychoanalysis, it is worth noting the…distinction between Freud's intended meaning and [our own].
>
> (p. 108)

The authors go on to distance themselves safely from psychoanalytic thinking by asserting that the psychological processes they have in mind are not sub-conscious but rather *super-conscious*. It is precisely this sort of "epistemological prejudice" that encourages isolation among otherwise rich and productive schools of thought, and the very same prejudice has limited the usefulness and richness of the cognitive behavioral school because it has deprived the model of access to the very wellspring of human nature: a deep, inherited unconscious as described by both Jung and Freud.

The third proposed aspect of constructivist conceptualization involves self-organizing development of the personality. Guidano (1987) describes the idea this way:

> The essential feature of this perspective considers the self-organizing ability of a human knowing system as a basic evolutionary constraint.…The availability of this stable and structured self-identity permits continuous and coherent self-perception and self-evaluation in the face of temporal becoming and mutable reality.
>
> (p. 3)

The interpersonal, or social, context is increasingly a focus of theoretical concern among many cognitive schools, and this trend is mirrored within the psychodynamic school as well (see below). Recent studies have sought to examine the role of schemas or otherwise-named perceptual styles in social categorization, clearly an area of some importance. Quite apart from theoretical schemes designed to locate cognitive structures within a hierarchy, recent work has attempted to investigate orthogonal factors determining interpersonal and social behavior via schemas and related constructs. Such cognitive mediators have included affective motivation of behavior (Chiew & Braver, 2014), the role of belief updating in stress-related responses characteristic of Post-traumatic stress disorder (PTSD) (Linson et al., 2020), individual sensemaking (Harris, 1994), social categorization (Moskowitz, 1993), and many others.

The research literature inspired by constructivist theory has formed the basis for an empirically derived form of psychotherapy called coherence therapy (Chamberlain, 2023). This psychotherapeutic perspective assumes that new (contradictory) perspectives drive reconsolidation of memories, leading to reduction of symptoms, and is predicated on a therapeutic goal of "representational redescription":

> AIMCT posits that memory control bias against recall and reexperiencing of the associated physiological state, is a common cause of impaired inference that precludes representational redescription, experience of agency and contextual embedding. Policy selection in the moment of a childhood, emotionally urgent situation is unavailable for revision and optimization.
>
> (p. 9)

The expansion of constructivist theory into cascading levels of mental representation leading all the way to cortical function has resulted in a range of mental representations that overlap with several of the harmonic levels described by the Integrated Analytical Model. For example, Bazan (2011) draws upon both Freudian and Lacanian models of mental representation into a constructivist perspective in which language fragments (*material phoneme vectors*) seated in lexical brain areas mediate mental representation, which "always has an ambiguous structure, transiently and unconsciously activating its different meanings, followed by inhibition of the contextually inappropriate meanings" (p. 113), resulting in what Freud described as repression, and what we may more broadly classify as unconscious defensive operations in psychoanalytic language. Furthermore, despite the apparent reservations of some of its early proponents, constructivist theory has recently been evolving in an integrative direction with psychoanalytic theory more broadly, forming the basis for so-called neuropsychoanalysis (Solms & Turnbull, 2011).

Archetype to Schema: The Story So Far

Cognitive schema theory is remarkable and useful in its ready compatibility with neuroscience, developmental neuroanatomy, and biologically based theories of learning. In addition, it almost certainly owes part of its wide acceptance to the fact that cognitive theory generates scientific hypotheses more or less amenable to traditional experimentation under laboratory conditions. Generally, it is similar to related constructs described in the more psychodynamic schools, but as has been stated above, schemas are necessarily generated through interpersonal experience and do not represent "nativist" or "endogenous" factors, although some theorists have suggested that schemas may interact with such factors.

Hierarchical schema theory in particular approaches archetypal theory in further reducing cognitive schema to its most basic ingredients; however, the theory stops short of approaching inherent unconscious determinants of schemas because it is built within a cognitive-behavioral framework which assumes that behavior and experience are learned. Constructivism takes the argument a quantum leap forward by directly addressing sub-conscious (or "hyper-conscious" as it seems to be preferred) mechanisms for the generation of meaning.

Although cognitive schema theory at its "deepest" appears to approach the characterological/constitutional emphasis of the psychodynamic models, the former theoretical paradigm stops short of reaching characterological (in the psychodynamic sense) ground due to its emphasis on social learning. For example, Harris (1994) seeks to redress the apparent "neglect of the individual-level dynamics of organizational culture" by focusing on culture's manifestation in individual's "sensemaking structures and processes" (p. 318). The author concludes that individuals make sense of their experiences based on a "contrived mental dialog between themselves and other contextually relevant individuals of groups" (p. 318). This study may be taken as representative of cognitive schema research in general through its various assumptions and conclusions, which cluster closely among contextual grounds: neglect of individual dynamics is addressed by assessing how social vectors may influence the individual. Such theoretical postulates may be clearly seen as descending from the cognitive and behavioral roots that went before them, and one is reminded of Piaget's ducks imprinting on their unlikely human mother figure.

Constructivist perspectives, however, have been moving away from social learning models back toward an emphasis on the native properties of the brain and its methods of encoding reality at the cognitive level. This shift is consummated in the emergence of a theoretical perspective known as the Bayesian Brain Hypothesis (see Hipólito & Kirchhoff, 2023), which suggests that the neuronal organization of the central nervous system results in inferential sense-making comprised of competing mental representations. The Bayesian Brain Hypothesis provides a useful context for understanding the cognitive complexity that arises from cascading mental representations resulting in inside-to-outside hypothesis testing, depicting the brain as primarily an organ of inference that draws upon competing mental representations. Because this perspective provides a useful neurocognitive model for the integration of different levels of mental representation, we will continue to explore the implications of this model ahead in Chapter 9.

References

Bazan, A. (2011). Phantoms in the voice: A neuropsychoanalytic hypothesis on the structure of the unconscious. *Neuropsychoanalysis, 13*: 161–176.

Beck, A. T. (1967). *Depression: Clinical, experimental, and theoretical aspects.* Harper and Row.

Beck, A. T., Rush, A. J., Shaw, B. F., & Emery, G. (1987). *Cognitive therapy of depression.* Guilford Press.

Beck, A. T., & Weishaar, M. E. (1995). Cognitive therapy. In R. J. Corsini & D. Wedding (Eds.), *Current psychotherapies* (pp. 229–261). F.E. Peacock Publishers.

Bernstein, D. P., Keulen-de Vos, M., Clercx, M., de Vogel, V., Kersten, G. C. M., Lancel, M., Jonkers, P. P., Bogaerts, S., Slaats, M., Broers, N. J., Deenen, T. A. M., & Arntz, A. (2023). Schema therapy for violent PD offenders: A randomized clinical trial. *Psychological Medicine, 53*(1): 88–102.

Braver, T. S. (2012). The variable nature of cognitive control: A dual mechanisms framework. *Trends in Cognitive Science, 16*(2): 106–113.

Burns, D. (1990). *The feeling good handbook.* Plume.

Chamberlain, D. E., (2023). The active inference model of coherence therapy. *Frontiers in Human Neuroscience, 16*: 1–12.

Chiew, K. S., & Braver, T. S. (2014). Dissociable influences of reward motivation and positive emotion on cognitive control. *Cognitive, Affective, and Behavioral Neuroscience, 4*(2): 509–529.

Clark, D. M. (1986). A cognitive approach to panic. *Behaviour Research and Therapy, 24*(4): 461–470.

Guidano, V. F. (1987). *Complexity of the self: A developmental approach to psychopathology and therapy.* Guilford.

Guidano, V. F. (1995). A constructivist outline of human knowing processes. In M. J. Mahoney (Ed.), *Cognitive and constructive psychotherapies* (pp. 89–201). Springer Publishing Company.

Harris, S. G. (1994). Organizational culture and individual sensemaking: A schema-based perspective. *Organization Science, 5*(3): 309–321.

Hipólito, I., & Kirchhoff, M. (2023). Breaking boundaries: The Bayesian Brain Hypothesis for perception and prediction. *Consciousness and Cognition, 111*(3): 1–8.

Jacob, G., & Arntz, A. (2013). Schema therapy for personality disorders: A review. *International Journal of Cognitive Therapy, 6*: 171–185.

Kopala-Sibley, D. C., & Santor, S. A., (2009). The mediating role of automatic thoughts in the personality–event–affect relationship. *Cognitive Behaviour Therapy, 38*(3): 1651–2316.

Linson, A., Parr, T., & Friston, K. J. (2020). Active inference, stressors, and psychological trauma: A neuroethological model of (mal)adaptive explore-exploit dynamics in ecological context. *Behavioral Brain Research, 380*: 1–13.

Mahoney, M. J. (1995). *Cognitive and constructive psychotherapies.* Springer Publishing Company.

Mahoney, M. J., Miller, H. M., & Arciero, G. (1995). Constructive metatheory and the nature of mental representation. In M. J. Mahoney (Ed.), *Cognitive and constructive psychotherapies* (pp. 103–120). Springer Publishing Company.

Moskowitz, G. B. (1993). Individual differences in social categorization: The influence of personal need for structure on spontaneous trait inferences. *Journal of Personality and Social Psychology, 65*: 132–142.

Piaget, J. (1962). *Play, Dreams and Imitation in Childhood.* Norton.

Robins, C. J., & Hayes, A. M. (1995). The role of causal attributions in the prediction of depression. In G. M. Buchanan & M. E. P. Seligman (Eds.), *Explanatory style* (pp. 71–98). Lawrence Erlbaum Associates.

Schmidt, N. B., Joiner, T. E., Young, J. E., & Telch, M. J. (1995). The schema questionnaire: Investigation of psychometric properties and the hierarchical structure of a measure of maladaptive schemas. *Cognitive Research and Therapy, 19*: 295–321.

Simpson, S., & Smith, E. (2020). *Schema therapy for eating disorders: Theory, practice and group-treatment manual.* Routledge.

Solms, M., & Turnbull, O. H. (2011). What is neuropsychoanalysis? *Neuropsychoanalysis, 13*(2): 133–145.

Thase, M. E., Khazanov, G., & Wright, J. H. (2023). Cognitive and behavioral therapies. In Tasman, A., Riba, M.B., Alarcón, R.D., Alfonso, C.A., Kanba, S., Lecic-Tosevski, D.,

Ndetei, D.M., Ng, C.H., & Schulze, T.G (Eds.), *Tasman's Psychiatry* (pp. 1–38). Springer International Publishing.

van der Kolk, B. A., & van der Hart, O. (1989). Pierre Janet & the breakdown of adaptation in psychological trauma. *American Journal of Psychiatry, 146*(12): 1530–1540.

Young, J. E., Klosko, J., & Weishaar, M. E. (2003). *Schema therapy: A practitioner's guide.* Guilford.

Chapter 7

The Sixth Harmonic
Self

> The Self is all-pervading, hence It is that which sits still and that which travels, that which is active and that which is inactive. It is both stationary and moving, and It is the basis of all forms of existence; therefore whatever exists in the universe, whether joy or joylessness, pleasure or pain, must spring from It. Who is better able to know God than I myself, since He resides in my heart and is the very essence of my being? Such should be the attitude of one who is seeking.
>
> —Katha Upanishad 2.21

We emerge now at the upper reaches of the watery sphere of the complex adaptive mind, the final level of harmonic representation: the self. We shall have quite as much difficulty and complexity describing the sixth harmonic as we did the first harmonic (which was archetype, to remind you), because of all the varying ways in which the construct has been defined and debated. Some models of psychology have practically ignored the self harmonic: our old nemesis, B.F. Skinner (1953), didn't ascribe autonomous existence to the self at all, instead considering it "an organized system of responses" (p. 287) directed by environmental contingencies, and some behaviorists go so far as to claim that there is no self which can be said to be distinct from its environment or objects (Williams, 1986). Other models made elaboration of the self its central business (such as so-called self psychology) or a crucial organizing principle, as we shall discuss in this chapter.

From many angles, the search for the self, which has involved inquiry from philosophy, psychology, religion, and cognitive science, has been a search for what Daniel Dennett (1991) calls Cartesian Theater: a theoretical space within the brain or mind that provides self function. Dennett points out that Cartesian dualism (which we have, after all, gradually abandoned in favor of materialism) relegates consciousness to the realm an immaterial soul, which saves us from having to define consciousness in material terms but doesn't really explain anything. Dennett's critique of Cartesian Theater is predicated on the desirability of all of us agreeing to remain appropriately faithful to materialism. Hence, at this end of the ladder of representational harmonics, we again revisit Kant's (2003) distinction between Noumenal and Phenomenal realms (see Chapter 3). It seems that the problems

DOI: 10.4324/9781032708751-9

posed by the highest-order and lowest-order of mental representations invoke the controversy over dualism.

In one corner of the ring, we have perspectives that affirm and acknowledge the existence of a symphonic self, in phenomenological terms if not noumenal terms. These conceptualizations of self include more contemporary psychoanalytic perspectives emerging from self psychology, interpersonal psychoanalysis, and intersubjective theory, all of which either acknowledge or peacefully co-exist with phenomenological and, to some extent, teleological conceptualizations of selfhood. These perspectives, which are also upheld within humanistic and existential models of human psychology, acknowledge that an individual's selfhood is a crucial organizing principle in psychotherapy, that acknowledging and mirroring the selfhood of another is intrinsically healing, and that there is something about the intersection of the client's selfhood with the selfhood of the therapist which forms the very matrix of a psychotherapeutic relationship. Furthermore, these perspectives affirm that this intersection of selves forms the basis for attachment, which is central to human psychological functioning. Jung, of course, takes the centrality of the self even further: he specifically acknowledges the teleological development of a self as the primal motivation and organizing principle of psychological development.

On the other side of the argument, the unlikely bedfellows who reject the orthogonal and autonomous existence of the self include Freudians (who speak in terms of biologically based drives and rarely speak in terms of self, and it took Heinz Kohut to remind them that maybe a self exists in the first place), Buddhists (who hold that individual identity is delusional), and cognitive scientists (who do not deny the concept of mind but point out that the structure of the mind…that is, the brain…is decentralized and heterogeneous, and therefore tend to see self as an epiphenomenon of cognitive processes).

The question of selfhood, then, tends to cluster around philosophical assumptions, much as the question of archetypes does. For purposes of describing the self harmonic, I propose that this level of harmonic representation describes an individual's experience (whether it is illusory or not) as a single, conscious, symphonic, autonomous being that is orthogonally distinct from others, manifesting with continuity across time and place, which is the epiphenomenal outcome of layered affective, cognitive, cultural, interpersonal, and intersubjective forces bounded and shaped by defensive imperatives as well as teleologically shaped toward phenomenological wholeness. Di Francesco et al. (2016) put it in similar terms:

> The self as subjective identity is a construction with no metaphysical guarantee; it is not something guaranteed once and for all, but rather a precarious acquisition, continuously under construction by a human organism and constantly exposed to the risk of dissolution. This precariousness is the key to grasping the defensive nature of identity self-construction. The need to construct and protect an identity that is valid to the greatest extent possible is rooted in the primary need to subsist subjectively, and thus to exist solidly as a describable ego, as a unitary subject.
>
> (p. 174)

Furthermore, questions of the self and selfhood lead naturally to questions of consciousness, the relationship of consciousness to self, and ultimately how the central nervous system generates consciousness (if it does). I will limit myself here to considering selfhood as a level of psychological mentalization and will then briefly explore the problem of consciousness in Chapter 9. We shall therefore undertake a limited survey of especially the Jungian, psychoanalytic, and constructivist perspectives on selfhood, including some of the philosophical foundations upon which inspire the central assumptions of those models.

The Jungian Self

Jung (1970), significantly, predicates selfhood on consciousness, and, notwithstanding his emphasis on the presence of a collective unconscious, identifies the individual self as the sole carrier of consciousness:

> Without consciousness there would, practically speaking, be no world, for the world exists for us only in so far as it is consciously reflected by a psyche. Consciousness is a precondition of being. Thus the psyche is endowed with the dignity of a cosmic principle, which philosophically and in fact gives it a position co-equal with the principle of physical being. The carrier of this consciousness is the individual, who does not produce the psyche of his own volition but is, on the contrary, preformed by it and nourished by the gradual awakening of consciousness during childhood. If therefore the psyche is of overriding empirical importance, so also is the individual, who is the only immediate manifestation of the psyche.
>
> (Paragraph 528)

Joseph Cambray (2009) articulates the relationship between the individuation process and the Jungian Self

> Related to individuation is Jung's larger view of the Self, as the center and circumference of the entire personality, conscious and unconscious. For Jung the ego is merely the center of consciousness, while the Self is the archetypal potential from which the ego complex emerges. The Self serves as the deepest source of motivation for the unfolding and subsequent reunification of the personality; when expressed, its archetypal imagery coincides with the god image though it can also take the negative of this as in daimonic forms.
>
> (p. 34)

For our purposes, it appears significant that Jung ascribes both a "cosmic" as well as a physical aspect of being, a distinction that reinforces the continuity of the Archetypal Harmonic in continuous sequence with other levels of mental representation. From the Jungian point of view, self is both an experienced process and a developmental destination: June Singer (1994) writes that self is "both guide and goal" (p. 60). This theoretical expansiveness suggests to me the interrelationships among the levels of the harmonic self described in our current developing model.

To complicate matters, the Jungian model of self has undergone significant updates over time, both within and after Jung's lifetime. Jung originally conceptualized the self as itself an archetype and further explicated his idea of self as distinct from the agency of the ego, both of which were seen as "centers" of the personality. Development of the egoic self becomes the task of the first half of life and replaces an earlier felt sense of unity experienced early in life. The second half of life, which was the phase of most interest to Jung, involves a transcendent function leading back into a more holistic sense of self through a process of individuation. This process of emergence from unity into an egoic consciousness which is then transcended suggests to me the alternating ascending and descending pathways through the harmonic levels, as well as the different styles of therapy (e.g., supportive versus expressive psychotherapy), which we shall explore further in Chapter 10.

Edward Edinger (1992) sums up the Jungian position on self in this way:

> The Self is the ordering and unifying center of the total psyche (conscious and unconscious) just as the ego is the center of the conscious personality. Or, put in other words, the ego is the seat of subjective identity while the Self is the seat of objective identity. The Self is thus the supreme psychic authority and subordinates the ego to it. The Self is most simply described as the inner empirical deity and is identical with the imago Dei.
>
> (p. 3)

Taken altogether, it seems clear that Jung's conceptualization of the self does not correspond neatly to the sixth harmonic; instead, the Jungian sense of self transcends mere level of mental representation and corresponds to a broader teleological and ultimately metaphysical concept of being, which either is archetypal or has its basis in archetypal level reality. Jung reserved another, unfortunately equally murky concept called *persona* to describe the dissociable, object-facing facets of identity:

> It frequently happens that men who in public life are extremely energetic, spirited, obstinate, willful and ruthless appear good-natured, mild, compliant, even weak, when at home and in the bosom of their family...[representing] two collective personalities, which may be summed up quite simply under the name 'personae'.
>
> (Jung, 1986, pp. 98–99)

The word "persona" has a Latin root invoking theatrical masks worn by actors on stage, and therefore represents a kind of compromise between the perceptions of the world and the internal reality of the actor. Persona belongs to the domain of the conscious, and is readily perceived and identified from the outside, and therefore fits the bill as a descriptor for the sixth harmonic. Jung's perspective was that persona, as a representative of the conscious attitude, represents an appearance of selfhood that is to some degree at odds with the "true self" which is the legitimate goal of individuation:

> If the ego identifies with persona, the subject's centre of gravity lies in the unconscious. It is then practically identical with the collective unconscious, because the whole personality is collective. In those cases there is a strong pull towards the unconscious and, at the same time, violent resistance to it on the part of consciousness because the destruction of conscious ideals is feared.
>
> (Jung, 1972, paragraph 509)

Based on Jung's account of what happens during the first and second halves of the life cycle, the first half of life organizes around building a persona, and the second half of life involves transcending that persona as part of the individuating process. We shall discuss these implications in Chapter 10 as a function of the shift between ascending and descending the trajectory of harmonic levels: from this point of view, the "self" harmonic is both the final outcome of the manifestation of the self into the world and a starting point for its own reversal as the harmonic sequence reverses itself.

Psychoanalytic Models of Selfhood

Psychoanalysis has historically approached the subject of self with a curious kind of diffidence. Freud's original drive theory, has been called "hydraulic" because it resembled nothing so much as a liquid moving in a confined space under pressure (the unconscious urges and instincts), which has to be redirected, repressed, and contained by a complicated system of psychological dams, spillways, and canals that made up Freud's topographical model of the personality. This classical Freudian perspective cast the personality in particularly recursive and biological terms in which there wasn't much emphasis on the self as a teleological principle.

The concept of the self was introduced in a functional way by the self-psychologists who broke away methodologically from Freud's original drive theory. Heinz Hartmann (1950) suggested that in the example of pathological narcissism, the "self" becomes cathected with libido rather than the ego, resulting in a magnification of the sense of self-worth. From this point of view, healthy narcissism fortified by the empathic support of significant figures in early life supports and enhances the development of a sense of self (and that narcissistic developmental arrest results in a fragile or incoherent self, see Chapter 14).

The other Heinz, Heinz Kohut, elaborated a movement within psychoanalysis that would come to be called self psychology. A staunch conservative psychoanalyst who was reluctant to break with drive theory, Kohut found himself schooled by a 25-year-old woman whom he was treating, who took him to task any time she felt that Kohut was misinterpreting her (and therefore failing to perceive her sense of self).

Kohut's determination to take such patient feedback seriously led to his focus on empathy and "experience-near" psychotherapeutic work, which involved accepting that he himself might be misunderstanding clients rather than chalking up such feedback to resistance to analysis. These perspectives, initially taken by the psychoanalytic community as quite heretical, led to Kohut's (1971) focus on the selfhood of the client as having its own center of gravity in the psychotherapeutic frame, and to his seminal work on mirroring and the mirroring self-object transference, especially in the context of narcissism:

> I began to entertain the thought that these people were not concerned with me as a separate person but that they were concerned with themselves; that they did not love me or hate me, but that they needed me as part of themselves, needed me as a set of functions which they had not acquired in early life; that what appeared to be their love and hate was in reality their need that I fulfill certain psychological functions for them and anger at me when I did not do so.
>
> (2011, pp. 888–889)

However, Kohut never went much further than this in defining the self as such and appeared to approach the self as a quality of internal experience rather than a "thing" with autonomy.

Our discussion so far underlines the tendency of early psychoanalysis to eschew Hegelian-style descriptions of self as an emerging intersubjectively in the context of a relationship with an object (see Kirshner, 1991); instead, the self is seen as the composite results of the internal mathematics of drive states, phantasy, and ego functions. One of the first to anticipate a more relational and then intersubjective perspective on selfhood was Donald Winnicott, who drew a distinction between the natural spontaneity of babies and the defensive compliance that emerges in childhood in response to significant empathic failures with the parent. This strategy of compliance lays the foundation for a so-called "false self" in which natural dependency needs are defensively denied. Winnicott's (1990) elaboration of true versus false self systems begins to approximate the competing representational systems described by constructivist perspectives within cognitive neuroscience, which we described in Chapter 6, pointing to a continuity between the self harmonic and some of the underlying schema-level representations which underlie self representations.

The intersubjective movement, a defining feature of contemporary psychoanalysis, radically shifted the idea of selfhood in the direction of so-called two-person psychology. Robert Stolorow et al. (1987) was one of the first and most prominent theorists to move in the direction of redefining psychotherapeutic space as an interpenetrating field of subjective states, including both the patient and the therapist. From this point of view, bridging the realms of self psychology and intersubjective psychology, the intersection of the self-object needs of both therapist and client co-create a unique field experience that has been characterized as the "therapeutic third." Stolorow's perspective is that a central goal of selfhood is managing affect, and the attachment field is the primary way in which a child learns to differentiate among affective experiences, to reconcile and synthesize experiential mismatches between different states, and to develop psychological strategies for tolerating strong affective states and to use them as self-signals.

In Stolorow's perspective, we arrive at some of the most important contributions of contemporary psychoanalysis with the problem of selfhood: the intersubjective and relational context of the development of self, which differentiates this perspective from the biological determinism of Freud's perspective as well as the recursive brain functions at the center of the constructivist model. Phillip Bromberg (1996) similarly reinterpreted the psychoanalytic sense of self from a relational and dissociative perspective, depicting self as a constellation of discontinuous *self states*. By extension, the object relations which underpin a sense of self represent competing versions of the self dynamically interacting with competing versions of others. Bromberg's emphasis on the dissociative quality of self-state organization challenges earlier psychoanalytic emphasis on repression (see Howell, 2022), and highlights the ubiquity of dissociation in psychological life:

> I have argued that a flexible relationship among self-states through the use of normal dissociation is what allows a human being to engage the ever-shifting requirements of life's complexities with creativity and spontaneity – from this vantage point, normal dissociation, a mind–brain mechanism that is intrinsic to everyday mental functioning, attempts to select a self-state configuration that is most immediately adaptive within the constraints of self-coherence. This flexibility is what gives a person the remarkable capacity to negotiate character and change simultaneously – to stay the same while changing.
>
> (2009, p. 90)

Multiplicity: Is There More Than One "Me"?

Although subtly different from the concept of intersubjectivity, psychoanalytic theory has also been experimenting with the concept of multiple selves to explain the apparent psychological diversity of integrated forces extant within a single person. Rustin (1994) argued that the increasing attention upon "multiplicity" is part of a general methodological tendency among clinicians to shift "from developmental history towards the subtleties and ambiguities of the interactions between patient and analyst, on both conscious and unconscious levels" (p. 114). In other words, psychoanalysts have come to pay more attention to the subtle and shifting aspects of the therapeutic relationship, including the various "selves" that become apparent during the intimate and intense clinical relationship. It is worth noting that Rustin and others have taken this theoretical shift as evidence of increased concern for scientific validity and verifiability (see Harris, 1996). Davies (1996) conceptualized the "multiplicity faction" in psychoanalysis as representing a "postclassical" stage which is currently one of the developmental descendants of pre-analytic developments. She states that the development involves a transition from seeing the self as "integrated, singular, internally coherent, structured linearly upon the accruing bedrock of phase-specific developmental crises" to conceptualizing the self as "a necessary illusion, a metaphoric, functional conduit, providing safe passage across more intrinsically discordant aspects of internalized but essentially irreconcilable aspects of self-other experience" (p. 553).

According to more recent descriptions of the theoretical multiplicity of selves, self-states "organize internal experience, establishing a set of coherences that may or may not appear as an overarching coherence for the individual" (Harris, 1996, p. 538). This conceptualization of the psychodynamic self-state is significant for this discussion for its resemblance to the cognitive schemas both in an operational sense (inasmuch as the self-state is an organizing principle with the function of making coherent sense of experience) and for its apparently hierarchical arrangement (inasmuch as the self-state may or may not act as an "overarching" theme). However, theoretical operationalization of multiplicity describes characteristics of self-states which hearken back to Jung's conceptualization of archetypes. Harris goes on to compare modern multiplicity theory with a more cognitively focused emphasis: "The mainstream Piagetian position holds that there is one core organizing set of structures that is adequate to describe any particular individual at any particular time....[multiplicity theory] constitutes a very different kind of theory, with multilinear lines of development and considerable indeterminacy" (p. 539). In this sense, the theory of multiple selves within the psychodynamic schools resembles the earlier impressions of Klein and Bion, who described indeterminate and kaleidoscopic, dynamic forces within the psyche. The dynamic and indeterminate aspect of multiplicity thus represents a departure both from Freud's mechanistic drive systems and cognitive theory's "irreducible ingredients," which comprise the cognitive schema, and rather resemble Jung's archetypes themselves. Jung (2014) stated strongly that the archetypes are "indefinite, that is to say they can be known and determined only approximately. Although associated with causal process, or carried by them, they continually go beyond their frame of reference" (p. 515).

An important point of departure between psychodynamic multiplicity and the archetypes relates to the former concept's focus on relational factors. As a development of more contemporary strains of psychodynamic theory, most adherents define multiplicity as manifest within the interpersonal sphere rather than as an intrapsychic phenomenon. Supporters of multiplicity theory go even further than that, positing that multiple selves are formed within the crucible of interpersonal experience. Davies (1996) states: "It is from the unique interpersonal experience of the child that meaning-generating fantasy is organized, not through a developmentally fixed, epigenetic unfolding of endogenously organized universal fantasy, such as that claimed within classical theory" (p. 556). Here Davies draws a strong line not only between contemporary multiplicity theory and classical psychoanalytic theory but also between multiplicity and archetypal theory. Indeed, her insistence that multiple selves do not arise from "endogenously organized universal fantasy" seems to discount the archetypal source quite directly, although it is clear that she meant to draw a distinction from classical psychoanalytic theory. In this particular case, archetypal theory more closely resembles psychoanalytic theory, in that it focuses on dynamic aspects of the psyche that are native to the psyche rather than arising from experience, interpersonal or otherwise.

Other "postclassical" thinkers have described theoretical bridges between older, classical ideas on one hand and more "cognitive" formulations on the other. Aron (1993) recasts internal object representations as representational schemata of self and other. Similarly, Irene Fast (1992) describes the development from part-object to whole-object representations as essentially a growing capacity to tolerate competing schemata. Davies (1996) notes with approval these theoretical bridges, which she claims move psychoanalytic theory "into compatible juxtaposition with contemporary cognitive psychology by setting the groundwork for a dynamically motivated psychology of consciousness" (p. 560).

The Constructivist Self

Constructivism represents an essentially post-modern perspective on selfhood, moving away from an "essentialized" vision of self. Philosophically, the constructivist view of self reflects the perspective of Hume (2000) that self is an illusion distilled from perceptions that vary widely across time and circumstance. On one hand, constructivist viewpoints tend to seek and reinforce sources for selfhood directly in the cognitive science of discrete brain function; on the other hand, they acknowledge cultural and interpersonal vectors in contributing to the range of experiential states that make up the self. According to Ge et al. (2022):

> The experience of self is chiefly shaped by and adapted to environmental stimuli, which render the structure of the self as less enduring and more subject to change. Furthermore, as the enduring aspect of the self is an illusion, the actual perceptions of the self are composed of distinct experiences succeeding one another rather than one single continuous experience. This integration of self and environment also fosters and reinforces a sense of interconnectedness between the self and all elements of the environment.
>
> (p. 32)

Constructivist perspectives resemble and overlap intersubjective models within psychoanalysis in that they cast the self as a process rather than an entity (Mahoney & Granvold, 2005), resulting in a "fluid coherence of perspective from which one experiences" (p. 74). True to the conceptual focus of constructivist modeling on mental representations organized at the schema harmonic, this perspective conceptualizes multiple self-states as psychological hypothesis-generators, or inferences: self states at the schema harmonic reflect the personality trying to figure itself and the world out, with an emphasis on the emergence of phenomenal consciousness, cognitive control, and agency (see Cleeremans et al., 2020). True to the behavioral and cognitive roots of constructivism, this model depicts a sense of self emerging as an epiphenomenon of brain functions taking actions that impact the environment and therefore allow it to develop conclusions: that is to say, the constructivist self derives from behavior (including language, which is classified within this frame as a kind of behavior). This perspective suggests that a primary motivation of "self-hood" is therefore creating agency through successful inference, and "disorders of the self" represent this process breaking down due to failed inferences. One of the primary operating principles of the constructivist perspective in the context of applied clinical psychology is that psychopathology, trauma, and personality disorder are complex results of unexpected uncertainty and complexity which undermines the brain's goal of effective agency.

Ge et al. (2022) offer four characteristics of the constructivist self:

> (1) *boundlessness*: the extent to which the self is embedded with other people as well as other things in the environment; (2) *impermanence*: the extent to which the self is constantly in flux rather than at its core unchanging; (3) *discontinuity*: the extent to which the self is a string of distinct phenomena from moment to moment rather than a continuous experience over the life span; and (4) *disentification*: the extent to which the self does not have an essence.
>
> (p. 32)

These characteristics partially overlap with certain psychoanalytic perspectives: the *boundless* quality reflects the intersubjective field perspective, and the *discontinuous* quality parallels Bromberg's particular take on the intersubjective experience of self. The dynamics of *impermanence* and *disentification* agree with post-classical assumptions of multiplicity discussed earlier in this chapter, and certainly support the movement within Jungian theory which criticizes Jung's foundationalism.

The Integrative Analytical Model offers a potential integrative framework for these different perspectives through its holarchic arrangement of different mental representations across a spectrum of theoretical contexts. By tracing the harmonics of representation from the archetypal level to the level of self, we assemble a conceptual map that allows crosswalk comparisons across disparate perspectives, while acknowledging that different theoretical, clinical, and philosophical conditions hold true at different levels. As we shall explore over the next three chapters, the spectrum of mental representations represents "levels of reality" that range from the noumenal, phenomenological, and even metaphysical archetypal harmonic to the empirically observable and brain-based schema harmonic and beyond. In Chapter 9, we will explore an integrative overview of the six harmonics, and in Chapter 10 we will consider some broader applied implications for the six harmonics in clinical practice.

References

Aron, L. (1993). Working toward operational thought—Piagetian theory and psychoanalytic method. *Contemporary Psychoanalysis, 29*: 289–313.

Bromberg, P. M. (1996). Standing in the spaces: The multiplicity of self and the psychoanalytic relationship. *Contemporary Psychoanalysis, 32*: 509–535.

Bromberg, P. M. (2009). Truth, human relatedness, and the analytic process: An interpersonal/relational perspective. *The International Journal of Psychoanalysis, 90*(2), 347–361.

Cambray, J. (2009). *Nature and psyche in an interconnected universe.* Texas A&M University Press.

Cleeremans, A., Achoui, D., Beauny, A., Keuninckx, L., Martin, J.-R., & Muñoz-Moldes, S. (2020). Learning to be conscious. *Trends in Cognitive Science, 24*: 112–123.

Davies, J. M. (1996). Linking the pre-analytic with the postclassical: Integration, dissociation, and the multiplicity of unconscious process. *Contemporary Psychoanalysis, 32*: 553–575.

Dennett, D. C. (1991). *Consciousness explained.* Little, Brown & Co.

Di Francesco, M., Marraffa, M., & Paternoster, A. (2016). *The self and its defenses: From psychodynamics to cognitive science.* Palgrave MacMillan.

Edinger, E. F. (1992). *Ego and archetype.* Shambhala.

Fast, I. (1992). The embodied mind: Toward a relational perspective. *Psychoanalytic Dialogues, 2*(3): 389–409.

Ge, F., Syropoulos, S., Gensler, J., Leidner, B., Loughnan, S., Chang, J.-H., Harada, C., Mari, S., Paladino, M. P., Shi, J., Yeung, V. W. L., Kuo, C.-Y., & Tsuchiya, K. (2022). Constructivist self-construal: A cross-cultural comparison. *Cross-Cultural Research, 56*(1): 29–61.

Harris, A. (1996). The conceptual power of multiplicity. *Contemporary Psychoanalysis, 32*: 537–552.

Hartmann, H. (1950). Comments on the psychoanalytic theory of the ego. *Psychoanalytic Study of the Child, 7*: 9–30.

Howell, E. (2022). Philip Bromberg and the revolution about dissociated self-States. *Contemporary Psychoanalysis, 58*(2): 299–309.

Hume, D. (2000). *A treatise of human nature.* Oxford University Press.

Jung, C. G. (1970). *Civilization in transition* (R. F. C. Hull, Trans.). Princeton University Press.

Jung, C. G. (1972). *Two essays on analytical psychology* (R. F. C. Hull, Trans.). Princeton University Press.

Jung, C. G. (1986). *Selected writings* (A. Storr, Ed.). Fontana.

Jung, C. G. (2014). *The structure and dynamics of the psyche* (R. F. C. Hull, Trans.). Princeton University Press.

Kant, I. (2003). *Critique of pure reason* (M. Weigelt, Trans.). Penguin Classics.

Kirshner, L. A. (1991). The concept of the self in psychoanalytic theory and its philosophical foundations. *Journal of the American Psychoanalytic Association, 39*(1): 157–182.

Kohut, H. (1971). *The analysis of the self.* International Universities Press.

Kohut, H. (2011). Letters – 1961-1978. In Ornstein, P. (Ed.), *The Search for the Self: Volume 2: Selected Writings of Heinz Kohut 1978-1981* (pp. 851–930). Routledge.

Mahoney, M. J., & Granvold, D. K. (2005). Constructivism and Psychotherapy. *World Psychiatry, 4*(2): 74–77.

Rustin, M. (1994). Psychoanalysis, philosophical realism and the new sociology of science. *Free Association, 11*: 102–135.

Singer, J. (1994). *Boundaries of the soul.* Anchor Books.

Skinner, B.F. (1953). *Science and human behavior.* Macmillan.

Stolorow, R. D., Brandchaft, B., & Atwood, G. E. (1987). *Psychoanalytic treatment: An intersubjective approach.* Analytic Press.

Williams, J. L. (1986). The behavioral and the mystical: Reflections on behaviorism and eastern thought. *The Behavior Analyst, 9*: 167–173.

Winnicott, D. W. (1990). *The maturational processes and the facilitating environment: Studies in the theory of emotional development.* Routledge.

Chapter 8

Complexity Theory

I cannot fix on the hour, or the spot, or the look or the words, which laid the foundation. It is too long ago. I was in the middle before I knew that I had begun.

—Jane Austen, *Pride and Prejudice*

In this chapter, we will briefly consider the symbolic function of the human mind (and brain), especially as described by various cognitive and neurocognitive models. Taken together, the emerging consensus from scientific inquiry spanning actual brain structure to epiphenomenal functions like language suggests that the human brain is a symbolizing force that combines primordial elements grounded in central nervous system function into progressively complex and unpredictable cognitive systems. From this perspective, human cognition (and by extension, mental representation) results from interpenetrating dynamical systems governed by principles of "deterministic chaos" (see below). The neurocognitive components of complex mental representation, therefore, can be seen as a function of "a set of specialized modules, massively parallel and hierarchical, that progressively integrate and elaborate features of the environment in more and more complex and abstract representations" (Mesulam, 1998, as cited in Dehaene-Lambertz & Spelke, 2015, p. 98).

The idea of nested hierarchies generating increasing complexity is a very old idea and is reflected in such venerable sources as Pythagoras' quadrivium, Plato's microcosm, Leibniz's monads, Mandelbrot's fractal structures, and so on. Contemporary advancements in mathematical modeling, computer imaging, and other advancements have resulted in several overlapping and highly sophisticated models of complex systems in so-called phase space.

It appears that over time, human philosophy first discovered the symmetrical beauty of primordial forms, and only more recently have we discovered the profound ways that breakdowns and violation of beautiful primordial forms create a kind of creative chaos resulting in new iterations of reality. The history of science, in many ways, appears to represent the viewpoints that defended primordial order and represent chaotic change. Nicolaus Copernicus in particular struggled with the dynamic tension of these perspectives, attempting to reconcile the harmonious

DOI: 10.4324/9781032708751-10

and uniform circular models anticipated by Ptolemy with the actual complexity he observed in the sky:

> Yet the widespread [planetary theories], advanced by Ptolemy and most other [astronomers], although consistent with the numerical [data], seemed likewise to present no small difficulty. For these theories were not adequate unless they also conceived certain equalizing circles, which made the planet appear to move at all times with uniform velocity neither on its deferent sphere nor about its own [epicycle's] center…Therefore, having become aware of these [defects], I often considered whether there could perhaps be found a more reasonable arrangement of circles, from which every apparent irregularity would be derived while everything in itself would move uniformly, as is required by the rule of perfect motion.
>
> (Copernicus & Rosen, 1992, in Rabin, 2023, p. 81)

I can sense a certain amount of anguish in Copernicus as he endeavors to find a "more reasonable arrangement of circles" in order to preserve the symmetrical assumptions of the ancients, and yet this anguish resulted in his proposal of the heliocentric cosmos, that the Earth orbits around the Sun. In a sense, the history of modern science has been an attempt to model increasing degrees of observable chaos and complexity that emerge as we peer ever closer into the nature of reality. As we discover that breakdowns in primordial symmetry lead to the birth of new forms, it is almost as if we are approaching a scientific theory of creativity.

Deterministic Chaos

In 1887, King Oscar II of Sweden offered a prize of 2,500 crowns to anyone who could answer the question: "Is the solar system stable?" French mathematician Henri Poincaré responded by demonstrating that Newtonian mechanics could demonstrate that one astronomical body orbiting another, like the Moon around the Earth or the Earth around the Sun, represents a stable system. However, adding a third body (e.g., the Moon orbiting the Earth orbiting the Sun) introduced complexities that could not be shown to demonstrate stability by those same Newtonian principles. Although it might be argued that Poincaré did not really answer the question, his response demonstrated a kind of chaos theory, which would significantly widen the scientific understanding of complex systems. Poincaré (1905) sums it up in the following way:

> A very small cause that escapes our notice determines a considerable effect that we cannot fail to see, and then we say that the effect is due to chance. If we knew exactly the laws of nature and the situation of the universe at the initial moment, we could predict exactly the situation of that same universe at a succeeding moment. But even if it were the case that the natural laws had no longer any secret for us, we could still only know the initial situation

approximately. If that enabled us to predict the succeeding situation with the same approximation, that is all we require, and we should say that the phenomenon had been predicted, that it is governed by laws. But it is not always so; it may happen that small differences in the initial conditions produce very great ones in the final phenomena. A small error in the former will produce an enormous error in the latter. Prediction becomes impossible, and we have the fortuitous phenomenon.

(pp. 66–67)

Although Poincaré uses the mathematical and statistical term "error," as we shall see in the following subsequent accounts of complexity, error is not just an error but a kind of ultimately creative divergence that is not *random* but *chaotic*. The term deterministic chaos, which seems contradictory on the surface, reflects the fact that collectively, chaotic systems derive unpredictable results from primordial elements, which originally have predictable and deterministic relationships with each other. Chaos theory suggests that chaotic systems result from the interactions of *attractors*, which are driving forces representing a set of states toward which the system is evolving, and *dissipators*, which represent limitations or resistance to the changes invoked by the attractors (so-called *strange attractors* seem to have a fractal structure, that is, they exhibit self-similarity at different scales). Chaotic systems show *initial conditions* which reflect the original state of the system, and *boundary conditions* which define the limits of a system, beyond which the system will become unstable and change fundamentally. Later in this chapter, we will explore parallels between the boundary conditions described in chaos theory and the so-called Markov Blankets described in Bayesian networks.

Some additional features of chaotic systems are as follows:

- In chaotic systems, variations occurring within the original system become amplified at an exponential rate, which precludes predictions about the end state, even in the medium term.
- Chaotic systems can not be coerced: an environmental change in one instance will result in different outcomes than the same environmental change in another instance.
- Chaotic systems are irregular in time (that is to say, aperiodic).

Chaos theory is a promising scientific and mathematical framework for understanding some of the complex systems we will continue to discuss below, and as such approaches and approximates the kinds of ontology involved in describing the philosophical foundations underlying models of psychology and ultimately, personality. We will revisit some of the characteristics of chaos theory in the rest of this chapter as well as in Chapter 9, in which we will apply some of the features of chaos theory to the interrelationships of the harmonic levels of mentalization, which can be seen as dynamic and chaotic systems.

Complex Adaptive Systems, Symmetry, and the Emergentist Paradigm

Chaotic systems, as we have just discussed, can be seen as illustrating a deeper cross-disciplinary principle that has been called *emergence* (Newman, 1996). Emergence is a feature of so-called Complex Adaptive Systems (CAS) which describe the behavior of dynamical systems. Dynamical systems are phenomena in which initial conditions change exponentially over time, resulting in complex outcomes that could not be predicted based on initial conditions, but which *emerge* as a result of increasing complexity. As we discussed above in the context of chaos theory, dynamical systems are *chaotic* but not *random*; each individual shift in circumstances follows a deterministic logic, but the overall outcome of exponentially increasing change over multiple levels of magnitude creates new properties that do not relate in a linear way to initial conditions. Somehow, it seems that deterministic relationships among variables result in chaotic and unpredictable states when the interrelationships among those variables exponentially increase in number, magnitude, and quantity. For example, a stalled car at a particular intersection causes a local traffic jam whose consequences multiply and complexify, causing gridlock in a local neighborhood, unusual traffic patterns elsewhere caused by other vehicles avoiding the area, secondary accidents caused by the initial accident, and people arriving late for work or appointments with various consequences and outcomes. At some point, theoretically, the very fabric of reality is significantly altered in complex and unpredictable ways by that stalled car: jobs lost, opportunities missed or gained, chance encounters that happen or do not happen, relational impacts, shifting emotional states in the humans involved, and so forth, and each of these secondary and tertiary outcomes becomes the origin of another complex web of outcomes rippling outwards into space and time. Each individual outcome was logical and perhaps predictable, but the sum total of the complexity caused by the initial event transcends deterministic relationships that can be quantified, calculated, or predicted. Other examples of CAS might include economic systems, metabolic and cellular systems within the body of an organism, the human brain (and mind), ecosystems, weather systems, human and animal migratory patterns, and so on.

The term *emergence* describes phenomena that result from the turbulence of a CAS, which are greater than the sum of their parts. Therefore, complex epiphenomenal outcomes (such as human behavior and use of language) cannot be reduced to discrete causes that have a direct relationship with outcomes; rather, such outcomes can only "emerge" in the context of the complexity resulting from the dynamic interaction of many variables on multiple levels of scale. Emergentism occupies a philosophical space that mediates between reductionism and dualism, making the field an appealing one for transtheoretical perspectives in the study of complex systems (such as human psychology and sociology).

In characterizing the constructivist take on self-organization, Mahoney et al. (1995) invoke the concept of *autopoieses*, involving spontaneously self-ordering complex phenomena. The authors recall the work of Manfred Eigen, who described autocatalytic "hypercycles" intended to bridge biological systems and patterns of thinking

(Eigen & Schuster, 1979). *Hypercycles* are described as fundamental events which allow a process to become robustly self-organizing. Eigen's conceptualization is just one way of operationalizing the emergence of stable knowledge systems from "random energy dynamics." Ilya Prigogine (1980) approached the same problem from a somewhat different perspective by introducing "dissipative structures." This formulation resembles modern chaos theory in that functional disorganization at a fundamental level serves to effect deep structural reorganization of knowledge systems.

Mainzer (2005) elaborates on the dissipative self-organization of processes that lead from early symmetrical forms into systems of greater complexity:

> Dissipative self-organization is the phase transition of irreversible structures far from thermal equilibrium. Macroscopic patterns arise from the complex nonlinear cooperation of microscopic elements when the energetic interaction of the dissipative ("open") system with its environment reaches some critical value. The stability of the emergent structures is guaranteed by dynamical balance of nonlinearity and dissipation.
>
> (p. 13)

From this point of view, symmetry represents the stability of primordial systems. Those primordial systems actually evolve by devolving: they break down (develop "asymmetries") through complex and unpredictable interaction with the environment, allowing dissipative features of the original elements of the primordial symmetry to reorganize. In a sense, chaotic systems are the result of broken symmetry (Mainzer, 2005), and broken symmetry is therefore an agent of change and evolution. Symmetry breaks down through so-called phase transitions and transformative reorganizations of the system, which permit the manifestation of new forms. Jungian scholar Joseph Cambray (2009) applies the concept of symmetry shifting through phase transitions to individual psychology:

> In a truly complex system no single aspect has adequate information to represent the whole, nor can any single part statistically predict the dynamic behavior of the system, especially when it self-organizes. Symmetry is broken in what are called phase transitions, rapid, abrupt reorganizations in a dynamic system that radically restructure the system, allowing new forms to emerge. Bearing the psychological equivalent of phase transitions and reorganizations can be highly stressful for an individual even if ultimately positive in transformative effect.
>
> (p. 64)

Memes: The Epidemiology of Ideas

Yet another interesting line of inquiry focuses on "memes," a construct coined by Richard Dawkins in his book *The Selfish Gene* (1976). Dawkins defines the meme as "a unit of cultural transmission or a unit of imitation" which functions as "self-replicators" much as a virus does:

Just as genes propagate themselves in the gene pool by leading from body to body via sperm or eggs, so memes propagate themselves in the meme pool by leaping from brain to brain via a process which, in the broad sense, can be called imitation... Memes should be regarded as living structures, not just metaphorically but technically. When you plant a fertile meme in my mind, you literally parasitize my brain, turning it into a vehicle for the meme's propagation in just the way that a virus may parasitize the genetic mechanism of a host cell.

(p. 24)

The meme construct as described by Dawkins already bears a striking resemblance to archetypal theory, with the significant difference that memes are assumed to travel from person to person without any of that messy mucking about with genetic transmission...that is to say, a significant "idea-contagion" (meme) may travel from an individual to others in a room, down the corridor, and into the outside world within the course of hours. More recent authors since Dawkins have even explored the possibility of meme-networks which may comprise the basic cognitive-perceptive field of the human mind. Gabora and Aerts (2009) write:

It may be that the emergence of this kind of complex, adaptive self-modifying, self-mending, self-regenerating (i.e., autopoietic) structure is the critical step in the origin of any kind of evolutionary process, be it biological, cultural, or some other sort that we may not have identified. The evolution of culture involves not just creativity, nor just imitation, but a proclivity to put our own spin on the inventions of others, to use them for our own purposes and adapt them to our own needs and desires, such that the process becomes cumulative, adaptive, and open-ended.

(p. 37)

Gabora explores the possibility that cognitive autocatalysis of memes may even represent a scenario for the origins of culture. This same theme is picked up by Clewley (1998), who investigates "modern theories of nonlinear spatially-distributed dynamical systems to indicate how it may be possible to rigorously connect levels of mathematical representation in a model hierarchy" (p. 4). Clewley concludes by encouraging the adherents of mimetic theory to undertake ontological integration with comparable conceptualizations of "emergent structures" within psychology. Both cognitive theory and archetypal theory are particularly compatible with the thinking of the memeticists.

Biological Perspectives and the Bayesian Brain

A particularly relevant development is currently taking place in the literature on pre- and perinatal cognitive evolution. These research developments suggest considerable cognitive sophistication in the fetal and infant brain, which appears to be socially oriented and predisposed to pattern recognition from the start (see

Grossmann et al., 2007). If social pattern recognition is present in newborn infants, it seems reasonable to presume that the brain and its complex neural association networks come equipped with pre-programmed "patterns." Unfortunately, science has not yet progressed far enough in this direction to more fully explore this promising realm. However, neuropsychological investigation has begun to seek out the neurological substrates for some "higher-order" psychological functions, including neonatal mental representation. Berlucchi and Aglioti (1997) have investigated the brain mechanisms that may constitute a mental representation of the body, derived from spontaneous movements observed in neonates and in data from phantom-limb phenomena:

> Imitation of movements by neonates suggests an implicit knowledge of the body structure that antedates the adult body schema. This can include inanimate objects that bear systematic relations to the body, as shown by the elimination from self awareness of a body part and its associated paraphernalia after selective brain lesions.
>
> (p. 560)

Such findings seem to bolster the hypothesis that genetic transmission of certain mental representations, given the broad array of basic psychological functions, can be found to have a neuropsychological substrate even before birth.

Current understanding of the neurological substrate for intentionality, motivation, and consciousness suggests that such high-level cognitive processes are not seated in any single area of the brain but instead seem to arise from complex feedback loops based on neural pathways linking numerous neuropsychological functions. This kind of system allows a perceptually driven field of consciousness, in which input from the sensorium is selectively attended by attentional resources, based on feedback originating in complex motivational systems. Such mechanisms may play a part in the formation of schemas based on patterned tendencies built into the brain. Several recent studies have implicated the cingulate gyrus in determining hierarchical relationships in cognitive processing (see Patel et al., 2006), especially in the top-down organizational scheme which is evident in priming tasks (Gutchess et al., 2010). Such discoveries encourage the hypothesis that the mind functions largely categorically, with "nested" subroutines based on deeper and more fundamental systems.

The so-called Bayesian Brain Hypothesis (Hipólito & Kirchhoff, 2023), as we briefly discussed in Chapter 8, models brain function on dynamic analysis of data resembling statistical hypothesis testing. Bayesian analysis calculates probabilities based on new data to update prior hypotheses, resulting in new hypotheses which then become the prior hypotheses from an additional round of Bayesian "updating." From this perspective, the brain generates and tests hypotheses against incoming data, and continuously updates cognitive representations based on successive observations. The result of this process is a kind of fine-tuning of perception and behavior, driven by the goals of minimizing surprise (or "free energy") and uncertainty. This perspective is different from the kind of reinforcement learning assumed by cognitive-behavioral models of psychology, in that it assumes that mental representations are used to anticipate new perceptions and experiences, rather than just being shaped by them. The Bayesian Brain is an inferential device, motivated to reduce free energy states by constructing efficient and successful hypotheses…not by adapting to the environment, but by adapting the environment to fit the expectations of the system.

Mark Solms (2021), both a neuroscientist and a psychoanalyst, builds the Bayesian Brain Hypothesis into a more general model of consciousness itself. He describes the cognitive self-organizing systems that exist inside a Markov Blanket, which can be described as the boundaries containing orthogonally organized cognitive systems that act in concert. Within these Markov Blankets, self-organizing systems form inferences in the Bayesian manner, with the goal of maintaining their own homeostasis and avoiding disruption in the form of "surprise" (as measured by free energy which results from slippage among representations). According to Solms, the management of free energy (and therefore by extension, surprise-containment) is the central mechanism for consciousness itself. Therefore, consciousness is a function of our attempt to minimize uncertainty in the service of creating behaviors that address needs. Interestingly, Solms states that the default affect involved in gathering information to update internal representations is one of Jaak Panksepp's seven primary emotional systems, called SEEKING (see Davis & Montag, 2019). SEEKING can be interpreted as curiosity and openness to new information, an affective state long established as an indicator of mature object relations functioning in the psychoanalytic model (see Bion, 1959).

Complexity from Primitives: Constructivist Learning

Another branch of research into infant cognitive development has focused more on behavioral research. One of the most fruitful lines of inquiry in the past decade or so has been constructivist learning, which is a part-to-whole methodology in which discrete units of learning (termed schemas) are acquired and incorporated into increasingly complex structures of "knowledge," leading to more and more flexible responses.

Constructivist learning relies upon so-called self-organizing maps (see Kohonen, 2013), or SOM, which are actually based on human infant cognitive development. We have heard the term "constructivism" before…it is an essentially associationist paradigm in which "units" of learning and experience are acquired directly from the environment and used to construct more complex associations. In the constructivist learning sphere, and in Piaget's learning research which represents its intellectual ancestor, these "primitives" are assumed to represent sensory and motor data. Recent research into infant learning has built upon Piaget's earlier work and has resulted in a number of useful conclusions about the hierarchical nature of mental representations, and how learning results from a combination of native architecture and empirical experience. Cohen et al. (2002) suggest the following conclusions illuminated by such research, which I paraphrase:

1. *Infants are born with access to an innate information processing system.* Such innate systems provide "architectural guidance" which determines the rough patterns by which learning will be acquired. Like the glial cells which nudge the developing neurons that make up the central nervous system into their proper precise locations, there is something inherent and native in the newly created human brain which prepares the dim shape of future learning. While the nature and scope of such native content is controversial and the larger subject of this book, Cohen et al. limit their inquiry to such "low-level information" as orientation, sound, color, texture, and movement.

2. *Infants form higher schemas from lower schemas.* As it lays the groundwork for a lifetime of learning, the human mind does more than just throw information on top of an ever-growing pile. Rather, the learning system is structured in a hierarchical manner. New information becomes more and more complex, building upon prior processed information due to a nascent ability to integrate the lower-level schemas into more complex, higher-level schemas. Constructivist learning suggests that such hierarchical organization is based upon *correlations* in activity of those lower-level schemas.

3. *Higher schemas serve as components for still-higher schemas.* The hierarchical development of schemas allows for quantum leaps in complexity and increasingly rich networks of associations. The process of ever-higher integration of information is itself repeated throughout development and across domains.

4. *The individual shows a tendency to process using the "highest" available schemas.* When two or more layers of schemas have been formed, infants will tend to process additional information using the highest level available. "Lower-level" information remains available to the individual (and may be resorted to when the system is stressed, as we shall see below), but processing information at the highest possible level takes maximum advantage of the richness of acquired strategies and associations.

5. *Where higher schemas are not available or the system becomes distressed, the individual resorts to lower-level schemas.* As we shall discuss below when we look more closely at certain principles of artificial intelligence, this strategy of resorting to more primitive processing has been described as "fallback." Reasons for system distress include stimulus overload, presence of irrelevant material or "noise," or converting a simple object or event into a category of objects or events. When the individual resorts to a "fallback" mode of processing, it will attempt to regain equilibrium and accommodate, with the goal of moving back up to the next higher level.

6. *The strategy of hierarchical schematic processing is utilized throughout development and across domains.* In other words, the schema-based constructivist learning strategy is domain-general and is likely to represent how humans master a wide range of tasks throughout their lifespan and in a variety of contexts.

Some Concluding Thoughts about Complexity

One important conclusion from all this complexity, which I shall carry into the next chapter as we sum up an integrative account of the various levels of harmonic representation as anticipated by the Integrated Analytical Model, is that we are approaching mature and powerful scientific conceptualizations of complexity which transcend the deterministic models of either psychoanalytic drive theory or cognitive behavioral learning theory. Although we cannot mathematically prove that the solar system is stable, it certainly seems to be so, at the macrocosmic level. Although we cannot isolate the molecular structures or even the neural circuits that make up selfhood, we persist phenomenologically in experiencing ourselves in symphonic and unitary ways, illusory or not. Although we continue to wrangle over the true nature of archetypes, or whether they exist or are necessary, we relate to them intimately and intuitively in our everyday lives through story, song, symbol, and dream life. Although we debate the nature of God, the human (and natural) world continues to be profoundly shaped by what we think about Him, Her, It, or They. The promise of these contemporary models of constructive complexity is that they suggest a model of the human mind as a hypothesis-tester, an agent of inference, and above all, a creator (and co-creator, at the interpersonal level) of reality. The human mind does not just discover reality, the human mind creates reality. I can think of no better way to conclude Chapter 8 than with a citation by fantasy writer Terry Pratchett (2015):

> Stability is not about what a system is actually doing: it is about how the system would change if you disturbed it. Stability, by definition, deals with 'what if?'. Because a lot of science is really about this non-existent world of thought experiments, our understanding of science must concern itself with worlds of the imagination as well as with worlds of reality. Imagination, rather than mere intelligence, is the truly human quality.
>
> (p. 12)

References

Berlucchi, G., & Aglioti, S. (1997). The body in the brain: Neural bases of corporeal awareness. *Trends in Neurosciences, 20*: 560–564.

Bion, W. R. (1959). Attacks on linking. *International Journal of Psychoanalysis, 40*: 308–315.

Cambray, J. (2009). *Nature and psyche in an interconnected universe.* Texas A&M University Press.

Clewley, R. (1998). Emergence without magic: The role of memetics in multi-scale models of evolution and behavior. *Proceedings of the 15th International Congress on Cybernetics* (Association Internationale de Cybernetique, Namur). Retrieved at http://www.cam.cornell.edu/~rclewley/conf.html

Cohen, L. B., Chaput, H. H., & Cashon, C. H. (2002). A constructivist model of infant cognition. *Cognitive Development, 17*: 1323–1343.

Davis, K. L., & Montag, C. (2019). Selected principles of Pankseppian affective neuroscience. *Frontiers in Neuroscience, 12*: 1025.

Dawkins, R. (1976). *The selfish gene.* Oxford University Press.

Dehaene-Lambertz, G., & Spelke, E. S. (2015). The infancy of the human brain. *Neuron, 88*(1): 93–109.

Eigen, M., & Schuster, P. (1979). *The Hypercycle: A principle of natural self-organization.* Springer.

Gabora, L. & Aerts, D. (2009). A model of the emergence and evolution of integrated worldviews. *Journal of Mathematical Psychology, 53*: 434–451.

Grossmann, T., Johnson, M. H., Farroni, T, & Csibra, G. (2007). Social perception in the infant brain: Gamma oscillatory activity in response to eye gaze. *Social Cognitive and Affective Neuroscience, 2*(4): 284–291.

Gutchess, A. H., Hedden, T., Ketay, S., Aron, A., & Gabrieli, J. D. (2010). Neural differences in the processing of semantic relationships across cultures. *Social Cognitive and Affective Neuroscience, 5*(2): 254–263.

Hipólito, I., & Kirchhoff, M. (2023). Breaking boundaries: The Bayesian brain hypothesis for perception and prediction. *Consciousness and Cognition, 111*: 1–8.

Kohonen, T., (2013). Essentials of the self-organizing map. *Neural Networks, 37*: 52–65.

Mahoney, M. J., Miller, H. M., & Arciero, G. (1995). Constructive metatheory and the nature of mental representation. In M. J. Mahoney (Ed.), *Cognitive and constructive psychotherapies* (pp. 103–120). Springer Publishing Company.

Mainzer, K. (2005). *Symmetry and complexity: The spirit and beauty of nonlinear science.* World Scientific.

Newman, D. V. (1996). Emergence and strange attractors. *Philosophy of Science, 63*(2): 245–261.

Patel, R. S., Bowman, F. D., & Rilling, J. K. (2006). Determining hierarchical functional networks from auditory stimuli fMRI. *Human Brain Mapping, 27*: 462–470.

Poincaré, H. (1905). *Science and method.* The Walter Scott Publishing Co.

Pratchett, T. (2015). *The science of discworld: A novel.* Anchor Books.

Prigogine, I. (1980). *From being to becoming: Time and complexity in the physical sciences.* W. H. Freeman.

Rabin, S. (2023). Nicolaus Copernicus. In E. N. Zalta & U. Nodelman (Eds.), *The Stanford encyclopedia of philosophy* (Winter 2023 ed.). Stanford University. https://plato.stanford.edu/archives/win2023/entries/copernicus/

Solms, M. (2021). *The hidden spring: A journey to the source of consciousness.* W.W. Norton.

Chapter 9

Integrative Overview
of the Harmonic Systems

E pur si muove ("And yet, it moves").

-Attributed to Galileo Galilei

As discussed in Chapter 2, analytical psychology tends to view modern and post-modern modes of thought as phases of human experience no more (or less) valid than previous modes of thought that prevailed in antiquity and among traditional cultures. Some of the other systems we have carefully considered, such as psychoanalysis, constructivism, emergentism, or chaos theory, are intrinsically rooted in postmodern assumptions that explicitly reject essentialist metanarratives. Therefore, it will be quite tricky to envision a transtheoretical perspective that encompasses these various points of view. In fact, to do so, we must do as Jung did: to back way up and encompass the historical sweep of human philosophies even as we survey the various levels of mental representation.

I noticed in the writing (and I wondered if you noticed in the reading) that describing the various harmonic levels of mental representation in order, from archetype to self, also involved a chronology. Discussions of archetype inevitably lead backward in time: to Leibniz, to Plato, to Augustine, to Kant. Moving through the early Jungian perspectives on the symbolic function and into the early psychoanalytic perspectives on object relations led to more contemporary citations on complex and schema, and especially with the latter harmonic, we emerged into current models of cognitive neuroscience, which deign to concern themselves with the schema harmonic if not the archetype or symbol. In Psychology and Alchemy, Jung (1993) writes about the foundational ideals that have been discarded in the modern and postmodern age:

> The demand that we should follow the ideal and seek to become like it...ought logically to have the result of developing and exalting the inner man [individual psychology]. In actual fact, however, the ideal has been turned by superficial and formalistically-minded believers into external objects of worship...Western man is held in thrall by the 'ten thousand things'; he sees only particulars, he is ego-bound and thing-bound, and unaware of the deep root of all being...

DOI: 10.4324/9781032708751-11

The Western attitude, with its emphasis on the object, tends to fix the ideal...
in its outward aspect and thus rob it of its mysterious relation to the inner man.

(p. 232)

As I researched, composed, and wrote the content of the past few chapters, I
became aware of my own reactions, and the anxious tugging of some part of my
own mind to bring this book into a place of "scientific" respectability. Unfortunately for me, and for us all, to take archetypal reality seriously is to rebel against
the spirit of the age, which requires us to resist anything smacking of metaphysics. As Jung (2005) elaborated, "to think otherwise than our contemporaries think
is somehow illegitimate and disturbing; it is even indecent, morbid or blasphe-
mous, and therefore socially dangerous for the individual. He is stupidly swimming
against the social current" (p. 175).

Well, here I go, and I appreciate you joining me in swimming against the current,
stupidly or not. For the rest of this book, I will suggest a construct of primordial
symmetry, a primal structure of mental representations that starts with the vertical
stratification of harmonic layers and then shifts to the horizontal rotational energy
of specific archetypal themes. In this chapter and the next, I will summarize the
vertical model of harmonic representation, and consider some of its clinical applications and implications, in particular as a central organizing feature of personality.

A Harmonic Progression

Parallel with the discussions that spanned Chapters 2–8 of this work, the vertical
aspect of the Integrated Analytical Model describes a range of mental representations which I call harmonics, after a musical metaphor. I do not mean to suggest that
there are six of them; harmonic levels of representation likely exist on a spectrum,
which itself is the epiphenomenon of a lot of nested complexity, which is then further
modified by how we perceive and talk about them. For example, how many colors
are there? We might count the seven traditional colors of the visible light spectrum:
red, orange, yellow, green, blue, indigo, and violet (ROYGBIV), or the many forms
of red-green shades and yellow-blue shades according to some sources. The RGB
model used in display screens uses combinations of red, green, and blue to result
in 16,777,216 possible colors. To complicate matters, the naming and grouping of
colors are culturally relative: Americans consider "yellow" as the color adjacent to
green without orange tint, but the German word for "yellow" (*gelb*) is associated with
colors ranging from the "American" yellow to yellow-orange. In music theory, the
functional equivalent of color is the *octave*, and I am suggesting that in psychological space, the functional equivalent in mental representation is the representational
harmonic. Just as the naming of colors is culturally relative, we have encountered
many "cultural" traditions that slice the harmonic pie up in different ways. The six
that I have named are no more or less arbitrary than any other system, but these six
have the advantage of representing frequently named categories of mental representation within the literature and applied practice of psychodynamic psychology.

The six harmonic levels of mental representation were presented in this book in a particular progression, ranging from inchoate, primal, and unconscious aspects to the most highly differentiated, measurable, and conscious ones:

1 Archetype
2 Symbol
3 Object
4 Complex
5 Schema
6 Self

Consistent with the chaos and complexity models considered in Chapter 8, each harmonic level should be considered a Complex Adaptive System, a self-organizing system operating in fractal phase space, driven by principles of deterministic chaos described in Chapter 8. Using the terms of chaos theory, both the levels of mental representation described in Chapters 2–7 (the six harmonics) and the representational themes described ahead in Chapters 12–16 (the representational axes and resulting quadrants) represent *attractors* in the chaotic system: they are the raw organizational principles which drive the kinds of thematic inferences motivating the so-called Bayesian system. Other forces in the phase space of mental representation represent *dissipators* that delimit and disrupt the continuity of the attractor vectors. Psychodynamic theory has generally described these dissipators as defensive systems, and in Chapter 10, we will explore defenses as *radical discontinuities* within the phase space of the representational system. One of the complications that faces us in constructing an Integrative Analytical Model is the fact that Jungian theory has culturally focused on attractors, while psychoanalytic theory has emphasized the effects of dissipators.

The harmonic progression recapitulates Lacan's (1993) conceptualization of *signifying chains*, trajectories of representation that represent a desired meaning by the subject. A signifying chain represents an underlying intended meaning, expressed across a related system of signifiers, through the mechanism of *metonymy*. *Metonymy* describes the process of one signifier scaffolding onto another within a single chain, similar to Freud's notion of displacement (as opposed to metaphor, which refers to connections across chains, as we shall discuss in Chapter 11 in the context of the Circumplex Model). Meanwhile, a progressive amount of slippage occurs in the system of signifying chains since the difference between the signifier and the signified can only increase across iterations. Lacan used the term *glissement* to describe this slippage, or divergence of meaning between what is intended or desired and what is received. *Glissement* should now remind you of the dissipators described by complexity theory. Furthermore, Lacan's assertion that the mechanism of signification, central to language and therefore to human psychology, represents expressions of *desire* on behalf of the subject, parallels the intentionality inherent in Complex Adaptive Systems as we discussed in Chapter 8.

For purposes of the Integrated Analytical Model, I will refer to the trajectory of themes across the various harmonic levels as *harmonic vectors*, which each represent their own phase space and exist within their own kind of Markov Blanket. The harmonic progression of the Integrated Analytical Model, by means of harmonic vectors which represent archetypal themes across the various harmonic levels, can be understood as analogous to both Lacan's signifying chains,[1] which are essentially expressions of desire, and the "engine of inference" suggested by the Bayesian Brain Hypothesis, which are motivated attempts to approximate a goal inherent to the subject. In Jungian terms, the harmonic progression represents the outcome of libidinal expression, where libido is defined as a kind of psychic energy (rather than sexual as Freud originally held). Jung (1972) writes that "Libido can never be apprehended except in a definite form; that is to say, it is identical with fantasy-images. And we can only release it from the grip of the unconscious by bringing up the corresponding fantasy-images" (para. 345).

The harmonic progression is a primordial symmetry with an archetypal basis. We encountered the notion of "symmetry" in this chapter, in the context of how Complex Adaptive Systems evolve through the breakdown of symmetry. The breakdown of symmetry actually reflects the attempts of the psyche to represent crucial inner truths (and desires and goals related to those inner truths) while also making inferences about how successfully those goals are being met. The attractors of the system are primordial symmetrical models of desired end states (and therefore instinctive), and the dissipators of the system represent the array of reasons the symmetry breaks down or fails to be successfully represented...whether as the result of defenses (radical discontinuities within the system), Lacan's *glissement* (the ultimate impossibility of successful signification), or even the intervention of mental illness, which represents patternistic ways in which representation and intentionality break down.

As I have mentioned above, the developmental scaffolding of the harmonic levels and the circumplex model which we will discuss in the second part of this book represent a symmetrical precursor state representing archetypal probability fields which generate the "raw material" of unconscious content, the "fundamental frequency" from which subsequent keys of consciousness derive. As we shall see by the end of this book, the Integrated Analytical Model proposes both a vertical trajectory inherent in the harmonic levels and a rotational energy inherent in the circumplex model. As Mainzer (2005) puts it in the context of Complex Adaptive Systems, "with increasing velocity we get a birfurcation tree of increasing complexity" (p. 14).

To make a point similar to that of Mark Solms (2021) about the role of affect in consciousness (see Chapter 8), affect (as a manifestation of libido, Lacan's desire, or complexity theory's motivated inferences) provides a teleological impetus to develop progressively "realistic" mental representations which will ultimately prove instrumental in getting one's needs met in the external world of people, relationships, and things. But the harmonic progression (again, similar to Lacan's signifying chains or the adaptive intentions of complexity theory) operates not just by learning about the environment, as suggested in cognitive behavioral paradigms, but by generating inferences (signifiers) in an attempt to *shape* reality, or even *create* reality. Here the Jungian concept of archetypes becomes crucial: *the archetypal harmonic provides thematic probability fields which serve as the source for the psyche's creativity in generating its own narratives.* The psyche isn't just empirically investigating external reality, it is telling a story. *It is trying to tell a better story.*

A Hierarchy of Holons

At the beginning of this book, I mentioned holons and the idea of holarchy: an arrangement by which parts of a whole are paradoxically wholes themselves, such that the developing personality rebuilds its world and environment anew with each successive layer of representation. Each harmonic is therefore fractally structured, recapitulating itself, its neighboring harmonics, and the system as a whole itself. Each harmonic represents a kind of language, and like actual languages in the world, each harmonic has its own ways of expressing similar themes in different ways. And again like actual languages, some harmonics are better suited than others at approximating certain aspects of psychological reality: it would be much easier to negotiate a corporate merger in English than in Latin, even if everyone concerned were fluent in both languages, because of the ways in which modern English has adapted in the direction of communicating such ideas. All languages are capable of richly depicting the human experience, but they do it in different ways. The same is true of the harmonic levels.

The progression of the harmonic sequence is hierarchical, chaotic, and reversible. Similar to the conclusions drawn from constructivist models of infant cognition near the end of Chapter 8, the Integrated Analytical Model suggests that higher-order harmonics evolve from lower-order ones, and in turn form the basis for even higher levels of organization beyond itself as a result of increasingly available complexity. The psyche tends to prioritize the implementation of the highest harmonic level available to it (I will term this the *representational horizon* and discuss it further in Chapter 10), but when the system becomes distressed, it will resort to lower-level harmonic representations (regression). As we shall see in Chapter 10, psychotherapeutic intervention with serious mental illness, personality disorder, and trauma can be seen as an "upwards progression" of successively complex and embodied iterations of harmonic representation, whereas psychotherapy with high-functioning and "neurotically organized" personality structure follows a path of deconstructing higher-level harmonics in order to gain phenomenological access to lower-order ones.

With ascending differentiation and theoretical "distance" from the archetypal harmonic, primordial symmetry and symbolic representation increasingly collide with, and are challenged by, new perspectives entering the system from within and from without. We have previously discussed examples of such "dissipative" forces as defenses (radical discontinuities in the harmonic vector which represent the system challenging itself) and Lacan's slippage called *glissement* as a breakdown of meaning; however, one of the most primary sources of "dissipation" in archetypal representation is attachment and the intersubjective fields emerging from human relationships. As we shall discuss elsewhere, attachment and relational fields represent important challenges to the symmetry of the core psychic system, in both positive and negative senses, as dramatically evidenced by Grotstein's (1981) "primal split" (see Chapter 17). Relationships and attachment disrupt the system and also enrich it; both kinds of experiences have to be metabolized through adjustments in various levels of mental representation, as anticipated by relational psychoanalysis and intersubjective perspectives within psychotherapy.

The harmonic progression, as we shall see, is fractal: each level represents an inferential universe all of its own, and in our example, each harmonic recapitulates a common theme, which is the harmonic vector, like a Lacanian signifying chain, representing themes that have archetypal roots which become organized at higher and higher harmonic levels while still "working through" the foundational themes. The harmonic progression is therefore holographic: a projection of archetypal themes into fractal space. Grotstein (2004) takes up this theme in relation to Bion's conceptualization of O:

> May we not consider that the unconscious is holographic in so far as it can be considered to be holistic and ubiquitous, on one hand, and implicate (divided) (Bohm, 1980), on the other? I am postulating the possibility, to accommodate Bion's theories, that O can be considered to be paradoxically both beyond and within the embrace of the unconscious and consciousness—or both inside and outside the self.
>
> (p. 1097)

Jungian analyst Joseph Cambray (2009) approaches the same theme from the direction of Leibnitz's "reflected universe":

> Leibniz's monads also share this same fundamental image, his mirror thesis insists that each monad reflects all others, that is, the whole universe in itself. A holistic, radically interconnected, reflective universe has been a recurrent imagining of humanity, and Jung's theory of the Self together with the collective unconscious offer a psychological reading of this archetypal pattern. Synchronicity becomes a particularly potent manifestation of the field with the resonant reflections of internal and external events.
>
> (p. 44)

Elsewhere, Cambray (2009) summarizes

> A transpersonal psyche with a collective unconscious composed of the sum of all of the archetypes as Jung's model proposed would have features of a scale-free network structure. His methodology for approaching the unconscious, especially amplification, similarly can be seen to map and understand the psyche as such a network.
>
> (p. 50)

Integration of Affect

So far, in laying the foundations for the progression of harmonic levels of representation, we have focused primarily on the mental representations that comprise the "glial cells" of the system, providing a dynamic structure of complex inter-relationships of increasingly complex representations. Yet in the psychodynamic models of the mind, affect (that is, emotions) represents the "royal road" into the unconscious, and tracking affect is widely held as a *sina qua non* technique. Affect bears the "white heat of relevance," to use a term used by Lorna Smith Benjamin (1996, p. 83). Jung (1968) certainly prioritized the role of affect in understanding and communicating with the psyche:

> Emotions themselves are always in some degree overwhelming for the subject, because they are involuntary conditions which override the intentions of the ego. Moreover, they cling to the subject, and he cannot detach them from himself... Emotions are not detachable like ideas or thoughts, because they are identical with certain physical conditions and are thus deeply rooted in the heavy matter of the body.
>
> (p. 24)

Jung here is making a particular point that affect plays a qualitatively different role from ideation, is not "detachable," and somehow springs from the "heavy matter" of the body. This perspective is intriguingly consistent with Solms' (2021) hypothesis, explored in Chapter 8, that affect represents a kind of consciousness itself...a perceptual consciousness that is rooted in the cortex and different from the affective consciousness mediated by the periaqueductal gray, the superior colliculi, and the midbrain locomotor region of the brain. In fact, Solms' perceptual versus affective consciousness suggests two dynamic systems representing affect and ideation, thinking and feeling, both synergizing to create a kind of layered consciousness. From the perspective of the harmonic progression of the Integrated Analytical Model, I would suggest that affect plays a significant role in providing the motivational impetus for complexified expansion of mental representations. If thinking tells us what a thing *is*, feeling tells us what a thing is *worth*. Feeling determines our valuative relationship with ideas, perspectives, memories, outcomes, and mental representations of all kinds. Furthermore, affective experiences likely strongly accompany the transition from one harmonic representation to another, confirming the deeply held psychodynamic perspective that emotional catharsis accompanies psychological growth.

Psychoanalytic theory has been beautifully articulated about affective states and their complex roles in attachment and the formation of personality. Theoretical overlap between contemporary psychoanalysis and attachment theory defines attachment as dyadic regulation of emotion (Schore, 2000, p. 26). In other words, one of the most crucial outcomes of attachment is to establish the capacity to tolerate strong emotional experiences. Fonagy et al. (2017) identify "epistemic trust" as one of the primary functions of attachment: "defined as trust in the authenticity and personal relevance of interpersonally transmitted knowledge about how the social environment works" (p. 176). These perspectives collectively suggest complex feedback loops between affect and ideation, in which affective states drive mentalization through motivating perceptual sets and behaviors predicted to lead to fulfilling needs, and by providing real-time feedback about the relative effectiveness of mentalization strategies.

Historically, psychoanalytic theory in particular has identified basic anxiety states which can be conceptualized as drivers for successive levels of both attachment and mentalization. Taken together, these basic anxieties can be seen as occurring in a sequence, with one form of anxiety replacing the previous form. *Annihilation anxiety* (Hurvich, 2003) represents one of the most elemental of anxiety states and represents affective reactions to impending destruction, death, overwhelm, loss of body integrity, embodiment, or disintegration. Other colorful descriptors which resemble annihilation anxiety include organismic distress panic (Mahler, 1968), the destructive force within (Klein, 2002), prey/predatory anxiety (Grotstein, 1984), dissolution of boundedness (Ogden, 1989), unthinkable anxiety (Winnicott, 1965), Biotrauma (Stern, 1972), nameless dread (Bion, 1959), fright without solution (Hesse & Main, 2006), disintegration anxiety (Kohut, 1971), and others. We can think of annihilation anxiety as a natural result of the primitive helplessness of the human infant, which experiences primitive anxiety states in the absence of any agency or self-efficacy. Annihilation anxiety is mediated by attachment when an infant or child has repeated experiences of encountering annihilation anxiety, crying for help, and getting help such that annihilation anxiety becomes an experience that is not deadly (or at least, has never been) and therefore can be increasingly tolerated. Again, in this sense, primitive anxiety states are therefore motivators (they inspire help-seeking), the successful navigation of which results in additional means of mentalizing ("you never get too cold or hungry or sick; someone always comes along to help") which create a capacity to tolerate the anxiety.

The successful mediation of annihilation anxiety naturally leads to the next level of anxiety, which is *abandonment anxiety*, or fear of loss of the object that helped mediate annihilation anxiety in the first place. Abandonment anxiety, in turn, is mediated by the development of an agentic and positively valued sense of self, after which the ambient form of anxiety becomes *moral anxiety*, or the fear of inadequacy of the self ("What if I fail?"). This developmental scaffolding of anxiety states, as we can see, parallels and interacts with, and is an outcome of, increasing sophistication of object relations and mentalization systems. As we shall explore in Chapter 10, the appearance and prominence of different anxiety states therefore correlate with different levels of harmonic representation and by extension, different personality organizations. For example, borderline states organize especially around abandonment anxiety, and abandonment anxiety is simultaneously an outcome of the borderline (or, as I will call it, histrionic or Third Quadrant) personality's relatively intact capacity for attachment, which is less prominent in the more psychologically impoverished narcissistic personality (Second Quadrant) which is comparatively more vulnerable to annihilation anxiety.

The Harmonic Vector: Linking Internal with External

From a constructivist point of view, the progression of increasingly sophisticated mental representations that increasingly successfully represent the realistic outcome of psychic goals as measured by outcomes in the external world (a harmonic vector) serves the purpose of reducing basic anxiety and increasing control. The harmonic progression can be seen as a trajectory of increasingly elaborated phase space resulting in the potential for greater consonance between one's inner experience and one's outcomes in the world: linking internal and external experience, back and forth in both directions.

Let us take an example of a man who is invited to the home of a love interest for dinner, but gets spooked during the encounter and ends up leaving early, resulting in a relational conflict. The progression of harmonic representation might therefore progress something like this:

1   Subject makes an excuse and abruptly leaves a home dinner engagement.
    This is a behavior rather than a representation, and as we shall see, dissipates a mental representation without metabolizing, processing, or verbalizing it. In psychodynamic models, this kind of behavior is called an enactment, and it signals a failure of mentalizing.

2   Subject explains on the phone later that evening: "I went home early because I got uncomfortable, and you got so mad that I didn't feel like talking to you afterwards."
    A lower-order harmonic is employed to represent the experience; the subject begins to name a self state (at the crude level of comfortable/uncomfortable) but then externalizes the affect onto the object.

3   After several intense conversations over a couple of days, the subject is able to state retrospectively: "I got nervous because I was afraid you were losing interest in me, and when I get nervous, I avoid things."
    A higher-level harmonic is invoked, which comes closer to naming a crucial internal state (anxiety) despite misgivings about vulnerability, and even is able to name a defensive tendency of the system (avoidance).

4   The next week the subject is able to get here in a therapy session: "I got anxious because I'm developing very strong feelings for her, and so I don't want to lose her. But that makes me look for evidence that she's about to reject me, and to reject her first, before she gets the chance to hurt me. I can tell that I hurt her feelings, and I have to learn to trust her feelings for me."
    An even higher-level harmonic representation allows more complex, comprehensive, and relationally framed insight. This level allows enough complexity that intentions of the self, defensive operations of the self, and affective states of self and others are all available to be represented effectively.

The harmonic progression of mental representations is the psychological scaffolding that is central to crucial areas of human psychological functioning, such as the development of mature object relations, attachment, and successful adult adaptation to a complex interpersonal world. The harmonic progression, leading upwards and downwards, represents the intersection of one's own emotional honesty with one's willingness to trust an interpersonal process with another person in ways that risk the integrity of one's own "symmetrical" system.

Let us now trace the trajectory of a harmonic vector across the levels of mental representation we have discussed so far. I will briefly trace a trajectory of harmonic progression from the archetypal to the level of selfhood. Note that in keeping with my own sensibilities about how lower-order harmonics like archetype may and may not be represented, my style of writing will adapt accordingly:

Archetypal Harmonic

aaaa
   there is
   there is unboundedness
   there is encirclement
   Unboundedness and Encirclement, not-encirclement and not-unboundedness
   there is also a softness, and hardness…not-hardness and not-softness
   Encirclement, not unboundedness, restrains
   there is a restraining
   The restraining prevents
   is also encirclement
   encirclement protects against hardness
   restraint and softness
   Comments: *Note that, consistent with our discussion in Chapter 2, I have depicted archetypal content in a very protean way, which cannot be directly represented in language, image, or behavior. The themes are primordial and nearly geometric, but show the foundational tendency toward supporting thematic emergence. The emerging themes represent continua, suggesting a framework for organizing experience.*

Symbolic Harmonic

Encirclement encases and shields, like a seed, and contains nutrients. This encircling force loves and protects, brings safety, and feeds. It organizes inner soft, safe things from outer, hard things.

Encirclement is also controlling. Within it, there is softness and safety, and it limits danger. Dangers are possibilities. Encirclement prevents danger and possibilities.

Danger brings terror, a frightening emptiness and disappearance, a nothingness. The original unboundedness brings terror, and encirclement prevents this with softness.

Unboundedness is terror, and also freedom. Freedom is outside the encirclement, so freedom brings terror and threatens encirclement and softness.

The encirclement protects and brings softness, costs boundedness, and is safe inside and hard outside.

Comments: *At the symbolic level, archetypal themes show patternistic emergence but are not yet associated with objects, nor are they primary organizers of affect (although they provoke affect). The symbolic exists in a realm beyond the "I" and "thou," remaining in the realm of narrative content.*

Object Harmonic

The woman (mother) protects and brings love. She encircles and feeds, also preventing unboundedness which is freedom. I came from her, lived inside her, and was made safe by her. She provides safety with comfort and containment. But she also delimits. She offers safety through closeness, which undermines freedom (unboundedness).

The man (father) is powerful and free. He does not encircle and feed, and he brings hardness. He protects me also, like the mother, but his safety comes from his power and his freedom. He is not available, not present, like her. Because he is free. This is power.

The mother loves me by containing me and feeding me. The father loves me with separateness and with power.

I am like the mother, have a body like hers. I could be, can be, am like her. I enter into her softness and closeness for safety, a merging. I am not like the man, do not have a body like his. I do not have power and unboundedness like he does.

Comments: *Object representations of self and others emerge, initially experienced as functions but eventually associated with external objects, evolving from part object to whole object representations. Increasingly, object representations of self and others are imbued with affective valence (classified as good or bad, for example). By this level of mental representation, attachment experiences in and of themselves gain enough complexity and permanence to bind and modulate affect. For example, primary attachments gain the power to bind primitive anxiety states. Conscious awareness of this level of dynamics is generally not directly possible but can be described in indirect and imaginal ways.*

Complex Harmonic

My mother's control over me is both frustrating and familiar. I can see how she has the same effect on my father, through all the games she plays. She pretends to be helpless, tosses her hair, and it works every time. My father is frustrated but also fascinated by her helplessness. His attraction to her has something to do with saving her. It's what men do. They get the power, and women have to trick them into loving them, into sticking around.

I remember when my dad started backing off, getting distant. One day you're playing in the yard and reading stories in his lap, the next day he's too busy to give you the time of day. But that's all right, because not long after that, I started to get my own kind of attention.

Comments: *Object representations increase in complexity and are linked into constellations organized around similar themes and affective tones. Representations of objects continue to complexify, and by this level of organization, libidinal energy, affect, and projective content are categorized not just to individual object representations but to categories such as social groups. The progressively rich interpersonal field both results from and encourages the developmental imperative for more sophisticated mentalizing. Perception and behavior increase in representational complexity, but remain categorical and somewhat dichotomous. At this level, psychological dynamics can increasingly be identified and verbalized consciously.*

Schema Harmonic

My boyfriend thinks I'm clingy. I've heard that before; it must be some kind of theme with me. Or is it a problem with *him*? I guess I don't see what's so bad about wanting to be close to the person you love. Do I have to apologize for caring about him? I sure wish he'd return the favor, instead of hitting me with all this criticism. I'm tired of hearing about how I haven't finished my degree, or how I'm stuck in a dead-end job. I mean, excuse me for putting all my energy into this relationship. Isn't that what's most important? Anyway, like I keep telling him, he can keep the office job...I want to have a family.

Comments: *Mental representations at the schema harmonic increasingly integrate affect and ideation. Self-states, cognitive styles, attributional biases, and other forms of mental representation increasingly are experienced as subroutines available to the psyche, rather than just experiences associated with objects. Increasingly abstract representations of different perspectives of both self and others become possible. At this harmonic level, "observing ego" function becomes reliably present, resulting in more accurate, flexible, and reality-based means of conceptualizing self states. The psyche becomes increasingly aware of its own defensive operations and is able to notice its own distortions.*

Self Harmonic

I'm feeling pressured by this promotion. Sure, part of me is thrilled...I mean, it's nice to be appreciated. And I certainly worked hard for it. I care a lot about what I do, and I think it's good for my daughter to see an adult woman making it in the world, even if it means some gravel in your gut. Sometimes that's what it takes. But I'm surprised how scared I am. Part of me just wants my husband to come hold me and say "there there," and take this all away. So much for my own autonomy! Part of me worries that I'm not going to make it. And then part of me is angry for being scared, like it's a kind of weakness. I just never seem to know the answers anymore...like somehow, the more responsibility I get, the more lost I feel. And when my employees look at me, I know they're counting on me to be strong and figure things out...just like my daughter does. So this is what they call an existential crisis, I guess. Well, bring it on! On second thought, bring me a white wine spritzer.

Comments: *Smoothly integrated, symphonic abstract representations of self and others can be considered, evaluated, and modified at need, based on experience. Core experiences of self and others have settled into systems that are stable enough to be relied upon in order to navigate complex interpersonal reality, such as long-term intimate relationships, parenting, and the development and maintenance of professional and occupational identities. Conceptualizations of self and others are experienced as reliable enough to hold lightly, allowing for default states of curiosity and continued growth. In fact, at the level of the Self Harmonic, the organizational themes of the psyche become actually harder to identify, because there is so much complexity expressed at so many levels, and with so much nuance. Mature defensive systems reliably emerge, accessible to observing ego function, and therefore subject to self-analysis. Note the emergence of perspectives which are more philosophical and predicated on a capacity for humor.*

Note in our example the influence of what I will call representational vectors or themes that transcend the various levels of mental representation (again, like Lacan's signifying chains, or the inferential cognitive processes suggested by complexity theory). In this case, one transcendent theme organizes around questions about the adequacy and safety of the self, which is experienced as in conflict with the availability of safety and love. As a psychotherapist, I would associate these representational vectors with either depressive or histrionic themes (Fourth or Third Quadrant, as we shall see in future chapters).

As we round out this chapter, I would like to draw particular attention to a particular characteristic emerging from the harmonic progression: with increasing complexity, the adaptive utility of each harmonic in serving as a set of organizing principles for navigating adult life is progressively more robust, agentic, and effective in representing the needs of the self, and also in consolidating the capacity for curiosity and creativity. As we shall see in Chapter 10, the degree of sophistication of mental representation available to the psyche becomes an important correlate of what we call "mental health." In the next chapter, we will explore this and other important clinical applications and implications of harmonic progression.

Note

1   It seems noteworthy that Lacan sometimes discussed signifying chains in linear terms, and in other contexts as circular; a distinction that anticipates the vertical organization of the harmonic representations and the circumplex model which we will explore in future chapters.

References

Benjamin, L. S. (1996). *Interpersonal diagnosis and treatment of personality disorders.* The Guilford Press.

Bion, W. R. (1959). Attacks on linking. *International Journal of Psychoanalysis, 40*: 308–315.

Bohm, D. (1980). *Wholeness and the implicate order*. Routledge.

Cambray, J. (2009). *Nature and psyche in an interconnected universe*. Texas A&M University Press.

Fonagy, P., Campbell, C., & Bateman, A. (2017). Mentalizing, attachment, and epistemic trust in group therapy. *International Journal of Group Psychotherapy, 67*(2): 176–201.

Grotstein, J. (1984). A proposed revision of the psychoanalytic concept of the death instinct. In R. J. Langs (Ed.), *The yearbook of psychoanalysis and psychotherapy* (pp. 299–326). Gardner Press.

Grotstein, J. S. (2004). The seventh servant: The implications of a truth drive in Bion's theory of 'O'. *International Journal of Psycho-Analysis, 85*(5): 1081–1101.

Grotstein, J. S. (1981). *Splitting and projective identification*. Jason Aronson.

Hesse, E., & Main, M. (2006). Frightened, threatening, and dissociative parental behavior. *Development and Psychopathology, 18*(2): 309–343.

Hurvich, M. (2003). The place of annihilation anxieties in psychoanalytic theory. *Journal of the American Psychoanalytic Association, 51*: 579–616.

Jung, C. G. (1972). *Two essays on analytical psychology* (R. F. C. Hull, Trans.). Princeton University Press.

Jung, C. G. (1993). *Psychology and alchemy* (R. F. C. Hull, Trans.). Princeton University Press.

Jung, C. G. (2005). *Modern man in search of a soul*. Routledge.

Jung, C. G. (1968). *Analytical psychology: Its theory and practice*. Vintage Books.

Klein, M. (2002). *Envy and gratitude and other works*. The Free Press.

Kohut, H. (1971). *The analysis of the self*. International Universities Press.

Lacan, J. (1993). *The seminar. Book III, the psychoses, 1955-56.* (R. Grigg, Trans.). Routledge.

Mahler, M. S. (1968). *On human symbiosis and the vicissitudes of individuation*. International Universities Press.

Mainzer, K. (2005). *Symmetry and complexity: The spirit and beauty of nonlinear science*. World Scientific.

Ogden, T. H. (1989). On the concept of an autistic-contiguous position. *International Journal of Psychoanalysis, 70*(1): 127–140.

Schore, A. N. (2000). Attachment and the regulation of the right brain. *Attachment & Human Development, 2*(1): 23–47.

Solms, M. (2021). *The hidden spring: A journey to the source of consciousness*. W.W. Norton.

Stern, M. M. (1972). Biotrauma, fear of death and aggression. *International Journal of Psychoanalysis, 53*(2): 291–299.

Winnicott, D. W. (1965). *The maturational processes and the facilitating environment: Studies in the theory of emotional development*. International Universities Press.

Chapter 10

Clinical Implications of the Harmonic Progression

Don't be afraid! We won't make an author of you, while there's an honest trade to be learnt, or brick-making to turn to.

—Charles Dickens *Oliver Twist*

In a Complex Adaptive System, such as the harmonic progression suggested by the Integrated Analytical Model, holographic levels of mental representation progressively model perception, mediation, and ideation in increasingly complex iterations. Affective (emotional) experiences provide motivational impetus to the evolution of harmonic vectors along with vectors that represent the evolution of specific themes, which become represented in increasingly complex ways. Each harmonic vector represents an attempt at modeling reality, contextualizing experience, and generating both hypotheses and behavioral interventions designed to increase the likelihood that needs can be met. In a larger sense, however, as we have discussed, the purpose of this complex adaptive system is not just learning and re-acting: the symphonic epiphenomenal outcome of all that mentalizing represents a creative process such that the system generates reality as much as it assesses reality.

Functionally speaking, although harmonics represent fractal recapitulations of the entire system, that is, each harmonic level calculates and generates reality *in toto*, and deals with every aspect of the experiential field at every level, no single harmonic level has adequate information to effectively represent the whole, because each representational level mentalizes in a unique way. Similarly, no single part of the Complex Adaptive System can effectively predict the outcomes of the system. Borrowing language from chaos theory, we have described the self-organizing features of the harmonic progression as *attractors*, which collectively generate and maintain representational symmetry across the system, which explains the final shape that our model will take, which is a circumplex navigated by a spiral (see Chapter 11). On the other side of the psychological ledger book, we recognize *dissipators*, which are change agents that undermine, oppose, or restructure the primordial symmetry of the system, which not only causes entropy (i.e., suffering and symptoms) but also allows new forms to emerge. As we shall discuss below, dissipators include endogenous forces such as the defensive operations

DOI: 10.4324/9781032708751-12

of the personality, as well as exogenous factors like attachment and interpersonal relationships, the effects of trauma, the pervasive impact of culture, and even psychotherapy, among others.

The central idea of this chapter will be that the successive layers of mental representation comprising the harmonic succession, the so-called Vertical Model, represent a trajectory toward psychological integration and therefore mediate the overall level of what we call "mental health." In other words, the harmonic progression represents the level of organization of the personality.

The Representational Horizon and the Harmonic Progression

I have attempted to conceptualize the development of harmonic progression as a developmental spectrum of increasing complexity, which allows increasing depth, complexity, efficacy, and agency in psychological functioning. The evolution of the harmonic progression is progressive and builds upon itself such that one level of complexity begets another level of higher complexity due to the complex interaction of attractors and dissipators. Each quantum leap from one harmonic level to another represents a trauma to the system, in a sense, because of the breaking of symmetry which leads to new forms. Psychological growth, as we have learned, is painful.

Otto Kernberg (1975) contributed an enduring classification scheme describing three developmental layers of personality: the psychotic, borderline, and neurotic levels of organization. As Nancy McWilliams (2011) notes, this developmental dimension for personality organization allows a useful level of resolution in contextualizing psychological functioning at different levels, even within specific clinical symptoms such as phobias:

> People in a psychotic state seemed fixated at an unindividuated level in which they could not differentiate between what was inside and what was outside themselves; people in a borderline condition were construed as fixated in dyadic struggles between total enmeshment, which they feared would obliterate their identity, and total isolation, which they equated with traumatic abandonment; and people with neurotic difficulties were understood as having accomplished separation and individuation but as having run into conflicts between for example, things they wished for and things they feared, the prototype for which was the oedipal drama. This way of thinking made sense of numerous puzzling and demoralizing clinical challenges. It accounted for why one woman with phobias seemed to be clinging to sanity by a thread, while another was oddly stable in her phobic instability, and yet a third woman was, despite having a phobia, otherwise a paragon of mental health.
>
> (p. 54)

Kernberg's use of the word "borderline," which McWilliams adopts (and so do I), is different from the "borderline personality disorder" as described in the DSM

(American Psychiatric Association, 2013). The distinction between the "DSM borderline" and the "psychodynamic borderline" has confusticated, perplexed, and confounded graduate students of psychology (and probably most licensed clinicians) since the publishers of the DSM decided to change a complex, dynamic phase of psychological development into a static laundry list of dichotomous symptoms.

The harmonic progression we have explored in the past few chapters underwrites and contextualizes these differentiations. *Representational horizon* refers to the highest harmonic level that an individual personality is capable of generating and maintaining. The representational horizon therefore is epiphenomena of the Complex Adaptive System of mental representations as depicted in the harmonic progression, and a developmental achievement that reflects a personality's degree of capacity for complexity, ambivalence, and sophistication of mental representation. Because the harmonic progression ranges from its origins in the archetypal sphere and progressively manifests with increasingly mature object relations, affect tolerance, reality testing, and capacity for attachment, the dynamic system builds one harmonic on the foundations of the other.[1] Therefore, the representational horizon of a personality reflects which level of complexity of mental representation is able to be maintained over time and across situations, as well as the lower levels. For example, a personality with a representational horizon at the complex harmonic will also be able to mentalize the complex, object, symbol, and archetypal harmonic.

Furthermore, I would suggest as a hypothesis that roughly speaking, Kernberg's developmental levels of personality organization map onto the harmonic progression in this way: psychotically organized personalities show representational horizons at the archetypal and symbolic level, borderline personalities at the object and complex level, and neurotic personalities at the schema and self level.

There's a lot going on in Table 10.1, which amounts to an organizing principle for understanding the function of personality dynamics at different levels of organization, and the corresponding affect states. Note that the particular vector path through the harmonic progression will modify and complexify this scheme. For example, histrionic versus narcissistic personality disorders (both theoretically organized at the "borderline" level) will differ in their relationship to abandonment

Table 10.1 Representational harmonics mapped onto levels of personality development, with associated basic anxiety states

Level of Personality Organization	Representational Horizon	Anxiety State
Psychotic	• First Harmonic (Archetype) • Second Harmonic (Symbol)	Annihilation Anxiety
Borderline	• Third Harmonic (Object) • Fourth Harmonic (Complex)	Abandonment Anxiety
Neurotic	• Fifth Harmonic (Schema) • Sixth Harmonic (Self)	Moral Anxiety

anxiety (see Chapters 14 and 15). Narcissistic personalities (which I will call Second Quadrant personalities in Chapter 14) show a characteristic impoverishment in object relations which reflects their "pre-relational" status along the developmental trajectory. Narcissistic (and psychopathic and paranoid) personalities employ relatively primitive defenses which result in relational impoverishment and resistance to relational vulnerability, which has the secondary effect of (temporarily) saving them from abandonment anxiety, which would otherwise become the work of the borderline level of personality organization.

In a larger sense, the psychotherapeutic work of the psychotic level is developing patterned coherence in the face of annihilation anxiety, which is sometimes described in psychotherapeutic contexts as a process of re-parenting. I deeply appreciate the way Nancy McWilliams (2011) contextualizes working with psychotically organized people:

> They are wonderful in their attachment and terrifying in their needs. They are not yet oppositional and irritating, but they also tax one's resources to the limit. I should not work with a schizophrenic, a supervisor once told me, unless I was prepared to be eaten alive.
>
> (p. 63)

The work of the borderline level is attachment (including dealing with resistance to attachment), which ultimately both conjures and then contextualizes abandonment anxiety. Psychotherapeutic work at the borderline level is, therefore, typically highly boundaried and predicated on a lot of containment. Because of the centrality of attachment, the dialectical field in psychotherapy will tend to place the psychotherapist on center stage in all kinds of consuming and distorting ways, with the result that many psychotherapists are reluctant to work with this population.

The work of the neurotic level of development introduces a qualitatively different set of challenges. At the neurotic level of development, an individual has developed the capacity to hold a pattern, tolerate strong affect, and remain conversant with consensual reality. However, all this adjustment and settlement typically also results in a loss of connection with the archetypal center, and therefore the dynamic life-giving core of the psyche. For this reason, psychotherapy with neurotically organized persons often involves expressive, uncovering work that results in the restoration of a dynamic content with archetypal realities. In subjective terms, this kind of work often looks and feels like uncovering, in which the structure of the psyche is encouraged to dissipate and relax a bit rather than lean further into achievement, obligation, duty, or accomplishment.

This final point about the nature of psychotherapy with neurotic states raises two important questions. The first important question is: where do we go from here? If neurotic functioning is the best we can do (see the second important question), how does the harmonic progression continue? My best answer is that the harmonic progression then reverses its valence, cycling back toward the archetypal core in an attempt to reestablish the bright karmic thread of connection to origin, to cosmos, to meaning. True to the nature of uncovering work, this kind of process might feel like a deep willingness to question all the deeply held assumptions about life, which is consistent with Jungian and post-Jungian conceptualizations about the nature of the second half of life (see Hollis, 2006).

I once encountered a bumper sticker out in the world, whose ultimate provenance has defeated my research acumen to determine.[2] The bumper sticker read: *My job is to comfort the afflicted, and to afflict the comfortable.* I think this sentiment nicely captures our discussion about harmonic progression: how it starts as an ascent into higher complexity and presence in the world, and then cycles back into deconstructing itself. It is my own belief that this is the psychological heartbeat of life: an eternal cycle of growth, decay, and rebirth.

Our conceptualization of the harmonic progression thus far leads to conclusion that, consistent with the language of object relations theory, the Complex Adaptive System of the psyche will evidence the following properties:

1   The harmonic progression (when functioning optimally) results in new, qualitatively different cognitive and affective ways of representing internal realities and external realities.
2   These new capacities are initially mediated by attachment, then by adulthood are mediated by internal capacities for representational flexibility and regulation.
3   The manifestation of basic anxiety as a motivating factor in progressively sophisticated mental representation shifts as the mentalization system gains adaptive capacity, leading from annihilation anxiety states to abandonment anxiety states to moral anxiety states.
4   The succession of basic anxiety states do not replace each other but add to each other such that "neurotically" functioning people retain access to all of them.
5   The harmonic progression is both a driver and a result of increasingly mature defensive systems such that more mature (flexible and reality-based) defensive systems predominate at the upper harmonics.
6   The outcomes of successful harmonic progression include more consistently reliable reality testing and affect tolerance, which becomes clinically useful markers of personality functioning.
7   One of the most crucial outcomes of the harmonic progression is an integral, agentic, symphonic, and positively valued sense of self.

Let us consider now a crude example of the lineage of representational vectors, ranging from the archetypal harmonic to the Self Harmonic. As we do so, let us acknowledge that this diagram is a gross oversimplification of a chaotic system, which to be represented accurately would have dozens or hundreds of threads forking and spreading across the levels of increasing complexity.

Table 10.2 presents the phase space of a representational vector associated with a neurotically organized depressive personality. As we can see, archetypal dynamics relate to the experiences of the "archetypal mother," which involves unrepresentable dynamics describing a containment field associated with a force that is

Table 10.2 A simplified example of representational
vectors evolving through harmonic levels

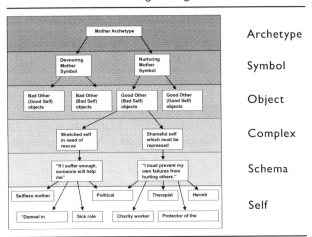

	Archetype
	Symbol
	Object
	Complex
	Schema
	Self

experienced as powerful and closely associated with feeding and containing. At the symbolic level, the experience of a mother can constellate as nurturing and protective, or devouring (being fed and being devoured being two aspects of a dynamic that is probably unified at the archetypal level). Based on early "phantasy" experiences including physical interaction and contact with a mother in embodied form, the potential object representations that show up might organize around the "good breast" and the "bad breast" versions of the mother's manifestations, resulting in affective reactions to different representational sets of encoded experiences with the mother. In our example, it appears that the "good breast" has outcompeted other parallel representations of the mother, and our subject closely identifies with the "good breast" associated with the mother, while the self is valuated in a more negative way, perhaps weak or helpless or selfish, compared with the mother's essential goodness. An object relations template therefore emerges at the Object Level which suggests encoding the self as bad and others as good; however, note that an alternative object representation, a Bad Other, has been encoded but remains nascent at the object level and does not evolve further into higher-order mental representations beyond the Complex Harmonic.

At the Complex Harmonic, negatively valued object representations of self become the center of gravity for a range of relational and interpersonal experiences which share that affective resonance and cognitively encoded theme: many experiences with others in the world serve to reinforce and continue to elaborate an emotionally charged configuration of mentalization relating to idealized others compared to a shameful, defective sense of self. Such a configuration at the object level encourages interpretations of relational space in the direction of expecting others to be stronger or smarter and anticipating failure experiences on the part of the self. Elsewhere at the Complex Harmonic, negative attributes of others that have been introjected and turned against the self result in a split-off contingent of sadistic, attacking mental representations, which generally turned against the self at the Complex Harmonic and have their origins in the bad self/bad other configuration at the Object Harmonic.

A number of themes are generated at the Schema Harmonic which receives the vector emerging from the "shameful self" complex, and each of these schema systems inspires self systems downstream. One of them relates to ideation about compensating for one's own shameful inadequacy by serving others, resulting in self states centered around helping and healing others (a therapist persona), or volunteering or intervening on behalf of the needy or weak (personas organized around volunteering for charity purposes, or political activism on behalf of disenfranchised others). Another thematic structure emergent at the Schema Harmonic has to do with "quarantining" one's badness and preventing it from affecting others, which leads to avoidant behavior and relational styles resulting in disconnection (a "hermit" persona) or else perhaps a self-state organized around committing to a role that appears to fight for justice against evil, which both allows the shameful self to be eclipsed and also serves the purpose of the other schematic structure about serving others. Finally, note that another schematic system has generated a hypothesis about possibly gaining self-esteem and support or nurturing from others through suffering in an obvious and noble way, leading to configurations at the self level which attract rescue or sympathy from others. This particular example seems to depict an introjectively depressive personality who has some self-defeating (masochistic) features; what we will come to refer to as an early Fourth Quadrant personality in later chapters.

Defenses as Radical Discontinuity

Psychological defenses are intrinsic features of the psychoanalytic worldview since the advent of ego psychology and ultimately rooted in the model's roots in drive theory. The idea of defenses describes the results of forces within the personality acting against other forces, in a way that delimits, modifies, or eliminates the other force. The index narrative within psychoanalytic theory is that defenses develop as ways of coping with anxiety-provoking aspects of early experience, which then carry over into adult life as a defining feature of personality, which end up psychologically counterproductive in some way. What originated as a defensive adaptation to conditions in childhood sometimes persists in rigid or obdurate ways later in life. To put it another way, the first goal of psychological life is to survive childhood, and we often end up hanging on to those ways in which we survived childhood even when it is no longer strictly necessary.

Among some psychodynamic models, psychological defenses define personality organization *per se*. A narcissistically organized personality evidences certain sets of defenses (i.e., primitive idealization and primitive devaluation); a depressive one is a characteristic other set (i.e., introjection). The defenses primarily act as narratives designed to accommodate, contain, limit, or deny some kind of anxiety: as we have seen, the kind of anxiety that is defended against tends to evolve over the trajectory of developing object relations. I would argue that defenses function to mediate ideation as well as affect, and therefore defenses shape how we perceive reality, what we think about, what we remember, how we prefer to conceptualize ourselves, and so forth.

To return to the language of dynamic systems theory, defenses represent dissipative forces endogenous to the psyche, and therefore they limit, delimit, and modify both the vertical evolution of representational vectors from one harmonic to another, and also the horizontal evolution of themes (see Chapters 11 and 12). In this sense, defenses operate as radical discontinuities in the structure of the harmonic progression: the influence of which mental representations are "allowed" to progress and evolve into higher and more complex forms, and which ones are "snuffed out." As a result of these radical discontinuities, certain emotional states, memories, beliefs, or associations never reach the outer harmonics, and therefore the content never becomes represented in the personality in some mature and integrative way. A "hole" is evidenced in the behavioral, emotional, interpersonal, and adaptive repertoires of the individual in question. The forbidden idea or feeling becomes what Jung (1969) described as "the rock against which we are broken":

> The patient who comes to us has a story that is not told, and which as a rule no one knows of. To my mind, therapy only really begins after the investigation of that wholly personal story. It is the patient's secret, the rock against which he is shattered. If I know his secret story, I have a key to treatment.
>
> (p. 117)

The function of defenses is the abnegation or contradiction of the content which invokes the defense. The defense known as *reaction formation* involves the defensive transformation of an idea into its opposite (e.g., attraction is turned into revulsion, or vice versa), and the defense of *repression* may serve to nip an entire developmental vector in the bud, preventing any of its more developed forms from ever-reaching conscious expression. Paranoid personality organization often comprises defensive transformations complex enough to throw off all but the most intrepid therapist: theoretically, felt experiences of love are defensively morphed into hatred, because the experience of love implies an intimacy too threatening for the fragile self to countenance; then that very feeling of hatred is itself projected onto the original object of the loving feelings because the hatred is itself intolerable (McWilliams, 2011).

Let us consider a crude schematic diagram of a representational vector ranging from the Object Harmonic to the Self Harmonic (Table 10.3).

Notice in this example how the defenses graphically represent a radical discontinuity in the trajectory of a harmonic vector, resulting in a personality organization that appears psychodynamically paranoid. The entire defensive system, in this case, is prophylactic against the "Craved-Other" object, specifically designed to submerse the entire subjective experience of being dependent on some needed Other. Among the significant implications of such defensive operations is the fact that the Craved-Other object entirely drops out of the system.

Table 10.3 Detail of a representational vector representing a paranoid personality

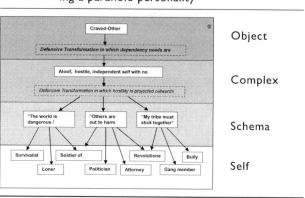

In other words, there are no higher-level mental representations reflecting the developmental necessity of interpersonal dependence on another. Such a radical "pruning" of a representational vector predicts a form of character pathology and portends a mode of interpersonal functioning dominated by mental representations that remain undeveloped at a lower harmonic state. An inability to register the developmental importance of a Craved Other, or put simply, a refusal to acknowledge that one needs others, will have all kinds of toxic implications for the individual across the lifespan.

It is worth pointing out here that "aloof, hostile, independent self with no needs" is not a "live" vector...in other words, it is not connected with the generative matrix of the archetypal and symbolic harmonics, and therefore, cannot be "healthy." One important implication of the Integrated Analytical Model is that a genuine inner life must intersect with a realistically perceived external environment such that affects, ideas, and perceptions are flexibly "connected" to their innate sources and perceptions of reality are rooted in actual reality (as opposed to delusions, fantasies, or distortions). Defensive content that cuts off and "replaces" representational vectors will lack the vitality, genuineness, and spontaneity of the archetypal and symbolic levels, and therefore feels subjectively dead, brittle, defensive, and fundamentally disconnected from reality to the observer. Such subjective deadness and brittleness are the outward and visible signs that some important developmental vector has been darkened. When representational vectors become cut off at relatively primitive levels of development, there are important functional implications for the personality as a whole.

Notes

1 I would compare the additive nature of the harmonic progression to how one learns mathematics: starting with arithmetic, and then algebra, and then trigonometry, and then calculus.
2 As near as I can tell, this citation comes in mutated form to a fictional character created by Chicago Evening Post journalist Finley Peter Dunne in 1902.

References

American Psychiatric Association. (2013). *Diagnostic and statistical manual of mental disorders* (5th ed.). Author.

Hollis, J. (2006). *Finding meaning in the second half of life: How to finally, really grow up.* Avery.

Jung, C. G. (1969). *Memories, dreams, reflections* (A. Jaffe, Ed., & R. Winston, Trans.). Vintage Books.

Kernberg, O. (1975). *Borderline conditions and pathological narcissism.* Jason Aronson.

McWilliams, N. (2011). *Psychoanalytic diagnosis: Understanding personality structure in the clinical process.* The Guilford Press.

Part 2

The Horizontal Model

Chapter 11

The Circumplex Model

The "horizontal" aspect of the Integrated Analytical Model shifts our focus from developmental layers, or stages, of the personality toward the organizing themes of the personality. In this sense, conceptualizing personality comes down to addressing two questions:

- How *developed* is the personality along a continuum (in our case, as measured by the progression of increasingly complex levels of mental representation)?
- What are the organizing *themes* of the personality?

In other words, conceptualizing personality means assessing the level and type of personality organization. Temperamental differences were of great interest to Jung and likely contributed to his break with Freud. Jung navigated encounters with archetypal figures and based his own typological models on his experiences with them (Odajnyk, 2013). Jung's typology describes two personality attitudes (extroversion and introversion) and four functions (thinking, sensation, intuition, and feeling); this typology was meant not to describe different kinds of people, but rather different kinds of consciousness (Jung, 1971). Jung's concept of *individuation*, similar to Maslow's *self-actualization*, involves an organic process of reconciling opposites.

Significantly, Jung's perspective on psychological types and the transcendent function which potentially integrates them differs from the psychoanalytic tradition in that Jung describes these processes as a *teleological agency* rather than an epiphenomenon of psychological forces within the individual. The psychoanalytic worldview generally casts personality as the messy result of internal drives or psychological forces interacting with psychological defense systems. One way to understand this difference is that the psychoanalytic narrative views the development of the personality as driven "from behind" by attachment experiences and primitive mental states, while the Jungian narrative describes the development

DOI: 10.4324/9781032708751-14

of the personality as if driven by a goal (the essence of teleology). In this sense, psychoanalytic versus analytic models of personality resemble the historical differences between Lamarckian and Darwinian evolution. The Lamarckian (Lamarck, 1914) view is that evolution is guided by adaptive inherited phenotypic adaptations, while the Darwinian model (Darwin, 2011) is that evolution is driven by random, undirected changes. You may notice that the Lamarckian reference is quite a bit older; just as psychoanalysis has "won" the debate about personality development, Darwinian evolution has become the consensual reality of contemporary modeling of evolution. The reasons for both outcomes are the same: teleology has been forbidden in empirical science since Francis Bacon published *Novum Organum* in 1620. The banishment of teleology presents all kinds of problems for Jungian theory, which thrives on teleology driven by archetypal forces. However, with your kind indulgence, reader, we shall continue here to engage in forbidden teleological practices.[1]

The Vertical and Horizontal models of Integrated Analytical Psychology represent an attempt to describe a geometric metaphor for the integration of level and type of personality organization, encompassing the developmental trajectory of the harmonic levels as well as the thematic relationships among types. The combination of the Vertical and Horizontal models results in a circumplex or circular depiction of related variables.

In previous chapters, we discussed six harmonics as a nested hierarchy of mental representations ranging from the harmonic of archetype to the harmonic of self. I shall now list them in descending order, to visually represent that the Self Harmonic is "on top," representing the outer skin of the psychic onion, and the Archetypal Harmonic is located "on bottom," representing its foundational structure, like this:

6   Self
5   Schema
4   Complex
3   Object
2   Symbol
1   Archetype

It is, however, ultimately likely that the more satisfactory visual depictions of self development are ultimately a circle or spiral. *The Book of the 24 Philosophers* (Liber XXIV Philosophorum) influenced Western medieval thought with the observation "*Deus est sphaera infinita cuius centrum est ubique, circumferentia nusquam*" (God is a sphere whose center is everywhere and whose circumference is nowhere, see Marenbon, 2001). Jung noted that the circle is one of the great primordial images of humankind: in *Memories, Dreams, Reflections*. Jung (1961) writes "There is no linear evolution; there is only circumambulation of the self" (p. 188). Circular models have similarly found their way into Western models of psychological and interpersonal functioning in a variety of ways (see Wiggins, 1996), inspired initially by Harry Stack Sullivan's (1953) clinical methodologies which became known as interpersonal psychoanalysis. In 1957, Timothy Leary published one of the first circumplex models based on two axes of power and love (later rephrased as dominance and affiliation), suggesting that any personality could be located at a particular coordinate of those two functions.

Adapting the table above listing harmonic levels of mental representation into a circumplex model, the six harmonics become nested concentric circles like this:

Next, we will add four orthogonal axes which represent archetypal teleologies guiding personality development with specific themes (which we shall elaborate in Chapter 12), which I have colorfully named the following:

1   The Axis of Transcendent Self, representing a perspective of self in an intersubjective context
2   The Axis of Unique Identity, representing a perspective of self based on holding a pattern
3   The Axis of Christ, representing an archetype of coherence and manifestation
4   The Axis of Lilith, representing an archetype of dissolving and adapting

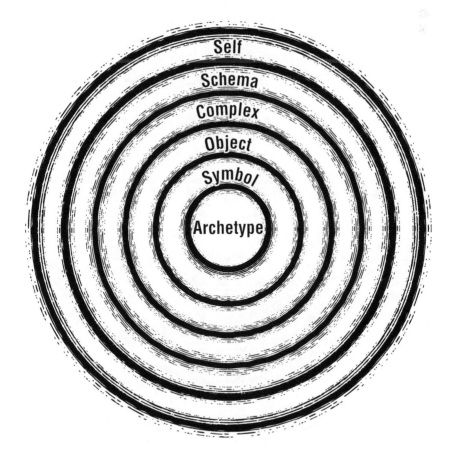

Figure 11.1 Six harmonic levels arranged on a circumplex.

We will explore these axes in more detail in the next chapter. Together, these themes comprise the basic rhythm of an alchemical transformation that navigates and ultimately reconciles and transcends dynamic opposites. Like the positive and negative ends of a battery, the archetypal axis generates motivational psychic energy through their dynamic differences. Mapping the four archetypal axes on top of the harmonic layers, our circumplex model evolves into something like this.

Now, let us behold the Circumplex Model in its fullness: the Axes of Christ and Lilith form the basis for what I will call the First Quadrant in the "north" position, the Second Quadrant in the west, the Third Quadrant in the south, and the Fourth Quadrant in the east. This more complex figure also includes the particular "aspects" of the Lilith and Christ Axes, developed further in Chapter 12. We will explore each of the four quadrants in Chapters 13–16 and summarize them again in Chapter 17.

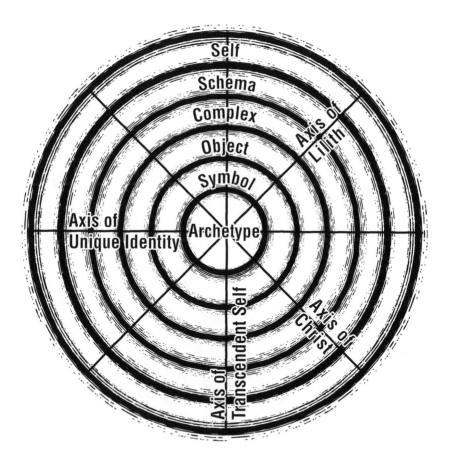

Figure 11.2 A circumplex figure showing four archetypal axes superimposed upon the six harmonic levels.

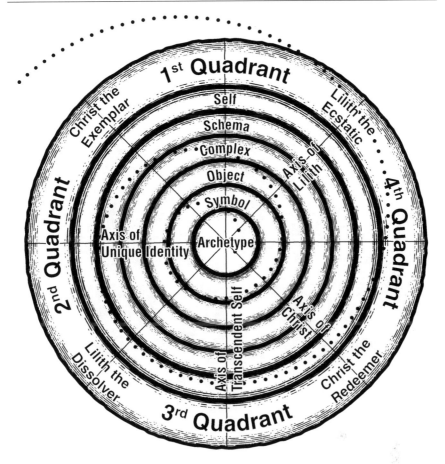

Figure 11.3 The full circumplex figure showing quadrants, harmonics, and axes with individual aspects.

The interaction of the four axes results in four possible semicircles or arcs. These arcs form the basis for characterological features described particularly in the psychoanalytic architecture. The Introjective Arc represents personalities organized around self-definition, comprising Quadrants 1 and 2:

The Anaclitic Arc represents personality organizations most powerfully motivated by dependency needs and intimacy, comprising Quadrants 3 and 4:

The Internalizing Arc includes personality styles which tend to handle conflict within the self, taking energetic responsibility for the conflict, representing Quadrants 1 and 4:

The Externalizing Arc incorporates personalities who tend to locate conflict outside the self, characterized by Quadrants 2 and 3.

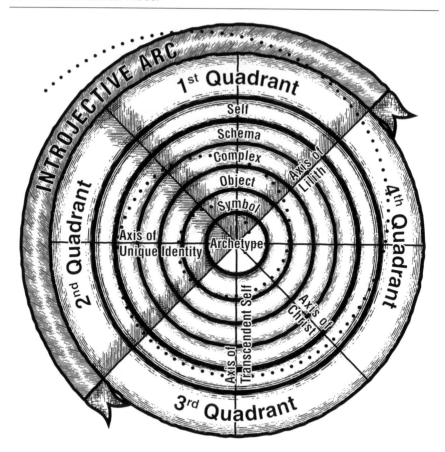

Figure 11.4 A circumplex figure showing the Introjective Arc.

Properties of the Circumplex

Our circumplex structure is intended to provide three useful functions in modeling the complexities of personality conceptualization. Firstly, it serves as a diagrammatic representation efficiently conveying complex ideas. Secondly, the circumplex implies a circular order in which personality styles located closer together on the circle are more related or correlated than those that are more distant, in which themes located at opposite sides of the circle are inversely related, and themes at right angles are orthogonal (unrelated to each other). Thirdly, locations around the rim of the circumplex structure can be understood as continuous, such that location and distance along the circle express meaningful ratios (Wiggins & Trobst, 1997).

In a symbolic and archetypal sense, the circumplex model, and the spiral journey that it depicts, elaborates complex energetic and psychological dualities and also reconciles and transcends them. Our circumplex describes the four interlocking

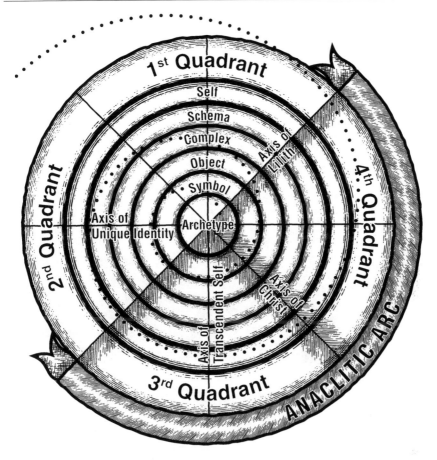

Figure 11.5 A circumplex figure showing the Anaclitic Arc.

thematic axes that radiate out from a central point, creating radial symmetry. Each thematic axis creates a potential hemispheric relationship between the resulting two sides of the circle, and an intersection between two axes results in four quadrants. The axes, hemispheres, and quadrants of the circumplex have a meaning, and the geometric relationships among them are significant. The circumplex maps out personality features based on the assumption that they can be grouped spatially in such a way that the spatial relationships imply morphological similarities or dissimilarities. Just as in Jungian typology, extroversion is the *opposite* of introversion, the Integrated Analytical Model suggests that introjective depressive defenses (which, as we shall see, are a function of the so-called Fourth Quadrant) are the opposite of narcissistic defenses (a function of the so-called Second Quadrant). Antisocial and narcissistic personality organizations are more similar to each other

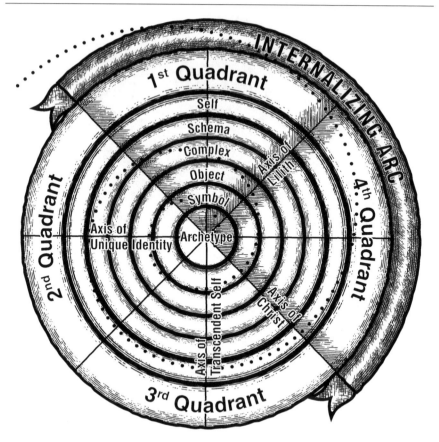

Figure 11.6 A circumplex figure showing the Internalizing Arc.

than to self-defeating personality organizations, therefore they are placed next door to each other and are located on the other side of the circumplex model from self-defeating personality.

More specifically, in our circumplex model, the center of the circle represents a *singularity*, a location equidistant from all points on the circumference, represented by a single point. The point has no dimensionality, and in keeping with the mathematical concept of a singularity or a point, lacks differentiability and analyticity. In our model, the singularity is also the origin point of the developmental path of the psyche, from which the spiral trajectory emerges. The point has location but no dimension, and cannot be quantified or added, subtracted, or divided. In terms of the language of geometry, the point is a "primitive" meaning it represents a basic form that cannot be reduced to other forms, and thus presumably make up other, more complex patterns. It becomes conceptually difficult to describe how points become shapes since they have no dimensionality. In other words, mathematical theories start with "primitive notions" which themselves cannot be defined, but everything that comes later is defined in terms of that primitive notion. Therefore, just as we

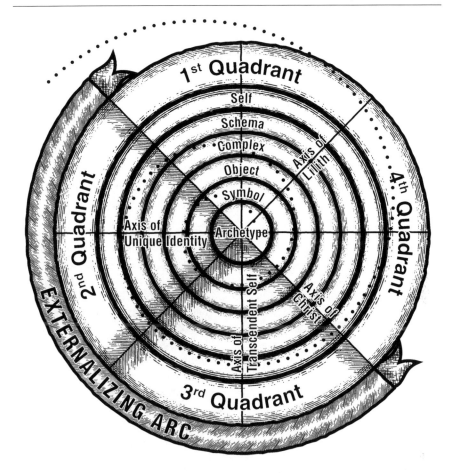

Figure 11.7 A circumplex figure showing the Externalizing Arc.

described archetype as the "fundamental frequency" of psychological reality in Chapter 2, the archetypal singularity at the center of the circumplex has no quantifiable geometric properties itself but serves as the starting point for the model.

In metaphysical terms, the singularity at the center of the circumplex represents a transition or inflection point at which reality can no longer be represented geometrically or verbally. Consistent with our discussion in Chapter 2, the singularity represents the fabled no-thing of the Zen traditions.

The Spiral Path

The complex interplay of metaphor and metonymy, condensation and displacement, suggests a complex, radiant, and radial flow of associated mental representations, arising up and out of the singularity, refracting and lensing through progressive harmonics, and also crossing categories from one archetypal axis to another. At the same time, this radiant and radial movement illustrates the dynamic tensions between Jungian and psychoanalytic points of view, as unconscious material manifests and ascends, and is refracted and refined through the filtering effects of defensive systems. In a sense, the Jungian model provides the horizontal content, represented by the archetypal axes, and the psychoanalytic model provides the vertical content, in its powerful and articulate depiction of energetic resistance, refraction, and displacement of unconscious content. How, then, shall we represent a developmental trajectory through the circumplex model which reconciles these two perspectives?

The spiral, another primordial image associated with so many parallel forms in nature and art, depicts a curvilinear relationship in plane space that relates the distance of a point from its origin (the singularity) to the angle at which it is rotated. The spiral describes a pathway in which distance from the origin increases while rotating around that origin. The spiral is a useful metaphor for psychological development, especially because it expands while keeping its shape. There are several different kinds of spirals; the most appropriate geometric metaphor for our purposes is the logarithmic spiral, with the formula $r = ae^{\theta \cot b}$. With a logarithmic spiral, successive turns increase in a geometric progression such that the space between turns continues to increase. The logarithmic spiral is also seen in the structure of spider webs, galaxies, hurricanes, and certain flowers, as well as the flight path of hawks pursuing prey, the approach of an insect toward a light source, and the nerves of the cornea. Consistent with the holarchic nature of the harmonic levels, logarithmic spirals are self-similar (the whole has the same shape as the parts, a fractal pattern). For purposes of modeling our circumplex, we shall adopt a logarithmic spiral with a growth factor representing φ, the golden ratio, in which the ratio of two different quantities (in this case, the radius, or distance from the center, and the angular position of the radius) is the same as the ratio of their sum to the larger of the two quantities. This ratio results in a so-called golden spiral, resulting in an aesthetically pleasing composition. The golden spiral looks and feels *right*, phenomenologically speaking.

The spiral path, in the case of our circumplex, describes a mathematical relationship between the level of mental representation along the harmonic sequence, represented by the radius of the spiral, and the symbolically meaningful location of a point on the curve relative to the archetypal axes, represented by the degree of rotation. Therefore, I would argue that the relationship between psychoanalytic and Jungian theory can be described as $ae^{\theta \cot b}$ as well.

The vertical aspect of the circumplex model (represented by the harmonic levels) and the horizontal aspect (represented by the archetypal axes and location along the circumference of the circumplex) represent a parallel with the concept of metonymy versus metaphor. Both metonymy and metaphor are examples of figurative representation of ideas or themes in language; they are symbolic means of representing ideas. Metaphor communicates figurative meaning by means of establishing a similarity between two different things, whereas metonymy communicates figurative meaning by establishing a contiguity between different things.

This linguistic concept is reflected in Freud's (2010) concepts of *displacement*, in which the psychological impact of one mental representation is transferred to another (which parallels metonymy), and *condensation*, in which a mental representation becomes associated with several others, across categories (which is similar to metaphor). Lacan (1993) considers metonymy to occur within a single signifying chain, while metaphor links mental representations across different signifying chains. Consistent with Lacan's take, the Integrated Analytical Circumplex implies that metonymy describes mental representations linked along representational vectors along the vertical, while metaphor describes "crossing over" from one archetypal axis to another, for example, from the First Quadrant to the Second Quadrant (see below).

The drivers are the spiral path, in our case, derived from the complex interplay between the representational vectors we described personally, which represent a "vertical" organizing force binding the harmonic levels, and the archetypal axes of the circumplex, which represent a "horizontal" organizing force.

The momentum for the vertical organization of the circumplex reflects the natural developmental progression of the psyche through the levels of harmonic representations: the harmonic vectors we discuss earlier in this book. This vector truly is an evolutionary process, up and out of a primal and primordial state into greater manifestation and differentiation in a way that parallels the development of consciousness as well as the structure of the brain itself. This evolutionary process, as we have discussed above, involves the emergence of thematically related ideas up (and back down) a trajectory of mental representations, and seems similar to Freudian displacement and Lacan's formulation of metonymy, *within* a representational vector or signifying chain.

Whence comes the momentum for the horizontal movement along the circumference of the circumplex? I have suggested four dynamic axes which represent archetypal themes that present as apparent dichotomies, as well as four quadrants representing the archetypal basis for character styles. I do not suggest that the axes and quadrants occur in any particular order; however, I do believe that the thematic organizing principles of the four quadrants build upon themselves and flow into each other in meaningful ways. For example, one might say that for a narcissistic personality (a Second Quadrant form), depressive dynamics (a Fourth Quadrant form) represents the direction of health and growth: therapeutic goals for a narcissistic personality may amount to developing a conscious capacity for tolerating guilt and shame, as well as self doubt, which is ordinarily split off through the narcissistic personality's "false self." However, the circumplex model would predict that the narcissistic personality cannot "teleport" across the circle into the depressive condition; they must instead "rotate" through intervening conditions that create the circumstances for the change. Integrated Analytical Psychology predicts that the trajectory for change in the narcissistic personality would, for example, lead across the Lilith line into the third quadrant, involving a willingness to surrender power in the name of intimacy and love. In other words, the Third Quadrant mediates the transition from the Second to the Fourth (and vice versa).

The phasic transitions that represent movement along the circumference of the circumplex are empowered by what we have called a metaphor, which allows them to jump from one axis to another. Within the language of Integrated Analytical Psychology, metaphor implies a leap from one harmonic vector to an entirely different harmonic vector, rather than up and down that vector. To return to the Lacanian language, the spiral rotation comes from shifting across signifying chains. It appears, then, that the rotational movement of the spiral path is not about a chronology, but a stepwise, additive evolutionary process in which psychological capacities are established, creating new creative, adaptive complexities.

Note

1 I cannot help but to interject here that there is some recent evidence of Lamarckian evolutionary process in antiphage defense systems in archaea and bacteria (Koonin & Wolf, 2009).

References

Darwin, C. (2011). *The origin of species.* William Collins.

Freud, S. (2010). *The interpretation of dreams.* Basic Books.

Jung, C. G. (1961). *Memories, dreams, reflections.* Fontana Press.

Jung, C. G. (1971). *Psychological types* (R. F. C. Hull, Trans.). Princeton University Press.

Koonin, E. V., & Wolf, Y. I. (2009). Is evolution Darwinian or/and Lamarckian? *Biology Direct, 4*(42): 1–14.

Lacan, J. (1993). *The seminar. Book III. The psychoses, 1955-56* (R. Grigg, Trans.). Routledge.

Lamarck, J. B. (1914). *Zoological philosophy: An exposition with regard to the natural history of animals.* Macmillan and Co.

Leary, T. (1957). *Interpersonal Diagnosis of Personality; A Functional Theory and Methodology for Personality Evaluation.* Ronald Press.

Marenbon, J. (Ed.). (2001). *Poetry and Philosophy in the Middle Ages: A Festschrift for Peter Dronke.* Brill.

Odajnyk, V. W. (2013). The Red Book as the source of Jung's psychological types. *Psychological Perspectives, 56*(3): 310–328.

Sullivan, H. S. (1953). *The interpersonal theory of psychiatry.* Norton.

Wiggins, J. S. (1996). An informal history of the interpersonal circumplex tradition. *Journal of Personality Assessment, 66*(2): 217–233.

Wiggins, J. S., & Trobst, K. K. (1997). When is a circumplex an "interpersonal circumplex"? The case of supportive actions. In R. Plutchik & H. R. Conte (Eds.), *Circumplex models of personality and emotions* (pp. 57–80). American Psychological Association.

Chapter 12

The Archetypal Axes

It is not down on any map; true places never are.

—Herman Melville, *Moby Dick*

The circumplex model represents a dynamic tension of archetypal forces that interact with each other, and in a fractal sense, also interact with themselves, and manifest in different aspects. We turn now to taking a closer look at the archetypal energies which act as profound motivational forces, the very engine of psyche. The Axes of Christ and Lilith represent dynamic opposites that invite reconciliation through deep interaction and energetic participation, as do the Axes of Transcendent Self and Unique Identity. Each of these axes also contains its own energetic dichotomy which must be reconciled, as we shall see below. The organizing principle of all this movement and transformation is Jung's transcendent function, a consummately Jungian principle which assumes a teleological psyche, a psyche which is going somewhere, a psyche with a destiny and a destination. Following the principle of the transcendent function, we will understand the dynamics and interactions of these archetypal axes as attempts to actualize and reconcile integral and orthogonal aspects of the human psyche which seem to strive for manifestation.

From the more psychoanalytic worldview, which has been more deeply ambivalent about teleologies from Freud onwards (Rychlak, 1981), the focus is more on ways in which the egoic self defends itself against certain primitive mental states, resulting in split-off content and repressed material which itself becomes the focus of psychotherapy.

Integrating the two perspectives, the dynamic that emerges is a highly psychically charged archetypal *telos* which serves as an unconscious instinct toward integration and wholeness, opposed and modified by a defensive system which is intrinsically related to temperament, attachment patterns, cognitive style, defensive style, cultural assumptions, and many other factors relating to the individual person's unique experiences and identity. In this sense, the archetypal axes described here amount to something that we are trying to be, or alternatively, trying not to be. Either way, each of these archetypal axes represents an experiential field implicitly available to the psyche.

DOI: 10.4324/9781032708751-15

As we shall see in subsequent chapters, some archetypal axes also mediate between the themes represented by the four archetypal quadrants (i.e., the Axes of Christ and Lilith), and some archetypal themes represent a modal theme of each of the four quadrants (i.e., the Axes of Transcendent Self and Unique Identity). Furthermore, each archetypal axis itself, consistent with the fractal and holarchic quality of the circumplex model, suggests a dynamic tension between one end of the axis and the other, which I will refer to as dynamic *aspects* of that axis.

The Axis of Christ

In *Ars Amatoria*, completed in the year 2 AD, Ovid writes, "It is convenient that there be gods, and, as it is convenient, let us believe there are." A world of human evolution is suggested in this sentence. In ancient human history and prehistory, modes of spiritual experience were characterized by primary symbolic participation in the natural world. This participation in the natural world, represented by divine forces identified as gods and goddesses, was not originally a matter of belief, but a mode of perception. To put the matter in contemporary neurobiological terms, spiritual experience was not a matter of cognition in the form of belief, which now appears to be mediated by the medial prefrontal cortex, along with the superior temporal gyri and hippocampal regions (Saxe, 2006). "Spiritual experiences" appear to be associated with activation of the nucleus accumbens (Ferguson et al., 2018), a part of the limbic reward system also implicated in attachment. I would argue, therefore, that spiritual experience has retreated across the evolution of human culture from an affective, affiliative, and evaluative experience to a system of codified doctrines. Ovid, who is otherwise known for his somewhat scandalous (by Hellenistic standards) depictions of the gods as sometimes petty and execrable, might be said to be noting a significant waypoint along this developmental trajectory: the gods and goddesses are no longer energetic means of participating in the natural world, but hypotheses that are now officially optional. Jung (1981) drives this point home in *Integration of the Personality*:

> All ages before ours believed in gods in some form or other. Only an unparalleled impoverishment in symbolism could enable us to rediscover the gods as psychic factors, which is to say, as archetypes of the unconscious. No doubt this discovery is hardly credible as yet.

(p. 72)

In fact, I would argue that Jung is being unreasonably optimistic here: we should be fortunate if the gods and goddesses were held as archetypal organizing principles in Western culture, instead of what they have become: something optional to believe in or not.

I can viscerally feel, and fully anticipate, the reaction of many readers in the Western world against the idea of expressing an important psychological function as an "Axis of Christ," both for reasons of implied cultural hegemony and because as contemporary humans, we have been trained to think of Jesus Christ as something to believe in (and therefore worship) or not (and therefore dismiss). I will instead attempt to maintain a decidedly Jungian perspective on the matter and acknowledge the archetypal quality of the Christ mythos, which has certainly towered over Western civilization for nearly 2,000 years. In keeping with the frame that I have set earlier in this book, the Christ mythos is too deep and powerful to be ignored, and anyway, in ignoring it, we should be depriving ourselves of some of the most influential organizing principles that have shaped the human world.

Jung approached the Christ mythos as an archetype of the Self. Significantly, Jung (1938) argued that the figure of Christ was not in itself sufficient to represent a Symbol of the Self because it lacks a dimension of evil (and therefore conflict); it took Christ's suffering and death at the hand of his society to imbue the Christ mythos with enough verisimilitude to serve as a metaphor for individuation. In other words, Christ became psychologically eligible to become a symbol of the Self through suffering. With the crucifixion of Christ, the cross becomes a symbol of selfhood through the opposing forces of good and evil, conscious and unconscious.

The Axis of Christ is an archetypal dichotomy reflecting different aspects of selfhood. Conceptually, the Axis of Christ is envisioned as a diagonal line running from the "northwest" to the "southeast" of the circumplex, differentiating the First Quadrant from the Second, and the Third from the Fourth. As such, the Axis of Christ also represents the transitional and interstitial space between those quadrants, and therefore mediates the psychological progression from one to the other. The Axis of Christ mediates the process of individuation, which is a supraordinate goal of analytical psychology, coming to fruition in the second half of life. Individuation represents the emergence of a separate psychological self, comprised of uniqueness. For our purposes, we will focus on two specific aspects of the Christ archetype: Christ as *exemplar*, and as *redeemer*. These two aspects reflect different manifestations of Christ as a transformative figure, symbolized as the blind eye of law and the open eye of love (McCloskey, 2001).

In his manifestation as *Christ the Exemplar*, Christ is the "Pattern Man," and the *imitatio Christi* represents one of the highest imperatives of Christianity. Early, Pre-Nicene Latin Christians conceptualized Christ as an exemplar of martial prowess; this vision of the Christ mythos, which is now returning culturally in politically motivated evangelical strains of Christianity in the United States, presents Christ as a kind of conquering hero who vanquishes evil, a power which flows from his own divinity. It must be acknowledged, therefore, that the *imitatio Christi* is therefore an attempt to approximate godhood or divinity in the self, with all the implied implications of the power that comes from selfhood. In this sense, the Christ mythos represents a metaphor for manifestation, which in psychological terms might be understood as the emergence of the psychological in an embodied way, resulting in a tethered entity that holds a pattern consistent across time and space. The biblical basis for Christ's status as an exemplar is well established: John 15:5 reads: "I am the vine, ye are the branches. He that abideth in Me and I in Him, the same bringeth forth much fruit, for without Me ye can do nothing" (King James Bible,

1769/2017). 1 Peter reads: "For even hereunto were ye called: because Christ also suffered for us, leaving us an example, that ye should follow His steps" (King James Bible, 1769/2017).

This capacity to hold a pattern does not necessarily result in the empty and recursive idealization of narcissism (although, as we shall see, narcissism may be a complex outcome of failure to successfully navigate the Axis of Christ at the Exemplar aspect), but rather a kind of coherence that enables and enhances the nascent development of a sense of self. In Jung's (1993) words, "The demand made by the *imitatio Christi* – that we should follow the ideal and seek to become like it – ought logically to have the result of developing and exalting the inner man" (para. 7). In this sense, crossing the Axis of Christ between the First and Second Quadrant invokes the alchemical concept of coagula: a process of transcending dualities and cohering into a solid state (in fact, in the alchemical tradition, the coagula represents the final step in a series of transformations resulting in the emergence of the Philosopher's Stone).

The second aspect of the Axis of Christ represents Christ as a redemptive figure: *Christ the Redeemer*. Redemption is one of the most powerful messages of the Christian mythic narrative, and Christ is held as a promise of the forgiveness of sins and of resurrection (rebirth and transformation). On the counterclockwise spiral rotation, transiting the Redeemer Aspect of the Axis of Christ suggests a reprise of the cohering, patternistic emergence of a tethered sense of self associated with the Exemplar Aspect, but this time with the proviso that perfection is not required. This aspect of the Axis of Christ mediates between the Third and Fourth Quadrants and marks a return to the evolution towards selfhood following the dissolving energies of the Third. This manifestation of the Christ ideal is a "kinder, gentler" one; this is the vision of Christ as a loving shepherd and savior. Consistent with Jung's comment on the *imitatio Christi* above, the Redeemer Aspect frames a sense of self based not on achievement, separation, resistance, and opinion, but rather on a more emotionally mature and empathic understanding of the pain and sacrifice associated with building a self.

If the Exemplar aspect of the Axis of Christ represents the capacity to muster an inner certainty, the Redeemer Aspect invites one into a vision of self which is inclusive of uncertainty, doubt, failure, and sin. The Axis of Christ, therefore, sets up a dichotomyous and dynamic sense of selfhood with thematically opposite but synergistic perspectives, invoking clinical distinctions between essentially narcissistic and essentially depressive versions of the self. Indeed, as we shall see, the Axis of Christ represents a psychological inflection point making both points of view possible.

The Axis of Lilith

The Axes of Christ and Lilith are, in a deep sense, synergistically and dynamically related interpenetrating visions of selfhood. Where the Christ Axis represents a "male" vision of selfhood predicated on the linear mathematics of progressive self-actualization, the Axis of Lilith illustrates a dark, feminine, curvilinear pathway of self-in-relation. The archetypal forces underlying the Axes of Christ and Lilith are the very psychic engines of what we call "the masculine" and "the feminine" in culture and in-depth psychology.

Originally a Sumerian succubus, Lilith becomes woven into Judaic mythology through midrashic interpretations into the backstory of the Torah. The Zohar (see Matt, 2003), a medieval work that represents the foundational text of Kabbalah, contains various accounts of Lilith, the most prominent of which depict her as the first woman and first wife of Adam. Lilith, the dark Madonna, quarreled with Adam and refused to "lie under" him; in other words, she refused to submit to him. Since this rebellion, Lilith has been demonized, and more or less been classified as a kind of night-demon and a stealer of infants. Historically, the Lilith archetype precedes the Christ archetype, both in terms of the historical context of the emergence of both myths, and in terms of the evolution of human culture from matriarchal to patriarchal, and from affective mythic participation in the natural world to cognitive hierarchies of abstract beliefs. Rachel Hillel (1997) describes the unconscious and cultural association of feminine modes yielding to the masculine:

> Of all feminine elements, erotic-sensuality, innately supported by Nature and earthly instinctuality, by definition has been most polarised to masculine consciousness. It represented an extreme opposite to an ideology that adored the spirit, an abstract male God. The inherent dichotomy between the original feminine cosmogony, and the later masculine cosmogony posed an existential threat to the survival of the newly established and still fragile monotheistic faith.
>
> (p. 28)

One of the cultural and psychological outcomes of the gendered division of consciousness has been a massive repression of the feminine to the shadow, as evidenced by the reassignment of Lilith from a primordial feminine being co-equal to Adam to a night hag who steals babies from cribs: an outrageous caricature of motherhood. Lerner (1987) notes the long eclipse of the feminine behind patriarchal thought:

> Yet, living in a world in which they are devalued, their experience bears the stigma of insignificance. Thus they have learned to mistrust their own experience and devalue it. What wisdom can there be in menses? What source of knowledge in the milk-filled breast? What food for abstraction in the daily routine of feeding and cleaning? Patriarchal thought has relegated such gender-defined experiences to the realm of the "natural," the non-transcendent. Women's knowledge becomes mere "intuition," women's talk becomes "gossip." Women deal with the irredeemably particular: they experience reality daily.
>
> (p. 224)

Psychologically speaking, therefore, we must address the "energy" of the Axis of Lilith as well as the relational way in which the Lilith archetype interacts in complex ways with the Christ archetype. As for the former, I would associate the Lilith archetype with the alchemical *solve* as opposed to the *coagula* of the Christ axis. Lilithian energy is protean, creative, and ultimately dissolving: it resists structures and hierarchies and insists on primal truths. Hélène Cixous (1997) depicts this energy as *jouissance*, calling it the feminine imaginal:

> Unleashed and raging, she belongs to the race of waves. She arises, she approaches, she lifts up, she reaches, covers over, washes a shore, flows embracing the cliffs least undulation, already she is another, arising again, throwing the fringed vastness of her body up high, follows herself, and covers over, uncovers, polishes, makes the stone body shine with the gentle undeserting ebbs, which return to the shoreless nonorigin, as if she recalled herself in order to come again as never before....

> (p. 15)

The Axis of Lilith represents a diagonal line from the "southwest," where it differentiates the Second Quadrant from the Third, and the "northeast" where it differentiates the Fourth from the First. The transit between the Second Quadrant and the Third Quadrant is of particular cultural importance, as we shall discuss elsewhere. The feminist critique of psychoanalysis, in particular, asserts that early psychoanalytic theory distorts what Cixous and others would call *jouissance* through a patriarchal lens, reframing it as hysteria and therefore an "interpretable" condition of suffering. Integrated Analytical Psychology reinforces the feminist critique by revealing the archetypal force underlying the Axis of Lilith and the Third Quadrant and differentiating this archetypal and symbolic reality from pathological forms of histrionic defenses which emerge especially at the third and fourth harmonic (see Chapter 15).

The Axis of Transcendent Self

In his Three Essays on Sexuality, Freud (1905) described a relationship between sexual drives and so-called self-preservative functions. From this early point of view, which was never extensively elaborated in his literature, Freud sets up a fundamental dichotomy between the essential integrity and sovereignty of the self (self-preservative functions) and the need to enter into a relationship with an object that can satisfy needs (libidinal functions). At first, in this early Freudian model, libidinal needs occur in the context of self-preservation, but later on in the developmental trajectory, they become orthogonal and implicit motivations on their own. Freud used the German word *Anlehnung*, which means something like "leaning on," to describe the mechanism by which libidinal needs "lean on" self-preservation. Traditionally, Freud's *Anlehnung* has been translated into English as *anaclisis*, borrowed from a Greek word.

By the by, you may note that Freud's distinction between the self-preservative and libidinal functions feels rather flat, as both functions ultimately serve a self-preservative function. This flatness has two sources. Firstly, the earliest cathexis of libido onto objects occurs at a time when there is not yet any effective perception of the other as an other (there is no other, there are only need-gratifying objects, like the breast). Secondly, Freudian theory was never truly relational, and it took the evolution from drive theory to object relations to self psychology to intersubjectivity to truly come into relational fullness.

More recently, Sidney Blatt and colleagues (2001) have refined and enriched the concept of anaclisis as a personality dimension which alternates with introjection as a thematic organizer. This distinction between the anaclitic and the introjective was originally proposed as representing two different types of depressive experience and has more generally been built into the Psychodynamic Diagnostic Manual (PDM, Lingiardi & McWilliams, 2017) as an underlying axis of personality dynamics.

Freud's original sense of Anlehnung, and his conceptualization that it originally occurs as a means of self-preservation, may be historically outmoded but suggests a critical aspect of the psychological import of anaclisis: that in developmental terms, the need for affiliation with others is originally experienced as a matter of survival of the self. The importance of anaclisis to survival is especially true in early childhood when the infant relies upon the connection with a mother or father for existential reasons. As a result, personalities that may be described as anaclitic experience their needs for closeness, intimacy, protection, and love in a pressured (or even desperate) kind of way. Furthermore, the shadow cast by this anaclitic need is very dark and frightening and is described in the psychoanalytic literature as abandonment or separation anxiety. Anaclitic (or sociotropic) personalities therefore are organized around a merger-hungry need for loving and protective affiliation from others and respond to the lack of availability of such affiliation with abandonment anxiety. The psychoanalytic literature suggests that anaclitic presentations thrive in more long-term expressive psychotherapies predicated on supportive mirroring (Blatt et al., 2001).

Integrative Analytic Psychology takes the perspective that anaclitic and introjective dynamics reflect meaningfully distinct psychological dynamics, rather than simply being opposites of each other. This perspective is consistent with Freud's original conceptualization of an "affiliative" system interacting meaningfully with a "self-preserving" (or rather, self-definitional) system. For purposes of our Circumplex Model, the anaclitic and introjective personality dimensions are each related to an axis, which is presumed to have an archetypal foundation, like the Axes of Lilith and Christ. Because the axis reflects an archetypal level of mental representation, rather than an object or complex level, the essence of the axis runs deeper than anaclisis as we've discussed it here. In fact, anaclisis, as a basic affective motivational dynamic toward interpersonal connection, is only an aspect of a deeper *transcendent* function. Jung's (1981) concept of transcendent function is central to his entire perspective, and generally relates more broadly to a teleological process of unification of opposites driving the development of the personality through what he described as an "irrational life process" (p. 289). Jung's transcendent function as a superordinate psychological process drives the spiral passage through the integrated analytical circumplex (see Chapter 17); in this more narrow instance, we refer to a kind of transcendence that describes shifting sets from a perspective of individual being to a perspective of relationship.

In *Being and Nothingness*, Sartre (2003) invokes the theme of transcendence to describe relations with others: the emergence of the other into the recursive and self-referential world of the self enables a shift from a pre-reflective state into pure reflection, or a deeper elaboration of the self. Sartre states that "the look" of the other shatters the self-referential pre-reflective state and is therefore shocking. In other words, an immediate experience of the other upends the previous phenomenological ordering of reality, and now nothing can ever be the same. As a matter of fact, "the look" from the other introduces a competing version of the you because the perception that the other has of you is not the same as your own understanding. Even worse, the gaze of the other undermines your own intrinsic reality because that gaze perceives you differently than you perceive yourself.

The tension introduced by Sartre's "look" is the central experience of the Axis of Transcendent Self, and anticipates both poles of the axis. At the "northern" end of the Axis of Transcendent Self, which forms the thematic center of gravity for the First Quadrant and the schizoid personality (see Chapter 13), the shock of being perceived, and the jarring disparity between the way that the other perceives you and your own idea of yourself, creates a state of eclipse. The First Quadrant personality shrinks from "the look" and defensively retreats to its own internal authenticity, a condition described by Lacan as aphanisis (2019; see Chapter 13). Therefore, the northern end of the Axis of Transcendent self may be seen as a resistance to anaclisis.

Sartre goes on to depict sex as a "double reciprocal incarnation," an attempt to reach a harmonious mutual recognition through intimacy of the body. Ultimately, sex is therefore an attempt to become more *real* through shared manifestation and the magical gestures of intimacy (kissing and stroking, and whatnot). This notion of double reciprocal incarnation reflects the "southern" end of the Axis of Transcendent Self, where it serves as the spine of the Third Quadrant (see Chapter 15). The Third Quadrant reprises anaclisis, the affective "leaning on" the other, as a bid for safety and love. The fact that Sartre points out that this attempt at symmetrical incarnation is ultimately doomed because it evaporates after the sexual climax, underscores the shadow side of Third Quadrant psychology, which in its more symptomatic forms may involve a pathological willingness to dissolve into relationships even at the cost of the sovereignty (and sometimes basic integrity and safety) of the self.

The Axis of Transcendent Self, therefore, reflects an archetypal theme of self-in-context, defining itself in terms of how it "fits in" to the world (or not). First and Third Quadrant personalities, therefore, tend to define themselves in terms of closeness versus distance with others. This axis governs a sense of self that is contextual, defined by the relational context, whether that context is characterized by anaclisis (the aspect of the Axis of Transcendent Self that characterizes the Third Quadrant) or aphanisis (the aspect characterizing the First Quadrant). To continue the mythological motif, the Axis of Transcendent Self has a Dionysian quality. Seen through Nietzsche's (2008) lens, the sons of Zeus, Apollo and Dionysus, are of archetypally distinct nature. Apollo, who as a god represents the sun, the arts such as music and poetry, also invokes themes of rational thought and order, logic, purity, and reason. Dionysus, who had a different mother, is the god of wine, dancing and pleasure, and is associated with instinct, ecstatic emotion, chaos, and irrationality. The Dionysian flavor is one of ecstatic merger and union, while the Apollonian ideal is one of individuation. One way to understand the Axis of Transcendent Self is that it is organized around Dionysian energies, ranging from defensive resistance of those energies (First Quadrant) to enthusiastic embodiment (Third Quadrant).

The Axis of Unique Identity

Shifting from the Axis of Transcendent Self to the Axis of Unique Identity, we shift from the anaclitic to the introjective, from an energy of relatedness to an energy of self-definition. Our theme in this axis of the circumplex is developing, curating, maintaining, and, where necessary, defending the boundaries of the self (and ultimately, multiple selves). Taken together, these concerns amount to a process Jung called individuation, invoking an Apollonian rather than a Dionysian energy, autonomy rather than sociotropy.

Returning to the Freudian distinction between the self-preservative functions and the libidinal functions, let us recall that the telos of both functions was the survival of the self, and in a broader sense, an elaboration of the being that is the self. Actual relationships with objects (whether we are attempting to merge with them or attempting to differentiate from them), and ultimately with other separate beings who are capable of inflicting us with "the look," was the business of the Axis of Transcendent Self. In Freudian language, the difference is reflected in *anaclitic object choice* versus *narcissistic object choice*. In the case of narcissistic object choice, libidinal energy is sucked back inwards and cathected to the ego, rather than leading outwards into a relationship with the object. In a way that could almost be described as a reversal of Sartre's "look," the identity of the object is eclipsed by the needs of the ego-self in order to reinforce and maintain the ego ideal. The central instinct of the Axis of Unique Identity is the conceptualization of the self.

Freud's notion of narcissistic object choice foreshadows the broadly used psychoanalytic term *introjection*, which shows a storied and sometimes contradictory range of definitions and usages across the literature. Klein (1940) elaborated on Ferenczi's (1994) conceptualization of introjection as a tendency to internalize qualities of external objects. Introjection is originally seen as the thematic opposite of projection, reversing the polarity from internal to external in a symmetrical way: aspects of the object can be either transferred into the self (introjection) or internal content can be placed outside into external objects (projection). These classical psychoanalytic takes on introjection (see Kcrnbcrg, 1976) cast introjection as a relatively primitive, or archaic, psychological operation (or at least, they are potentially primitive, or have primitive roots). The symmetry suggested by the projection/

introjection dichotomy is predicated on a state of relative undifferentiation between self and object.

Blatt's (1974) differentiation between *introjective* vs *anaclitic* personality structures, discussed above, drifts away from these earlier takes on introjection, defining it in terms of self-definition, autonomy, and personal standards, while anaclitic styles tend to be more attachment-oriented, organized around interpersonal relatedness. Blatt (2008) reprises this distinction as *self-definition* vs *self-in-relationship* (reflected in the Axis of Unique Identity and Transcendent Self, respectively). The introjective–anaclitic distinction parallels a similar theoretical model articulated by Aaron Beck as sociotropy vs autonomy (Bieling et al., 2000). Recent research into the introjective style suggests that when depression shows up primarily in introjective ways, the clinical picture is characterized by more "cognitive" indicators such as loss of interest and concentration difficulty, as well as self-criticism, self-attributions of worthlessness and dislike, and themes of defeat and failure (Marfoli et al., 2021). The PDM (Lingiardi & McWilliams, 2017) adopts the introjective vs anaclitic as dynamic polar dimensions across personality styles, consistent with the dimensional approach implied by spiral map we are exploring.

McWilliams (2011) notes another, deeply resonant take on introjection when identified with depressive dynamics in which an object's "positive attributes are generally remembered fondly, whereas negative ones are felt as part of the self" (p. 240). This emphasis interprets introjection with a particular piquancy that distinguishes it from mere self-definition, providing powerfully empathic ways of understanding the ways in which depressive personalities resist loss and collect "hostile introjects" over time by accumulating the darker qualities of lost or abandoning objects. There is a particular "human vacuum cleaner" quality to this type of introjection, in which the introjective personality sucks up into the self the qualities of especially loved objects as a way of continuing to idealize, and therefore love, those objects (keeping them "clean" by sucking up all their dirt into the self).

As we have seen, the term "introjective" has been used in psychoanalytic traditions in various ways: as a relatively primitive means of internalizing characteristics of objects (in the tradition of Klein and Ferenczi), as an intrinsic tendency to organize one's experience around self-definition (as described by Blatt), and as a particular strategy for taking responsibility for the feared or anxiety-provoking qualities of a loved object (as articulated by McWilliams). For purposes of the Integrated Analytical Model, the overall flavor defining the Axis of Unique Identity reflects introjection as a tendency to focus on self-definition (rather than self-in-context) in a way that prioritizes one's own structural integrity rather than melting or dissolving into, or compromising with, others in a more relational way.

The Second Quadrant aspect of this axis reflects the more impervious, impermeable, and intractable qualities of Freud's *narcissistic object choice*, which can be seen as an outcome of the introjective archetype constellating in the presence of a personality structure that prioritizes agency and volition over relational connecting. I will therefore refer to this aspect as the *narcissistic aspect* of the Axis of Unique

Identity. Schwartz-Salant (1982), in his depiction of narcissistic dynamics through a Jungian lens, writes:

> The narcissistic character rejects feelings of need for another human being, for experiencing such needs can unleash rage and envy that can flood the weak ego structure. Narcissistic characters often take pride in having no needs… If their own needs for sympathy of relatedness are kindled, this often is experienced as a blow to their self-esteem, and can lead to depression and loss of energy.
>
> (p. 39)

I might quibble with Schwartz-Salant's conclusion that the narcissistic implosion in the presence of intrusive dependency needs amounts to "depression"; I worry that this word blurs the (already quite blurry) line between narcissistic and depressive introjection, and even between narcissistic implosion and depression the mood disorder. However, this observation captures two levels of function of the narcissistic aspect of the Axis of Unique Identity: the organizing themes that delimit the anaclitic functions of the Axis of Transcendent Self through certain defensive structures (see Chapter 14), and the fact that the narcissistic aspect of the Axis of Unique Identity is a relatively more primitive and elemental manifestation of the axis (compared to the depressive aspect described below). At the narcissistic end of the Axis of Unique Identity, the question of self-identity is answered, consciously or unconsciously, as "I am the one who wins"

The Fourth Quadrant aspect of the Axis of Unique Identity reflects Blatt's introjective self-definition manifesting in a character structure that has both more relational capacity and a greater tendency toward self-doubt and intrapunitive affect. If narcissistic introjection is used as a bulwark against shame, depressive introjection is aimed pointedly at the self, reflecting a greater capacity and inclination to conceptualize the self in the first place (which is not a defining feature in a narcissistic personality). Depressive introjection remains introjective; it is ultimately an attempt at holding a pattern and self-conceptualizing. McWilliams (2011) names the "magnificent conceit" intrinsic to depressive introjection:

> Some guilt is simply part of the human condition, and is appropriate to our complex and not entirely benign natures, but depressive guilt has a certain magnificent conceit…." Bad things happen to me because I deserve them" may be a consistent underlying theme. Introjective depressive clients may even have a paradoxical kind of self-esteem based on the grandiose idea that "No one is as bad as I am."
>
> (p. 246)

Depressive vs narcissistic introjection is a useful meditation and helpful in differentiating depressive and narcissistic character styles and their associated personality disorders.[1] One of the principles that I have learned to reinforce with students and supervisees is to be careful of jumping to the conclusion that grandiose thinking necessarily spells a narcissistic character organization.

Note

1 Parenthetically, it is my belief that narcissistic vs depressive introjection is a foundational property in conservative vs liberal political ideology, respectively. At least in the United States, conservative politics comes down to protection of idealized self states (that's what's being "conserved"), while liberal politics tends to organize around confronting injustice in ones self and in ones own culture. The emotional impetus for Critical Theory and social justice is depressive introjection.

References

Bieling, P. J., Beck, A. T., & Brown, G. K. (2000). The sociotropy–autonomy scale: Structure and implications. *Cognitive Therapy and Research, 24*(6): 763–780.

Blatt, S. J. (1974). Levels of object representation in anaclitic and introjective depression. *Psychoanalytic Study of the Child, 29*: 107–152.

Blatt, S. J. (2008). *Polarities of experiences: Relatedness and self-definition in personality development, psychopathology and the therapeutic process.* American Psychological Association.

Blatt, S. J., Shahar, G., & Zuroff, D. C. (2001). Anaclitic (sociotropic) and introjective (autonomous) dimensions. *Psychotherapy: Theory, Research, Practice, Training, 38*(4): 449–454.

Cixous, H. (1997). Sorties: Out and out: Attacks/ways out/forays (B. Wing, Trans.). In A. D. Schrift (Ed.), *The logic of the gift* (pp. 148–173). Routledge.

Ferenczi, S. (1994). *Contributions to psychoanalysis.* Routledge.

Ferguson, M. A., Nielsen, J. A., King, J. B., Dai, L., Giangrasso, D. M., Holman, R., et al. (2018). Reward, salience, and attentional networks are activated by religious experience in devout Mormons. *Social Neuroscience, 13*(1): 104–116.

Freud, S. (1905). Three essays on the theory of sexuality. In J. Strachy & A. Freud (Eds.), *The standard edition of the complete psychological works of Sigmund Freud, Volume VII (1901–1905): A case of hysteria, three essays on sexuality and other works* (pp. 123–246). Hogarth Press.

Hillel, R. (1997). *The redemption of the feminine erotic soul.* Nicolas-Hays, Inc.

Jung, C. G. (1938). *Psychology and religion.* Yale University Press.

Jung, C. G. (1981). *The archetypes and the collective unconscious* (R. F. C. Hull, Trans.). Princeton University Press.

Jung, C. G. (1993). *Psychology and alchemy* (R. F. C. Hull, Trans.). Princeton University Press.

Kernberg, O. F. (1976). *Object relations theoryory and clinical psychoanalysis.* Jason Aronson.

King James Bible. (2017). Cambridge University Press. (Original work published 1769).

Klein, M. (1940). Mourning and its relation to manic-depressive states. *International Journal of Psycho-Analysis, 21*: 125–153.

Lacan, J., Miller, J.A., & Sheridan, A. (2019). *The four fundamental concepts of psychoanalysis.* Routledge.

Lerner, G. (1987). *The creation of patriarchy* (Women and History; V. 1). Oxford University Press.

Lingiardi, V., & McWilliams, N. (Eds.). (2017). *Psychodynamic diagnostic manual* (2nd ed.). The Guilford Press.

Marfoli, A., Viglia, F., Di Consiglio, M., Merola, S., Sdoia, S., & Couyoumdjian, A. (2021). Anaclitic-sociotropic and introjective-autonomic personality dimensions and depressive symptoms: A systematic review. *Annals of General Psychiatry, 20*(53): 1–30.

Matt, D. C. (2003). *The Zohar: Pritzker Edition*, Volume One. Stanford University Press.

McCloskey, L. J. (2001). *The heiroglyph of the human soul [painted studio library environment]*. Malibu.

McWilliams, N. (2011). *Psychoanalytic diagnosis: Understanding personality structure in the clinical process*. The Guilford Press.

Nietzsche, F. (2008). *The birth of tragedy*. Oxford University Press.

Rychlak, J. F. (1981). Freud's confrontation with the telic mind. *Journal of the History of the Behavioral Sciences, 17*(2): 176–183.

Sartre, J. P. (2003). *Being and nothingness* (H. E. Barnes, Trans.; 2nd ed.). Routledge.

Saxe, R. (2006). Why and how to study Theory of Mind with fMRI. *Brain Research, 1079*: 57–65.

Schwartz-Salant, N. (1982). *Narcissism and character transformation*. Inner City Books.

Chapter 13

The First Quadrant
The Sensitive Personality

Very funny this terrible thing is. A man that is born falls into a dream like a man who falls into the sea. If he tries to climb out into the air as inexperienced people endeavour to do, he drowns- nicht wahr?... No! I tell you! The way is to the destructive element submit yourself, and with the exertions of your hands and feet in the water make the deep, deep sea keep you up.

- Joseph Conrad
Lord Jim

Archetypal Themes of the First Quadrant

The First Quadrant represents liminal space and the origin point of the psyche. The idea of *falling into a dream* captures something essential about the First Quadrant: emergence from the archetypal singularity, leading to manifestation and embodiment into the world, not necessarily as a triumphant developmental achievement, but as a frightening or disorienting experience. The *Bardo Thodol*, or Tibetan Book of the Dead (Fremantle, 2001), describes a liminal state known as the *Sidpa Bardo* in which the consciousness of a dead person manifesting in a "radiant body" experiences a hallucinatory trip to the Six Realms of Existence in preparation for rebirth into the world. The "veil" between this world and others is thin within the compass of the First Quadrant, resulting in a dreamy and otherworldly archetypal quality.

The First Quadrant personality, therefore, stands at the very boundaries of this world. The psyche emerges into the material plane of existence through that gate, uncertain and ambivalent. The world is experienced as harrowing and intrusive, and the first psychological task becomes the nascent integrity of the emerging self. Faced with the bewildering, and inherently intrusive, experience of the external world into which it has been thrust, the emerging psyche has not yet accepted the idea of individual selfhood, much less accepted the challenge that selfhood requires. The First Quadrant personality is a spark of light in the midst of emergent chaos, and in such circumstances, it is challenging enough to remain lit and not be snuffed out.

The archetypal imperative of the First Quadrant is to become a tethered entity in the world. Human beings organized around First Quadrant archetypal themes are most profoundly motivated to preserve their own pattern, and this imperative

DOI: 10.4324/9781032708751-16

shows up as an energetic determination to "find" oneself, or tell one's own story, which also resists otherness. Otherness is the outer void, the creative matrix from which individual being must be hewn like a sculpture from stone. In one sense, the emergence of a stone sculpture can be seen as a matter of removing "excess" stone which is not integral to the emerging shape, but in another sense, the process is a matter of the intended shape itself emerging as an act of creation. In the vibrant and teeming internal lives of Sensitive personalities, the sensitive observer will notice both notes: resistance to *not-self*, and preoccupation with the task of one's own emerging authenticity. If we envision emergence into the First Quadrant as a culmination of navigating a harrowing *Sidpa Bardo* experience preceding arrival into the world, we can perhaps empathize with the tightness with which the migrating psyche clings to its shape.

The First Quadrant is the wellspring of human life and the origin story of the individual psyche. The organizing archetypal foundation for the First Quadrant is Ascension…not ascension up and out of this human world, but up *into* it. The instinctive imperative of the First Quadrant is emergence from the pleromic no-thing that precedes existence into the world of people, places, and things. The First Quadrant represents a commitment to *this world* and an expanding array of demands to *become*. This emergence is the first task of the developing psyche and is betokened by actual physical birth from the mother's womb. Grotstein (1981) depicted the psychological experience of separation from the mother as the "primal split," the first of many branching paths that navigate object relations and the development of a sense of self, from the first experiences of attachment into adult identity. Grotstein's terminology reminds us that the First Quadrant involves a split: a primordial vision of the self that exists beyond the vicissitudes of time and circumstance must be split up into a range of details. The First Quadrant demands that we emerge from the pleroma and become short or tall, introverted or extroverted, and rich or poor. Although we may combine and transcend some of these binaries, and achieve a full and flexible life, we must nevertheless navigate those binaries, and become *someone in particular*. Navigation of the First Quadrant represents the emergence from a pleromic oneness into increasingly forking paths and competing imperatives necessitated by adult life in the midst of the world. In the Tao Te Ching (Chan, 2015), we read: "Tao produced the One. / The One produced the two. / The two produced the three. / And the three produced the ten thousand things" (p. 176).

This transition from the oneness to the bewildering cacophony of the "ten thousand things," from the unnameable to the innumerable, represents the emergence from solitary and continuous existence of the self into the interpenetrating pathways of human relational complexity. The psychological challenge of the First Quadrant, then, amounts to tolerating the passage from one world to the next, like a traveler arriving in an alien culture, not as a sojourn but as a permanent resident. "Who is the dreamer and who dreams the dream?" asks Grotstein (2000), pointing to the primordial self which exists in a state of autochthony and which will become the basis for infantile grandiosity. Freud glancingly discusses a concept of *oceanic feeling,* which seemingly precedes and contextualizes birth, with French scholar

Romain Rolland based on teachings by Ramakrishna Paramahansa (Roland, 1986). Within the Jewish mystical tradition, the angel Lailah presses a finger to the upper lip of a newborn baby (creating, by the way, the philtrum) to induce forgetfulness of the child's prior existence:

> When at last the time arrives for his entrance into the world, the angel comes to him and says: "At a certain hour your time will come to enter the light of the world." He pleads with him, saying: "Why do you wish me to go out into the light of the world?" The angel replies: "You know, my son, that you were formed against your will; against your will you will be born; against your will you will die…". Thereupon he went out into the light of the world, though against his will. Upon going out the infant forgot everything he had witnessed and everything he knew. Why does the child cry out on leaving his mother's womb? Because the place wherein he had been at rest and at ease was irretrievable and because of the condition of the world into which he must enter.
>
> (Berman, 1996, Pekudei 3)

There is a lot to unpack in this mythic narrative. As we will discuss later on, grief over the loss of the womb will not manifest consciously until the advent of the Third and Fourth Quadrant, at which point in the archetypal cycle the loss of Grotstein's primal split comes full circle and is finally emotionally metabolized. The organizing theme of the First Quadrant is reflected in the phrase "he went out into the light of the world, though against his will," which may as well be engraved in the forlorn hearts of First Quadrant personalities everywhere. This reluctance, this *dynamic of resistance*, strongly accentuates the interpersonal and relational style of the schizoid personality, which has its origins in this sector of the spiral path.

The First Quadrant is a haunted quadrant because here we are still impacted by the trauma of *not being able to remember*, and yet knowing in some deep way that there is something that cannot be remembered. In the First Quadrant, we are haunted by something we know exists. There is heroism in the willingness to enter into this harrowing world with our senses intact. The First Quadrant, like the Third, reminds us that humankind is a heroic species. "Around the hero," writes Nietzsche (2008), "everything becomes a tragedy" (chapter 4, aphorism 150).

The First Quadrant personality represents qualities of the hierophant. In ancient Greek culture, the hierophant was an intermediary between the internal mysteries of the cosmos and the people, able to mediate messages from the unseen world. I chose to name the avatar of the First Quadrant the "Sensitive" personality because of the hierophantic functions they serve: their attentiveness to the "inner" realities often results in overwhelm, as if listening to too many channels at once. "I am large," writes Walt Whitman (2023), a consummate First Quadrant personality. "I contain multitudes" (p. 6). The First Quadrant preserves an androgyny of consciousness that becomes lost by the advent of the Second Quadrant (a tragic victim of the Axis of Christ), and the Sensitive Personality is fairly described as a pontifex… a bridge builder. The challenge of this dynamic, as we shall see, will be holding a pattern, or "boundedness" as Ogden (1989) would call it, the accomplishment of which represents the successful transit of the Axis of Christ at the Exemplar aspect.

There is no question of humility, or kindness, or self-effacement in infancy. The human psyche at its most basic developmental state, shortly after birth, is to manifest, take up space, consume, and need...to be. The needs of the self, its biological imperatives, are announced without awareness, much less concern, for the well-being of those tasked with supplying the needs of infancy. The needs of infancy are screamed aloud. However, much we smile tenderly upon the natural selfishness of infants, we all also recognize how necessary it is to climb down, developmentally, from what would become a pinnacle of unthinking tyranny in adulthood. In a sense, childhood, adolescence, and adult life can be seen as one long divestment of primal selfishness, and in its place a painstaking development of the complex social skills required to balance personal needs with the rights of others in a bewildering and ungentle world. This evolution from selfish certainty to sober doubt is the work of the spiral path.

Shall we call babies "selfish," given their circumstances? Their needs are so great because their helplessness is so absolute...and this logic also holds with adults who have not transcended childlike grandiosity, as we shall see. Infantile insistence on being fed and protected is developmentally appropriate and reflects the imperative not just to survive but to grow and become. Infants are in the process of *rising*, and at their stage of life, there is little to distract them, and few internal conflicts to undermine them, as their bodies do their silent work of completing the process of birth outside the womb. How have you, dear reader, managed not to lose yourself and your identity in the midst of the teeming purposes of the world? We can tolerate the *multiplicity* of adult life because we have psychologically labored to make ourselves a robust vessel capable of containing the human experience. The dichotomy between the internal authentic self and the protective coloration required by adjustment to adult life cannot be expected of the First Quadrant, in which *becoming* is an imperative. T. H. White (1976) describes knowledge of the world as a kind of seventh sense, the emergence of which marks a transition from the innocence of authenticity toward the stultifying compromises of adult life:

> There was a time when each of us stood naked before the world, confronting life as a serious problem with which we were intimately and passionately concerned. There was a time when it was of vital interest to us to find out whether there was a God or not. Obviously the existence or otherwise of a future life must be of the very first importance to somebody who is going to live her present one, because her manner of living it must hinge on the problem...
>
> All these problems and feelings fade away when we get the seventh sense. Middle-aged people can balance between believing in God and breaking all the commandments, without difficulty. The seventh sense, indeed, slowly kills all the other ones, so that at last there is no trouble about the commandments. We cannot see any more, or feel, or hear about them. The bodies which we loved, the truths which we sought, the Gods whom we questioned: we are deaf and

blind to them now, safely and automatically balancing along toward the inevitable grave, under the protection of our last sense.

(p. 213)

There is a kind of heroism in accomplishing such balance, in accommodating the self-doubt and humility that come with adaptation to the complexities of adult life. This kind of heroism allows us to retain our dignity even as we admit our sadness and the feeling of being *lost*. And a different kind of heroism is required to navigate the First Quadrant. Just as recognizing and naming the heroism of doubt will become important in the midst of the Fourth Quadrant, our duty to the First Quadrant archetype is to respect and hold space for its need to be true to itself. The human psyche stirs toward apotheosis, which is a greater manifestation.

The developmental arc of the First Quadrant is boundaried by the Axis of Christ to the left and the Axis of Lilith to the right, representing cohering and dissolving psychic functions, respectively. On the counterclockwise rotation, the spiral path leads across the Axis of Christ and into the Second Quadrant through a dynamic of resistance, from energy monism into duality, into configurations of the self that are able to hold a pattern and wield power (reflecting the mythic status of Christ as a "pattern man" or exemplar). On the clockwise rotation, the spiral path leads across the Axis of Lilith into the Fourth Quadrant, creating the conditions for melancholic and introjective assumptions leading to self-critique, and therefore also empathy. Therefore, the energetic and developmental resolution of the First Quadrant involves emergence either into a boundaried and potent sense of self capable of projecting power into the human world, or into a configuration of attachment, interdependence, and the capacity for doubt. In either case, emergence from the First Quadrant involves greater "incarnation" into the world in one form or another.

Defensive Correlates of the First Quadrant

If the energetic imperative of the First Quadrant is manifestation into the world, and holding a pattern, the developmental challenge becomes a matter of defending one's own selfhood and prioritizing one's own authenticity against forces which would undermine that effort (or appear to undermine it). Threats to authentic manifestation (both actual and perceived) therefore become the *bête noire* of the developing psyche. Sensitive personalities therefore guard their inner essences and resist influences, which would restrict or impinge their efforts to emerge as authentic separate entities…tethered in the world, but sovereign. Sensitive personalities attune to themselves and therefore tend to stand apart in ways that preserve their authenticity, often at the point of great personal and interpersonal cost.

Psychoanalytic perspectives on the defensive operations of Sensitive personalities tend to refer primarily to schizoid styles, and to a lesser extent, avoidant styles. Nancy McWilliams (2011), who has done more to give voice to the qualities and conditions of the First Quadrant than any other contemporary writer, notes that these individuals "may take the pursuit of authenticity to such extreme lengths that their isolation and demoralization are virtually guaranteed" (p. 205). For any of us who are personally conscious of our own deeply felt transit of the First Quadrant, or who love a person who has ended up stranded there, McWilliams' words power-fully capture the high cost of emotional, social, intellectual, spiritual, and psycho-logical honesty in a world, which values those things little. Sensitive personalities often suffer greatly during their lonesome vigils along their psychological watch-towers, but this suffering may not show up in conscious awareness in ways that can be traced back to a self-state. Rather, Sensitive personalities tend to chalk up their painful experiences to the cost of living in a world, which often appears shallow, ignorant, or garish rather than experiencing them as outcomes of their own way of inhabiting the world.

The Sensitive Personality's instinct to stand apart in the name of personal sov-ereignty is perhaps best summed up in the psychoanalytic literature by the term *aphanisis*. The word comes from the Greek ἀφάνισις, meaning "disappearance," and appears to have been originally applied by Jones (1927) to reference the dis-appearance of sexual desire in the context of Freudian drive theory. Lacan et al. (2019) reinterpreted aphanisis (which he also referenced with the English word "fading") not as a disappearance of sexual desire but an intersubjective process of personal identity being eclipsed by the signifier that represents that identity…that is to say, sense of self is eclipsed by the perceptions and expectations of others. Broadly interpreted, then, aphanisis can be understood as a kind of anxiety about subjectively disappearing into the perceptions, and by extension the expectations, demands, and needs, of others in the world. From this point of view, aphanisis is the fear of losing one's own sovereign identity in the midst of external expecta-tions. The Sensitive Personality can be understood to carry around the assumption that "the more I adapt to the world, the less of me there is." Therefore, compro-mising with the world's expectations becomes an existential threat that invokes a kind of annihilation anxiety. This "fear of fading" represents the central affective experience of the Sensitive Personality and drives its defenses and interpersonal style. Returning to our discussion of the Axis of Transcendent Self in Chapter 12, aphanisis represents a defensive retreat from what Sartre calls "the look," in which the defining gaze of the other threatens to overcome or overpower the nascent and insubstantial sense of self which prevails in the First Quadrant.

Consistent with McWilliams' formulation, Sensitive personalities are powerfully motivated to protect what feels like a fragile authenticity, which must be defended against the depredations and incursions of the outer world, resulting in defensive styles that are described in the psychoanalytic and clinical literature as avoidance, withdrawal, and retreat. Fairbairn (1952) and Guntrip (1969) described schizoid withdrawal in terms of splitting that reflects a conflict between a part of the self that wants to be in the world and a part of the self that needs protective space in-sulated from the cost of being in the world. Erskine (1997) underlines the sense of loss inherent in the compromise between withdrawal and fulfillment, although the defensive style of the Sensitive Personality tends to prevent such loss from being consciously experienced as sadness or melancholy. As McWilliams (2011) points out, the schizoid sense of self tends to result in internal needs and stressors being defensively reinterpreted as coming at them from the outside. In other words, the Sensitive Personality is less likely to admit loneliness and more likely to complain about demands placed upon them to come out of their shells.

There is a certain elemental purity to the psychological defenses manifesting in the context of First Quadrant archetypal realities. *If you withdraw*, according to an old psychoanalytic chestnut, *you don't have to distort*. In the 1984 film *The Karate Kid*, Pat Morita's character, Mr. Miyagi, advises his young protégé that the best way to avoid a punch is to not be there (Avildsen). First Quadrant defenses often amount to "not being there" in the sense of keeping a low profile in the world, and often have an appealingly honest quality to them. This defensive style lacks the cloying, manipulative, or emotionally dishonest defenses that will predominate especially in the Third and Fourth Quadrants. "I gotta be my dirty self," sings Nils Lofgren (1977). The Sensitive Personality therefore is more likely to come across as tactless, blunt, or emotionally unavailable as a way of cutting through the snares and webs of social contracts and interpersonal pressures, which might result in seductive or manipulative responses in the Third Quadrant personality, or in introjective self-denial in the Fourth Quadrant. The resulting pursuit of authenticity at any cost contributes to the experience of friends and family of the Sensitive Personality that they often remain distressingly out of reach and difficult to contact. The outcome of these defenses may result in what Laing artfully calls "Life, without feeling alive" (1969, p. 42).

The historical tendency to describe schizoid defenses as related to "withdrawal" from the world and consensual reality has ultimately been problematic. Words like "withdrawal" and "retreat" into fantasy or an internal world carry the implications that a person has encountered the world, did not like what they see, and has chosen to exit "stage left" from the stage of life. It is perhaps more helpful to conceptualize the defensive style of the Sensitive Personality as a *withholding*, or a resistance to emerging. In archetypal terms, the energy is not so much about avoidance but preserving the structural integrity of the self.

Diagnostic Considerations

The First Quadrant represents the archetypal foundation of defensive styles and personality structure described in the literature as schizoid. The term "schizoid" seems to have come from Bleuler (1911), who described it as a tendency to direct psychological resources inwards rather than out into the world. In keeping with the vertical model of harmonic representation, persons who qualify as "schizoid personality disorder" would include First Quadrant personalities with representational horizons in the third and fourth harmonic. Sensitive personalities organized at the fifth and sixth harmonics will show up as psychologically robust and relationally apt people who nevertheless exhibit personality characteristics including rich and intense private lives of great authenticity (including many who are gifted artists, writers, philosophers, and entertainers). Sensitive personalities organized at the first and second harmonics will exhibit more significant adjustment problems including symptoms of mental illness strong enough to disrupt interpersonal and occupational functioning.

Of all the personality styles described in the literature and parsed into the DSM, the schizoid personality disorder represents a particularly trenchant litmus test for the world-view of the observer. Formulations range from the sterile laundry list of behavioral deficits found in the DSM to Guntrip's (1969) insights about the importance of a relational capacity for human functioning to Nancy McWilliams' (2006) arresting depictions of the internal richness awaiting anybody who attempts to take the schizoid dynamic seriously.

The Diagnostic and Statistical Manual (2013), in unfortunately characteristic fashion, commits important empathic failures in describing the schizoid personality. Criterion one as articulated in the DSM V states that the schizoid personality "neither desires nor enjoys close relationships," which does deep injustice to the contemporary psychodynamic understanding that schizoid avoidance reflects a meaningful and dynamic tension between inner authenticity and the demands of the world, rather than a lack of desire to connect with others. Deeply attuned observers of the schizoid personality will notice within the heart of a schizoid presentation not a lack of desire for a relationship but a hungry desire for intimacy countered by fears of the psychological cost of actually obtaining it. Fairbairn (1941) identifies this central dynamic as "love made hungry." Indeed, it has been my anecdotal observation that many schizoid personalities are natural ectomorphs, sometimes eschewing food and the very experience of feeding.

The Psychodynamic Diagnostic Manual (Lingiardi & McWilliams, 2017) acknowledges the important characteristic of deep sensitivity, vulnerability to over-stimulation, shy relational style, and what Guntrip (1969) succinctly calls the *in and out programme, which* he describes as "the chronic dilemma in which the schizoid individual is placed, namely that he can neither be in a relationship with another person nor out of it" (p. 36). This painful psychic quandary elegantly captures the psychological conflict of being "between a rock and a hard place," in which the rock represents painful loneliness and isolation while the hard place represents an unwillingness to compromise one's own authenticity. The dichotomy captures the origins of the word "schizoid" whose root "schizo" comes from the Greek σχίζω, "to split."

The Jungian tradition is regrettably sparse on schizoid dynamics. Jung's (1971) descriptors of the introverted function captures a widely acknowledged feature of the schizoid personality, but as I have suggested above, the deeper motivation of the schizoid personality is not so much to turn away from the world but to titrate outer experience with inner. While the schizoid pursuit of authenticity often does result in a well-developed introverted function, the psychological adaptations characterizing schizoid people are much more complex than that, and some deeply schizoid people end up transcending their natural shyness to develop highly charismatic and engaging personalities sometimes referred to as "covert" or masked schizoid personalities.

The First Quadrant also comprises personality organizations which may be described as Avoidant or Schizotypal rather than Schizoid. As is most likely true with other personality organizations, it is likely that the DSM's emphasis on discrete traits belies a continuous relationship among these three personality styles which likely represents differences among levels of personality organization. All three personality styles reflect a general theme of defensive withholding with the purpose of protecting a core sense of authenticity. Personalities described as avoidant are likely to comprise relatively high-functioning ends of the schizoid continuum who nevertheless exhibit behavioral patterns designed to protect against external rejection and judgment. Schizotypal personalities are more likely to represent the lower functioning end of the schizoid continuum, manifesting as pervasive and overt challenges with fitting in or "passing for normal," and more likely to show up as "eccentric" in various ways.

Ogden (1989) describes a so-called *autistic-contiguous mode* of presymbolic experience which complements the Kleinian paranoid-schizoid and depressive positions and represents the "primitive edge" of schizoid experience. This mode of generating experience forms the basis for human boundedness based on locating sensory input like shape, temperature, texture, and hardness in body sensation. The so-called Highly Sensitive Person (Aron, 1997) represents another personality characterization based on First Quadrant sensibilities, including sensory processing sensitivity reminiscent of Ogden's formulation. Jackson (1963) similarly describes the formation of symbols and their precursors from an analytical perspective:

> At primitive levels symbolism is archaic and prelogical, the symbol having the same emotional value as the thing symbolized, and this stage has been called the symbolic equation. With further development this changes to symbolic representation, where the symbol represents rather than presents the thing symbolized, is a picture rather than a replica. When this change occurs in the treatment of schizoid patients, it is associated with a lessening of persecutory anxiety and an increased capacity for depression and for healthier object relations.
>
> (p. 156)

This formulation is consistent with the assumptions of the harmonic progression of the vertical model of Integrated Analytical Psychology, describing an evolution of mental representation to a higher "harmonic" as well as implying a hoped-for trajectory toward "an increased capacity for depression" (i.e., progress toward the Fourth Harmonic). Such primitive mental representations also invoke Bion's (1988) idea of "beta elements," which are raw, primal ingredients of undifferentiated experience that must be metabolized through "alpha function" (which implies a relational process).

The schizoid tendency toward Jackson's "symbolic equation," Ogden's "austistic-contiguous mode," or Bion's "beta elements," which suggest energetic identification with unconscious symbolic content that border on the concrete, paradoxically seems to result in a natural capacity for navigating perceptual sets, affective states, and other forms of mental representation in an unusually robust way. Schizoid people are ideational egalitarians who show a broad willingness to take on markedly different self-states and perceptions. This kind of internal fluency gives schizoid personalities a natural advantage to adopting Jung's transcendent function (Miller, 2004). Natural artists, dreamers, philosophers, and schizoid personalities are admirably able to move freely in the imaginal, allowing them to excel at the transcendent function through their capacity to "acknowledge the gap between what is imagined and what is actually present in the material world" (Colman, 2006, p. 22). "Facts," says Don Quixote in Man of La Mancha, "are the enemy of truth." (Hiller et al., 2004, scene 8.)

Maslow's (1968) conceptualization of self-actualization amplifies the intrinsic energy of First Quadrant personalities, as it describes an aspiration to preserve an inner life in the midst of outer realities:

> An important existential problem is posed by the fact that self-actualizing persons (and all people in their peak- experiences) occasionally live out-of-time and out-of-the- world (atemporal and aspatial) even though mostly they must live in the outer world. Living in the inner psychic world (which is ruled by psychic laws and not by the laws of outer-reality), i.e., the world of experience, of emotion, of wishes and fears and hopes, of love of poetry, art and fantasy, is different from living in and adapting to the nonpsychic reality which runs by laws he never made and which are not essential to his nature even though he has to live by them. (He could, after all, live in other kinds of worlds, as any science fiction fan knows.) The person who is not afraid of this inner, psychic world, can enjoy it to such an extent that it may be called Heaven by contrast with the more effortful, fatiguing, externally responsible world of "reality," of striving and coping, of right and wrong, of truth and falsehood. This is true even though the healthier person can also adapt more easily and enjoyably to the "real" world, and has better "reality testing," i.e., doesn't confuse it with his inner psychic world.
>
> (p. 213)

Harry Guntrip in particular championed the ubiquity of the schizoid condition and found it fundamental to the human experience. Where psychoanalytic thought (and the cultural trends which followed it) associated schizoid conditions with ego weakness (a misconception I am hoping to address in this chapter) and depression with guilt, Guntrip noted that human beings seem to prefer being bad than being weak. From this perspective, Guntrip (1969) considered the over-emphasis on depression to be humankind's "greatest and most consistent self-deception" (p. 134). Guntrip noted the (perhaps ironical) avoidance of schizoid truth, concluding: "It may be that we ourselves would rather not be forced to see it too clearly lest we should find a textbook in our own hearts" (p. 178).

Gender and Cultural Considerations

Redwood trees are exemplars of the schizoid style. They obtain most of their water from ambient amounts of moisture in the air, which they are able to absorb directly into their leaves through a process called foliar uptake, or directly through the bark, in addition to water absorbed by the roots. In this way, redwood trees sip ambient amounts of moisture from the air, which is a reason they thrive in foggy coastal areas. In the same way, schizoid personalities sip ambient amounts of intimacy as if from the air…they do not gulp it hungrily, as will happen in the Third and Fourth Quadrants. Just as the habitat of redwood trees is threatened by climate change (Sillett et al., 2015), Sensitive personalities inhabiting the First Quadrant remain exquisitely sensitive to the external cultural conditions in which they live. They can thrive in cultural environments in which their inner lives are respected and invited, but wither and withdraw into themselves in environments that demand that they denature themselves in order to fit in.

To attempt another metaphor: I find that it helps to understand the Sensitive Personality as existing at a great altitude…perhaps 35,000 feet or so, the altitude of a commercial aircraft in flight. At that altitude, we do not see people and cars and flowers and dogs; we see river systems, mountain ranges, and coastlines. Sensitive personalities have an intently cosmic point of view, such that the things they think are care most about tend to be big things, and deep things. For this reason, they are often alienated from, and uninterested in, consensual reality that governs the lives of most of us. Their cognitive style and perceptive style are often deconstructive, in the sense that they track and value what seems most true and valuable to them rather than following the existing pathways and patterns offered by their culture, and are often natural iconoclasts. There is therefore something *perpendicular* about them, as if they operate at right angles to what most of us consider reality. The 35,000-foot perspective, the intently cosmic point of view, gives Sensitive personalities an unusually broad perspective on human life at an existential level to which few of us attend. For this reason, we would be wise to listen to the Sensitive personalities in our midst. If anyone ever saves the world, it will be a schizoid personality.

Unfortunately, for all their intrinsic value, the world has never treated Sensitive personalities kindly. One of the central tragedies of the Sensitive experience is the lack of culturally sanctioned value and meaning extended to this arc of the spiral by Western culture.

The Sensitive style has layered relationships with cultural privilege, which intersect in complex ways with gender. Although men, women, and nonbinary persons all navigate a relationship with the First Quadrant, a decidedly schizoid presentation can, in many ways, require a position of some cultural privilege. It has been my anecdotal experience First Quadrant energy is most expected, normalized, and forgivable in men. Because Western patriarchal culture assigns greater thematic leeway to men (in terms of broadness of life choices), men may simply be given more cultural license to sink into a decidedly schizoid lifestyle. The "spinster" variant of the Sensitive Personality carries a more negative social valence than the stereotypical "absent minded professor" variant, which tends to assume the form of a male with relatively ascetic and solitary values who remains aloof from the more prosaic and textured requirements of daily life, such as childcare or housework. To put it bluntly, men are typically more free to treat the world as if it were optional. As Manon Garcia (2011) puts it:

> It does not come from the fact that women are naturally more able to perceive dirty laundry or that men are blind to housework but from the fact that perception has a social dimension and is shaped by the gendered division of labor: women perceive dirty socks more because they are the ones in charge of doing laundry.

(p. 91)

Garcia's point reinforces the fact that patriarchal forces tend to pull women deeper into embodiment and into the transactional requirements of life (both relegating women to their bodies and then commodifying those bodies), giving women comparatively less freedom to treat reality as optional or philosophical. Especially in cultures that provide no traditional vocational posture for the First Quadrant energies (for example, in American culture), the Sensitive Personality requires "being left alone" to some extent, and the degree to which one is left alone by the world intersects powerfully with identity including race, gender, and economic class.

References

American Psychiatric Association. (2013). *Diagnostic and statistical manual of mental disorders* (5th ed.). Author.

Aron, E. (1997). *The highly sensitive person: How to thrive when the world overwhelms you.* Broadway Books.

Berman, S. A. (1996). *Midrash Tanhuma-Yelammedenu.* KTAV Publishing House.

Bion, W. R. (1988). A theory of thinking. In E. B. Spillius (Ed.), *Melanie Klein today: Developments in theory and practice, Vol. 1. Mainly theory* (pp. 178–186). Routledge.

Bleuler, P. E. (1911). *Dementia praecox: Or the group of schizophrenias.* International Universities Press.

Chan, W. (2015). *The way of Lao Tzu.* Ravenio Books.

Colman, W. (2006). Imagination and the imaginary. *The Journal of Analytical Psychology, 51*(1): 21–41.

Erskine, R. G. (1997). *Theories and methods of an integrative transactional analysis: A volume of selected articles.* TA Press.

Fairbairn, W. R. D. (1941). A revised psychopathology of the psychoses and psychoneuroses. *The International Journal of Psychoanalysis, 22*: 250–270.

Fairbairn, W. R. D. (1952). *Psychoanalytic studies of the personality.* Tavistock.

Fremantle, F. (2001). *Luminous emptiness: Understanding the Tibetan book of the dead.* Shambhala.

Garcia, M. (2011). *We are not born submissive: How patriarchy shapes women's lives.* Princeton University Press.

Grotstein, J. S. (1981). *Splitting and projective identification.* Jason Aronson.

Grotstein, J. S. (2000). *Who is the dreamer who dreams the dream.* The Analytic Press.

Guntrip, H. (1969). *Schizoid phenomena, object-relations and the self.* International Universities Press.

Hiller, A., Wasserman, D., O'Toole, P., Loren, S., Coco, J., Andrews, H., & Castle, J. (2004). *Man of La Mancha.* Distributed by Metro Goldwyn Mayer Home Entertainment.

Jackson, M. (1963). Symbol formation and the delusional transference. *Journal of Analytical Psychology, 8*: 145–159.

Jones, E. (1927). The early development of female sexuality. *The International Journal of Psychoanalysis, 8*: 459–472.

Jung, C. G. (1971). *Psychological types* (R. F. C. Hull, Trans.). Princeton University Press.

Lacan, J., Miller, J. A., & Sheridan, A. (2019). *The four fundamental concepts of psychoanalysis.* Routledge.

Lingiardi, V., & McWilliams, N. (Eds.). (2017). *Psychodynamic diagnostic manual* (2nd ed.). The Guilford Press.

Lofgren, N. (1977). *I came to dance [Song]. On I came to dance.* Bias Studios; A&M Records.

Maslow, A. H. (1968). *Toward a psychology of being* (2nd ed.). D. Van Nostrand.

McWilliams, N. (2006). Some thoughts about schizoid dynamics. *Psychoanalytic Review, 93*(1): 1–24.

McWilliams, N. (2011). *Psychoanalytic diagnosis: Understanding personality structure in the clinical process.* The Guilford Press.

Miller, J. C. (2004). *The transcendent function: Jung's model of psychological growth through dialogue with the unconscious.* State University of New York Press.

Nietzsche, F. (2008). *The birth of tragedy.* Oxford University Press.

Ogden, T. H. (1989). *The primitive edge of experience.* Jason Aronson.

Roland, A. (1986). Ramakrishna: Mystical, erotic, or both? *Journal of Religion and Health, 37*: 31–36.

Sillett, S. C., Antoine, M. E., Carroll, A. L., Graham, M. E., Chin, A. R. O., & Van Pelt, R. (2015). Rangewide climatic sensitivities and non-timber values of tall Sequoia sempervirens forests. *Forest Ecology and Management, 526*: 1–36.

White, T. H. (1976). *The once and future king.* Berkley Books.

Whitman, W. (2023). *Leaves of grass.* Peter Pauper Press.

Chapter 14

The Second Quadrant

The Imperial Personality

White Fang could have become leader of the pack. But he was too morose and solitary for that. He merely thrashed his team-mates. Otherwise he ignored them. They got out of his way when he came along; nor did the boldest of them ever dare to rob him of his meat... White Fang knew the law well: to oppress the weak and obey the strong.

- Jack London
White Fang

One must be cunning and wicked in this world.

- Leo Tolstoy
War and Peace

Archetypal Themes of the Second Quadrant

Emergence from the First Quadrant to the Second is our first irrevocable step into Movement. The Axis of Christ in this arc of the spiral invokes Christ as the pattern-man and exemplar, and an archetype for nascent selfhood. This commitment to movement implies the loss of First Quadrant origins, including loss of Oceanic Consciousness, away from pure possibility and into an atomic form capable of holding its own pattern. Movement from the First to the Second Quadrant also shifts from the yonic opening of birth into a cross, which is a more stable pattern. Energetically speaking, emergence from the First Quadrant into the Second implies a shedding of pathways and outcomes that previously remained possible and instead, entering into patterned embodiment, a tethered entity in time and space. In other words, the shift from the First to the Second invokes a movement from spontaneous creation into formal operations of unique egoic experience, from unity to duality. At some point along this process, growing awareness of self-as-separate becomes a traumatic sundering of individual consciousness from the creative matrix of the archetypal origin, and self is now "dug in," a posture of opposition to Other and the Outer World.

Navigating the second quadrant involves developing an increasing ratio of resistance. Developmentally, the infant discovers its fingers and toes, reveling in its own newfound incarnation in the world. At the same time, the infant undertakes an archetypal shift from over-identification with Mother into identifying as a self,

DOI: 10.4324/9781032708751-17

and Mother becomes Other. In the Second Quadrant, there is no dwelling on the loss of the primal oneness and belonging of Oceanic Consciousness (although that loss will be discovered in the Third Quadrant and amplified into a major theme in the Fourth). There is instead a determined renunciation of innocence and a commitment to discovering and serving one's own truth. The Imperial personality discovers, and organizes around, a disconnect between one's own internal truth and the perceived falsity of the outside world. This disconnect creates the energetic conditions for splitting and conflict rather than defensive withdrawal into authenticity (as in the First Quadrant). The god of the Second Quadrant is an angry and jealous god.

Speaking of angry and jealous gods, mythically speaking (that is, symbolically speaking), the early transit of the Second Quadrant can be narrated as a discovery and fascination with dark magics, invoking legends of the dark sorcerers of Atlantis whose pursuit of forbidden knowledge doomed their civilization. Sociologically and anthropologically, the transition from the First to the Second parallels an evolution from traditional cultures that evolved around shared experience, ecstasy, and trance into formal religious structures defined as beliefs and dogmas. The organizing principle is control: there are those who are weak and those who are strong, and the strong should rule the weak. However, the Second Quadrant is still a relatively "early" stage of the circumplex, and "closer" to archetypal experience than the Third or Fourth Quadrants; that is to say, the Second Quadrant is available to lower-order harmonic representations (according to the curvilinear mathematics of the Spiral Path). There is therefore something primal and atavistic about the Second Quadrant.[1]

The second quadrant governs the evolution of a new, formal, agentic sense of self. In psychological terms, the development of an agentic self requires the capacity to independently make choices and to impose those choices on the outer world of other people, things, and events. Whereas the challenge of the first quadrant was to resolve ambivalence about manifesting in the social world at all, the second quadrant requires the psyche to take its presence in the world for granted, and moving on from there. The second quadrant psyche is no longer interested in whether or not things are "real," or "true." The second quadrant psyche is engaged in the process of influencing the world as a self-interested individual force. "Ready or not, here I come," says the second quadrant personality. From this point of view, the world is not an existential challenge or a frightening source of alienation, but a cake to be eaten ravenously (although as we shall see, awareness of one's own hunger is not a characteristic feature). This quadrant is home to the carnivore, the hunter, and the predator. The sobriquet "Imperial" captures some of the agentic, forceful, colonizing, grandiose, and externalizing qualities of this archetypal field. The Second Quadrant formalizes and consummates Jung's (1971) sensate function.

In terms of the cartography of the spiral path, emergence into the Second Quadrant from the First involves an energy of cohering upon a unified field of self. The arc involves rotation across the Axis of Christ through the "exemplar" aspect of that archetype, resolving First Quadrant's reluctance to manifest and fully accepting the transition from single-hearted authenticity (a Sensitive trait) to canny duality. In the Second Quadrant, origin is an irrelevant memory, authenticity of the self is a distraction, and we have fully embraced the "ten thousand things" and taken our rightful place in the marketplace (or battlefield) of the world.

As we will discuss, at the southern border of the Second Quadrant, the Axis of Lilith looms large. Indeed, Lilith and her ferocious feminine, dissolving energy, forms an effective barrier against forward motion that would transcend Second Quadrant perspectives and evolve onwards into the Third.

The clockwise rotation of the spiral path reverses this polarity, such that the psyche transcends the third quadrant in order to enter the second. This transition compellingly mirrors the counterclockwise rotation from the Third to the Fourth: both transitions involve an archetypal return to an ongoing journey of selfhood, and a concurrent energetic reframe and containment of relational commitments and dissolving anaclitic energy. However, the clockwise transition from Third to Second involves embracing a sense of self that is founded upon self-reliance, certainty, and personal power rather than the principled self-doubt of the Fourth Quadrant.

The psychological ingredients necessary to navigating the second quadrant include a capacity to faithfully represent the self in the interpersonal world. Second quadrant personalities are not troubled by doubts or internal conflicts (at least consciously) but celebrate their own realities in an elementally pure and forceful way. The second quadrant personality has claimed a patch of territory, staked out the boundary lines, and is fully prepared to defend those boundaries against encroachment. It is this psychological energy signature that allows a sense of what is "mine." This insistence on maintaining a pattern is both similar and different from First Quadrant conditions. Whereas First Quadrant patterning is organized around preserving an authenticity against the world's demands (in a manner that often places the self in a "one down" position relative to more powerful forces emanating from the outside), the Second Quadrant is based rather on a primary motivation to exert power on one's own behalf. In other words, the Second Quadrant's goal is power for its own sake rather than preservation of an inner vision. The transition from First Quadrant to Second involves moving out of a state and wonder and into a state of opposition.

Owning property, resisting trespass, and defending possessions against others requires a secure conviction that "I am the source of action and determination in the world." This conviction is not the same as believing that "I am in the right," or "I am morally justified," because second quadrant convictions are not based on moral calculus but on the exercise of power or representation of the self. The second quadrant personality is energetically clearing a space for itself without self-consciousness, like a hunter wielding a spear. The spear has a handle end, making it an extension of the hunter's will, and a business end, which is pointed at the intended target on the outside. In this quadrant, the personality becomes a source of power and discrimination, where self is the predator and desired objects in the world are prey.

Developmentally, second quadrant energy begins with an infant noticing itself and its capacities. Babies become fascinated with their own fingers and toes and rejoice in the discovery that they can move them, use them as tools, and impact the world with them. As any parent could attest, around the age of two years, children sometimes become tantrum-prone, aggressive, defiant, and bossy as they begin to experience the extent (but not yet the limits) of their own power. Research shows that even three-to-five-year-old children are unlikely to share if left to their own devices, and that only by age seven or eight do they begin to develop a more egalitarian perspective including empathy and sharing.

Ultimately, traversing the Axis of Christ from the first to the second quadrant represents an important achievement resulting in a secure sense of self which is powerful and agentic, able to affect the world. However, this psychological achievement comes with a cost. The developmental tasks of entering mortal adulthood require that some possibilities go unmet, and some promises remain unfulfilled. Of all the possible selves, one must be selected, anointed, and crowned as king. The result is an emergence into dualism, whereby one way of being and acting in the world achieves ascendancy over other ways of being and acting. The second quadrant, therefore, ultimately encourages dichotomies and black and white thinking, and a sense of self built at the expense of other ways of experiencing and being. "I am this and not that" cries the psyche at this stage of development. "I believe these things, which are good and natural, and not those things, which are evil and perverse." It is not difficult to see what important and complex realities are missing from this viewpoint, nor to recognize the potential for human evil implicit in this quadrant. The second quadrant contains energies that have proved difficult for the human psyche to metabolize successfully. The history of human civilization, in a sense, is one long struggle to come to terms with the Second Quadrant and its implications.

One useful metaphor for the Second Quadrant archetype is that of gardening. What is gardening, but the sheer expression of human will upon a tract of nature? The gardener approaches living plants on the property with a clear agenda, pulling up weeds and killing them while feeding and watering the more desirable plants. A garden represents the triumph of human will over nature based purely on our own arbitrary desires. What is a "weed" but a plant we have deemed undesirable? In this sense, the second quadrant is about weeding and gardening, and definitively clearing out a space for the self to inhabit, which will be defended against interlopers, invaders, and pests.

The metaphor of the gardener also reminds us of the archetypal and therefore intrinsically human quality of the Second Quadrant: although the dynamic may result in pathological narcissism or psychopathy, the foundational motivation of the Imperial is the capacity to become the center of one's own experience. Indeed, a quality of the narcissistically organized personality that has become universally admired in contemporary culture is its capacity to unselfconsciously promote its own agenda in an (apparently) guilt-free and doubt-free manner.

The interpersonal configurations resulting from the Second Quadrant focus on "this and that" rather than "I and Thou." Buber's (1971) sense of the "I and Thou" relationship reflects a genuine relational field in which the separate identity of the other is acknowledged and connected with (and even, according to Buber, a kind of portal into connecting with God). The Second Quadrant archetype, rather, reflects a sense of self still folded in upon itself. The medium is not connections and relationships, nor principles and possibilities, but rather the discrete world of things and tangible forces. The energetic imperative of the Second Quadrant is control and establishing what is *mine*. The Imperial personality is an engineer, dispassionately calculating the gearing of the world. As Leigh McCloskey (2003) puts it, in describing his illustration of the Devil, the 15th key in the Tarot Arcana:

> A man and a woman are each bound on the outer wheel. The Latin words "Et eritus Sicut Dii, Scientes Bonum et Mallum" which mean "Ye shall be as gods knowning good and evil" are also inscribed here. These words call to mind one of the important lessons of this archetype. The Devil signifies both the tempter and the redeemer, generating good and evil. These seeming opposites are part of the necessary lessons in discrimination that man must experience to appreciate fully the polarity involved in all thought, choice, and action. Without contrasting evil or resistance, there would be no struggle. This contrast keeps the desire of the intellect, which is to structure, from ever truly holding sway over the much more universal impulse towards the creative. The creative qualities of consciousness are unpredictable and therefore the intellect distrusts and desires to control these qualities. It is this struggle which disallows stasis, the conflict being a necessary catalyst for change and continual evolution.
>
> (pp. 191–192)

The god of the Second Quadrant is an angry, jealous god who commands that we divide and separate. The emergence of formal operations manifesting as power, opinion, and rule represents an attempt to contain spontaneous creation through formal thought. Historically, the emergence of the second quadrant empowered monotheism over the primal paganism resulting from a deeper connection with the natural world. The ascendancy of the Second Quadrant probably parallels periods of human history in which religion shifted from a mode of primary participation in the natural world to a formal system of encoded belief. Religious experience as a mode of experiencing and participating in the natural world encourages the mysticism and harrowing humility of the First Quadrant; formal systems of encoded belief which characterize the Second Quadrant allow for the collection and focus of power in some persons over other persons, and also create the condition for war and conflict.

Ovid's point that the gods are optional, dating back to the year 2 AD, exemplifies the transition from spiritual participation in the mysteries of the natural world to an enshrinement of human intellect and its discriminatory powers. Second quadrant energy is directive and transactional and gives rise to the executive functions of ego and the formal operations of the conscious mind, as an attempt to contain spontaneous creation through thought, opinion, and belief, along with other forms of unique egoic experience. The Imperial personality looks into the world for feedback, away from spontaneous creation (and away from traditional cultures with tribal sensibilities, trance, and celebration into formal religious structure). Following hard upon the transit of the Axis of Christ, the Second Quadrant lays the foundation for monotheism, in the form of an angry jealous god demanding obedience.

Speaking of Ovid, who also articulates the myth of Narcissus: in many ways, the term "narcissism" as a label for the Second Quadrant personality structure is an unfortunate one. Freud (1905) picks up use of the myth of Narcissus, who is cursed by the gods for spurning Echo and falls in love with his own reflection in a pool of water. This mythological parallel has engendered all kinds of misunderstandings about the nature of Second Quadrant conditions, especially in equating it with "self-love." The popular conceptualizations of narcissistic personalities "in love" with themselves have led the culture further away from understanding the pathological outcomes of developmental arrest in the First Quadrant. A better metaphor comes from the Buddhist tradition of the Hungry Ghost, which are beings driven by animalistic needs that can never be sated: the more a Hungry Ghost eats, the hungrier it becomes. Medieval mystic Jakob Boehme (Boehme & Erb, 1977) captures something intrinsic about Second (and Third) Quadrant dynamics in *Mysterium Magnum*:

> ...the will desireth to be something, and yet it hath nothing of which it may make something to itself; and therefore it bringeth itself into a receivingness of itself, and compresseth itself to a something; and that something is nothing but a magnetical hunger, a harshness.

(p. 15)

As we shall see, there is a *magnetical hunger* at the center of the Imperial personality, but it is a hunger that does not result in gaining nutrients, but a hunger that collapses on itself and results in a harshness.

Defensive Correlates

The psychoanalytic take on the archetypal qualities characterizing the Second Quadrant have focused on the narcissistic, psychopathic/antisocial, and paranoid personalities, along with their various defensive strategies. Key organizing principles articulated by the psychoanalytic literature describing these personality organizations include the characterological avoidance of shame, signature defensive styles known as primitive idealization and primitive devaluation, omnipotent control, and projection in particular, as well as the key concept of *selfobject* function.

The psychological common denominator among the various defensive styles related to Second Quadrant themes involve externalizing defenses against primitive affective states related to shame. Narcissistic, psychopathic/antisocial, and paranoid personalities follow various psychological, cognitive and affective, and relational strategies that generate Winnicott's (1992) "false self" with an "omnipotent, triumphant, vindicated" presentation (McWilliams, 2011, p. 223). Second quadrant defensive styles are intended to reinforce an inviolable sense of self. "I am the one who wins, by definition" may as well be engraved on the hearts of such personalities. Starting from this elemental proposition, anything which can be perceived as "weakness" is therefore an existential threat to the integrity of the self. The primitive affective states that prevail among Second Quadrant personalities therefore tend to reflect annihilation anxiety: the very undoing of the self is at stake. The consequences of failure, as with a child who fears catastrophic rejection by exacting parents who have made love conditional, necessitate any amount of pretzeling (of the self and of other people) in order to come out on top.

Because of their intrinsic psychological "shame-proofing," Imperial personalities end up locked out of the more relational capacities (and entanglements), which will to some extent characterize all the personality styles downstream from the Axis of Lilith. They can therefore be said to be "pre-relational." Technically, the Second Quadrant shares this pre-relational condition with the First Quadrant (it is the Axis of Lilith which creates the conditions for dissolving and love); First Quadrant personalities have more of an under-defended, "skinless" quality which preserves something foundationally authentic in them. By contrast, Second Quadrants are more powerfully eclipsed by their more rigid defenses, and their defenses are more likely to distort reality in important ways (for example, in clinging to the absolute power of the self and denying "weakness" in the form of vulnerability to either intimacy or shame). In fact, weakness emerges powerfully as a theme among Second Quadrant personalities, as a condition to be avoided courtesy of any amount of distorting defensive transformations. For this reason, psychotherapy with Second Quadrant personalities most likely will require the therapist to remain "inside" the client's defenses, riding out or gently interpreting them rather than taking them on directly. *Confront the borderline, interpret the narcissist* is an old psychoanalytic chestnut that reflects important realities of the Third versus the Second Quadrant. Similarly, psychotherapy in the Second Quadrant is more likely to track content over process, since the defensive styles of these personality organizations lack effective strategies for deeper attunement, which is prerequisite for more relational and process-based forms of talk therapy. Imperial defenses trade vulnerability and intimacy for self-efficacy, mastery, and shame avoidance.

Specific defensive styles among Imperial personalities are generally described as omnipotent control for psychopathic personalities, primitive idealization and devaluation for narcissistic personalities, and projection for paranoid personalities. In messy reality of course, there is no one-to-one relationship between defensive style and personality organization; all three defensive styles as well as others are shared among the Imperial styles. However, the defensive styles that tend to predominate among Imperial personalities are externalizing defenses, which seek to locate undesirable affective and ideational states outside of the self. Courtesy of externalizing defenses, the threats will always be *out there* rather than within the self, preserving a *good self / bad other* configuration of object relations. For example, given early childhood empathic failures with a parent involving abandonment (or perceived abandonment), introjecting defenses might narrativize the abandonment experience as a failure in the self ("I was abandoned because I'm abandonable"), while externalizing defenses leave the "onus" for the failure with the external object ("My parents failed me"). For these same reasons, the Imperial personalities are prone to acting out; that is to say, they are likely to manifest problems with reality testing and poor affect tolerance in their behavior in ways that generate additional levels of complication (a characteristic that is shared with Third Quadrant personalities, as we shall see).

Omnipotent control (Kernberg, 1995), the characteristic defense of the psychopathic personality, accomplishes this kind of externalization in an absolute way, by outsourcing primitive mental states into the external object ("I'm not scared; *you're* scared"). The mechanism of omnipotent control as a means of locating basic anxieties into a victim underline the poor affect tolerance of the psychopathic personality, as well. Primitive idealization and devaluation is a somewhat more complex defensive strategy assigning a winning vs. losing, dominant vs submissive context to the relational field with the ultimate purpose of keeping a relationship in an hierarchical configuration, which benefits the self: for example, the alternating phases of domination and reconciliation that mark the Cycle of Abuse (Walker, 1979) achieve the cumulative effect of controlling the victim and locating all the distress in the victim. Finally, projection as a defense mechanism fulfils a primary defensive function central to the Imperial strategy: extracting painful or forbidden emotional states from the self as a means of maintaining a posture of strength, confidence, or virtue in the self. Taken as a class, the externalizing defenses of the various Imperial personalities suggest the maintenance of self-states characterized by malignant grandiosity (Kernberg, 1995) through externalization of primitive mental states into other people and the social environment.

Imperial personalities' various defensive styles reflect a hunger for *selfobjects* (Kohut, 1971). Selfobjects are attachment figures who provide unconditional love, containment, and support, as with the role of a parent in childhood. The selfobject represents the modal experience of a young child craving the attention and approval of a parent figure who puts personal needs aside in the interest of promoting the wellbeing of the child. Imperial personalities remain developmentally arrested in this phase, relying upon narcissistic supplies to prop up self-esteem into adulthood. Developmentally speaking, it is easy to conceptualize Second Quadrant personalities as relying upon archetypal themes of power and control as a means of staving off the toxic effects of empathic failures in important early attachment relationships, which leave the developing psyche frozen in time, attempting to win parental approval. Psychopathic personalities respond to failures of selfobject function with primitive and omnipotent rage, narcissistic personalities with manipulative devaluation, and paranoid personalities with a profound denial of one's need to need in the first place.

Diagnostic Considerations

The three personality styles described in the DSM and the mainstream clinical literature which correspond to the Imperial personalities based on the Second Quadrant archetype include the psychopathic, narcissistic, and paranoid personality styles, in that "order" along the arc running from the Axis of Christ to the Axis of Lilith. The differences among the specific styles within the Second Quadrant represent variations in defensive style, underlying temperament, and relative relational capacity. Other personality traits and styles have been identified in the psychological literature which might be mapped onto the Second Quadrant space, including the so-called "dark personalities" generally termed Machiavellianism, narcissism, sadism, and psychopathy (Paulhus et al., 2021). Classic psychoanalytic takes on narcissism have included a formulation of a normal developmental stage described as "need satisfying" (Freud, 1969) or a manifestation of "magical omnipotence" (Mahler, 1968).

The narcissistic personality perhaps represents the modal Imperial style: self assured, worldly, authoritative, and relatively free from the ambiguity, self-doubt, or emotional entanglements that haunt the edges of the other three quadrants of the spiral. As I have previously alluded, our psychological understanding of the true nature of narcissism has been needlessly watered down and obstructed by confusing the defensive adaptations of narcissism with what it really is. In fact, popular and conventional understandings of narcissism, which might be personified as self-satisfied, doubt-free go-getters in love with themselves who "tell it like it is," sound more like marketing materials from the Narcissism Chamber of Commerce than a diagnosis, let alone an indictment of a pathological condition. The hidden truth is that narcissism is about Boehme's *magnetical hunger*: a craving for the soothing, safety, and containment of a selfobject without any real capacity to make use of those relational resources in order to grow and develop the capacity to reciprocate. As Nancy McWilliams puts it, "the most grievous cost of a narcissistic orientation is a stunted capacity to love" (2011, p. 183). Significantly, classical psychoanalytic thought long held narcissism to be essentially untreatable; this was largely because psychoanalytic psychotherapy's very engine operated along certain relational principles such as analysis of transference, and such interventions tend to fall flat with narcissistic personality disorders. It took some evolution in technique to discover that the methodology of psychotherapy merely had to be adjusted to accommodate for the lack of relational capacity in narcissistic personalities (see Kohut & Wolf, 1978).

Specific defensive styles that represent the psychopathic and paranoid styles may be seen as variations on the narcissistic theme. The common denominator is the Second Quadrant theme: construction of a grandiose, fortified self weatherproofed against shame and relationally impoverished.

The Integrative Analytical model implies that the psychopathic defensive style is a particularly "early" (closer to First Quadrant) version of the Imperial style, and organizes around more primitive mental states. In fact, the psychopathic personality can be seen as reflecting particular aspects of the turbulence prevailing around the border of the First Quadrant with the Second. In effect, the psychopathic personality combines the disaffected and intrinsically marginalized qualities of the Sensitive personality with the hostile encapsulation of the Second. Indeed, psychopathic personalities often wrap their destructive ideation and behavior around self-righteous "causes" reflecting the purity of inner convictions. Hollywood has provided us with many examples of movie villains who explain away mass murder with high-flown principles delivered in grand soliloquys. More distressingly, actual human history provides us with many tragic examples of psychopathic personalities whose primitive grievances are operationalized against victims who are used as scapegoats for the psychopath's intolerable experiences of humiliation and infantile rage.

The psychopathic personality manifests "early" in the Second Quadrant as a result of the complex confluence of First and Second Quadrant archetypal themes related to hostile and omnipotent encapsulation of one's psychological sovereignty. The psychopathic style therefore combines malignant grandiosity with a constitutional predisposition to wreak retribution upon the abandoning object and to express primitive mental states by invoking them in the object. Narcissistic personalities are less motivated to sadistically punish the abandoning object and more proximally motivated to extract soothing selfobject function as a means of staving off shame. Where narcissistic personalities seem motivated more purely by extracting selfobject function from adoring supporters, psychopathic personalities appear to get reinforcement from harming, humiliating, and controlling others. It is my experience that narcissistic personalities are willing to harm others to further their goals, but that's not what intrinsically motivates them. Psychopathic personalities do seem to get a charge out of their victim's suffering for its own sake (Meloy, 2001).

I am ambivalent about representing the psychopathic personality on the "main sequence" represented by the Spiral Path. How shall we differentiate the energetic, archetypal basis that leads to psychopathy from its behavioral outcomes? Is psychopathy "archetypally necessary?" The question invokes classic differences in perspective between Heinz Kohut's developmental model and Otto Kernberg's structural deficit model about whether narcissism represents a developmental waypoint or an intrinsically pathological syndrome. In a sense, I take the psychopathic personality as a tragic detour from the natural archetypal progression from the First to the Second quadrant. However, a major emphasis of the Integrated Analytical model is to draw attention to what is intrinsically human in these patternings. The specter of psychopathy and sociopathy challenges our philosophical and moral powers of accommodation. In Heauton Timorumenos, African Roman playwright Terence (2019) writes *homo sum: humani nihil a me alienum puto* (I am human: I consider nothing human as alien to me) (Act 1, scene 1, line 77).

There has been some welcome attention in recent years to the presence of higher functioning psychopathic personality in contemporary culture, reflecting Imperial personalities organized at the Fifth and Sixth Harmonic who exhibit omnipotent control as a defensive style. Babiak and Hare (2006) and Stout (2006) describe the implications of the omnipresence of psychopathic personalities in contemporary corporate culture, and the impacts they have on others.

Paranoid personalities may be conceptualized as occupying a more "late" Second Quadrant position, closing in on the Axis of Lilith. The location of the paranoid style "further down" the Second Quadrant arc represents something important about them: of all the Imperials, paranoid personalities typically possess the most robust capacity for empathic attunement and even love. I have come to view Paranoid personalities as essentially narcissistic personalities who feel the archetypal sizzle of Lilith's dissolving, and therefore are less internally empty and relationally inert. The paranoid personality's location in the "late" Second Quadrant, edging up against the Third, represents both the subjective agony of the paranoid person as well as their therapeutic promise. Nancy McWilliams describes the "Texas two-step" defensive transformation in the paranoid style, in which dependency needs are denied in the interest of avoiding dangerous vulnerability, and then the denial of dependency needs is externalized and projected outwards ("I want to be loved, but I can't risk it"). As McWilliams (2011) artfully puts it:

> Even though they may be terrified by their own dependent needs and wracked with suspicion about the motives and intentions of those they care about, paranoid individuals are capable of deep attachment and protracted loyalty. However persecutory or inappropriate their childhood caregivers were, paranoid clients apparently had enough availability and consistency in their early lives to be able to attach, albeit anxiously or ambivalently. Their capacity to love is what makes therapy possible in spite of all their hyperreactivity, antagonisms, and terrors.
>
> (p. 223)

McWilliams and other observers have noted the functional relationship between paranoia and politics, at least in US politics. The externalization and projection of the paranoid style results naturally in a remorselessly political world view, in which all the threats are easily identified "out there" and the self is therefore free to be innocent and vindicated. Richard Hofstadter's classic (1967) article "The paranoid style in American politics," has only become more trenchant over time.

Gender and Cultural Considerations

In many ways, the Imperial presents unique challenges to the methods and purposes of human civilization. The Second Quadrant represents the apogee of individual interest which must be collectively balanced with the requirements of the social contract. We are not free, as it turns out, to pursue unlimited individual self-interest, but must navigate the needs and perspectives of others. For those of us for whom the Second Quadrant represents a relatively harmless passage into the dynamic of resistance, that is, learning to set limits, stand up for ourselves, and express anger effectively, we bring our own internally generated limitations (generally developed courtesy of the fourth quadrant) that naturally tend to balance our individual interest with the world. For Imperial personalities with defensive styles reflecting narcissistic or psychopathic personalities in particular, there will be definition be conflicts of some kind between the exercise of individual power and the needs of others. In a deep sense, the very purpose of civilization is to keep the Second Quadrant dynamic in check. In a deep sense, the Second Quadrant is the challenge of human survival, and the reason why sometimes it seems that we may not collectively make it. It is therefore supremely ironic that Western culture tends to lionize narcissistic personalities…lionize them, vote for them, hire them, and seek relationships with them. One of the deeper problems with narcissism is that it works. We are all participating in it.

There are interesting parallels between Imperial Second Quadrant energy and the social and cultural forces of racism and colonialism. Fanon (2008) describes the essential narcissism of whiteness, and Simmons (2007) and Drichel (2018) note the energy of narcissism in colonialism. Simmons writes: "Subject peoples could be of immense psychic use to their conquerors, as they could be compelled in a variety of ways to reflect back to the imperialist a grandiose self-image" (p. 1). Second Quadrant energy provides a powerful and compelling affective motivational system that enables racism, xenophobia, gender discrimination, and any social phenomena organized around a privileged "aggressor" in a one-up position exerting power and control over a "victim" in a one-down position. I believe that frameworks for understanding and responding effectively to racism and colonialism would be powerfully enhanced by recognition of the archetypal and affective Second Quadrant roots of the phenomenon, rather than considering them to be primarily political, social, or cultural phenomena.

Let us name the pachyderm in the room: Narcissism and sociopaths are endemic in men, for complex reasons. The Second Quadrant is fertile ground for the kind of "toxic masculinity" that has long challenged the boundaries of the social contract. In the psychological literature, "toxic masculinity" is named in a more clinical way as "gender role conflict" (APA, 2018), which has four defining features: (1) an emphasis on success, achievement, control, power, and competition, (2) limited range of emotional responsiveness, (3) prohibition on expressing care and affection with other men, and (4) relational conflict (O'Neil, 2015).

Across cultures, men are more physically aggressive than women, and this consistent conclusion represents one the most significant gender differences in psychology (Archer, 2004). Research on the gender effects of aggression suggests that gender differences are negligible in early childhood, but that by middle childhood girls show a reduction in aggressive behavior compared to boys, suggesting that attachment and other social and interpersonal factors seem to mediate increased aggression in males in ways that become reinforced through long-term potentiation of neural circuits, which reflect the neuroplasticity of the central nervous system (Eliot, 2021).

By means of a complex interplay between cultural and interpersonal influence with brain neuroplasticity, boys get an engraved invitation into the Second Quadrant (the counterclockwise rotation), and girls are nudged into the Fourth (the clockwise rotation). In the childhood primary school classrooms and playgrounds of the world, boys are more likely to be encouraged to stand up for themselves (physically if necessary), while girls are nudged into the direction of finding protectors and gearing up for the long road of self-denial, which ultimately leads to childcare and other supporting roles. In fact, the patriarchy is a force that hands males an individualized invitation into the Second Quadrant and routes females away from it.

Primary narcissism in women and nonbinary persons is less comprehensibly described in the literature, and the popular imagination of narcissistic personalities as intrinsically male, just like the corresponding assumptions that borderline/histrionic personalities are female, provides support for the degree to which cultural perception frames Second Quadrant themes. Research does suggest some differences in patterning of narcissistic traits along gender lines, for example, highlighting the prominence of body appearance anxiety in narcissistically organized women, a finding that likely reflects cultural vectors involving objectified body shaming in women (Boursier & Gioia, 2020).

Unfortunately, no conversation about the cultural context of the Second Quadrant can be complete without recognition of the political forces inspired by the Second Quadrant archetype. A deeper point of this book, in case I am doing a poor job of expressing it, is that psychological patterns of defense mechanisms, personality patterns, and cognitive and affective bases of human experience flow from an archetypal energetic basis, which informs perception and behavior in complex ways. As we have discussed, the archetypal harmonic is in many ways the most deeply motivating harmonic, and that harmonic expresses itself most powerfully through affect. Political and religious demagogues throughout history have implicitly understood and cynically exploited the powerful role of archetype; ironically, while contemporary "scientific" psychology studiously ignores it. While psychology debates whether we can talk about archetypes or not, despots cheerfully use them to fuel massive social movements, justify war, and strangle democracy. While B. F. Skinner forbids research psychology from concerning itself with freedom and dignity, charismatic villains from cult leaders to captains of industry to political leaders are promising those very things to a willing audience that craves them and votes for people who promise them.

In order to engage authentically with the conditions and limitations of narcissism and the Imperial personality, and to once again honor the archetypal resonance underlying narcissism, let us recall Ernest Becker's (2011) willingness to name the relationship we all must negotiate with the Second Quadrant:

A working level of narcissism is inseparable from self-esteem, from a basic sense of self-worth … it is all too absorbing and relentless to be an aberration; it expresses the heart of the creature: the desire to stand out, to be the one in creation… If everyone honestly admitted his urge to be a hero it would be a devastating release of truth.

(p. 6)

Note

1   We see the primal and atavistic qualities of the Second Quadrant particularly in their sociological and political manifestation during our era, reflected in "traditional values" that reinforce fierceness in men and protective caretaking in women.

References

American Psychological Association, Boys and Men Guidelines Group. (2018). APA guidelines for psychological practice with boys and men. Retrieved from http://www.apa.org/about/policy/psychological-practice-boys-men-guidelines.pdf

Archer, J. (2004). Sex differences in aggression in real-world settings: A meta-analytic review. *Review of General Psychology, 8*(4): 291–322.

Babiak, P., & Hare, R. D. (2006). *Snakes in suits: When psychopaths go to work.* Regan Books/Harper Collins Publishers.

Becker, E. (2011). *The denial of death.* Souvenir Press.

Boehme, J., & Erb, P. C. (1977). *The way to Christ.* Paulist Press.

Boursier, V., & Gioia, F. (2020). Women's pathological narcissism and its relationship with social appearance anxiety: The mediating role of body shame. *Clinical Neuropsychiatry: Journal of Treatment Evaluation, 17*(3): 164–174.

Buber, M. (1971). *I and Thou.* Touchstone.

Drichel, S. (2018). The disaster of colonial narcissism. *American Imago, 75*(3): 329–364.

Eliot, L. (2021). Brain development and physical aggression: How a small gender difference grows into a violence problem. *Current Anthropology, 62*(23): 67–78.

Fanon, F. (2008). *Black skin, white masks.* Grove Press.

Freud, A. (1969). *Writings of Anna Freud.* International Universities Press.

Freud, S. (1905). Three essays on the theory of sexuality. In J. Strachy & A. Freud (Eds.), *The standard edition of the complete psychological works of Sigmund Freud, Volume VII (1901–1905): A case of hysteria, three essays on sexuality and other works* (pp. 123–246). Hogarth Press.

Hofstadter, R. (1967). *The paranoid style in American politics and other essays.* Vintage Books.

Jung, C. G. (1971). *Psychological types* (R. F. C. Hull, Trans.). Princeton University Press.

Kernberg, O. F. (1995). Omnipotence in the transference and in the countertransference. *The Scandinavian Psychoanalytic Review, 18*(1): 2–21.

Kohut, H. (1971). *The analysis of the self.* International Universities Press.

Kohut, H., & Wolf, E. S. (1978). The disorders of the self and their treatment: An outline. *The International Journal of Psychoanalysis, 59*(4): 413–425.

Mahler, M. S. (1968). *On Human symbiosis and the vicissitudes of Individuation.* International Universities Press.

McCloskey, L. J. (2003). *Tarot re-visioned.* Olandar Press.

McWilliams, N. (2011). *Psychoanalytic diagnosis: Understanding personality structure in the clinical process.* The Guilford Press.

Meloy, J. R. (2001). *The mark of Cain: Psychoanalytic insight and the psychopath.* The Analytic Press.

O'Neil, J. M. (2015). *Men's gender role conflict: Psychological costs, consequences, and an agenda for change.* American Psychological Association.

Paulhus, D. L., Buckels, E. E., Trapnell, P. D., & Jones, D. N. (2021). Screening for dark personalities: The Short Dark Tetrad (SD4). *European Journal of Psychological Assessment, 37*(3): 208–222.

Simmons, D. (2007). *The narcissism of empire.* Sussex Academic Press.

Stout, M. (2006). *The sociopath next door.* Harmony.

Terence (2019). *Heauton timorumenos.* Stage Door.

Walker, L. E. (1979). *The battered woman.* Harper and Row.

Winnicott, D. W. (1992). *The child, the family and the outside world.* Perseus Publishing.

Chapter 15

The Third Quadrant

The Radiant Personality

Look like the innocent flower, but be the serpent under it.

- William Shakespeare
Macbeth

Archetypal Foundations

And now the spiral crosses the Axis of Lilith. Passing the Lilith gate means crossing the waters of forgiveness in order to emerge from the propositions of the Second Quadrant. The Imperial personality who becomes pathological resists the Lilith gate and therefore remains stranded on the shores of time.

Leigh McCloskey (2003) identifies Third Quadrant archetypal energy with the Empress, the third key of the Tarot Arcana:

> The Empress symbolizes mother nature, the fullness of fertility, growth, prosperity, peace, and beauty. She is creative inspiration and the guardian of true magic. To her belong love, beauty, art, imagination, intuition, sensuality, and desire. She symbolizes love as the formative energy of the universe. She is the sustaining and nurturing mother of all creation.
>
> (p. 27)

Lilith herself, the Dark Madonna, is a hidden figure and the guardian in a sense of the borders of the Third Quadrant, perhaps creating space for the Empress to be possible. Lilith is a representative of androgynous energies of consciousness that are primarily archetypally feminine, flowing, interconnected, spherical, both creating and dissolving. Anticipating the transition from the Third to the Fourth, she births out of herself the masculine, the right angle, the geometrizer (McCloskey, 2001), and thus she is the dark feminine root system, the dark matter, and pure energy of consciousness. The Lilith archetype is a potent cosmic force, and the complex telos that motivates the patriarchy has been attempting to control her and dilute her for most of human history, certainly since humanity transcended the gods and abandoned the natural world. Lilith represents primal life vitality, the ferocious feminine; she is the lioness at the heart of the "masculine" energies emerging in

DOI: 10.4324/9781032708751-18

woman and inversely she is the powerful feminine energies emerging in man, as he attempts to become worthy of her, desiring again to be noble (for nobility was surrendered to the pursuit of power in the Second Quadrant). She is the yin in the yang and the yang in the yin. She is again the great serpent, who like Tiamat sunders herself to create the above and the below.

Lilith establishes Eve, the Mother of Generation, as wise and yet innocent of her true energies, and innocent of her origin. This wisdom comes from primal intimacy rather than knowledge, memory, or control. The Third Quadrant therefore represents an archetypal inversion, and the Radiant personality remains innocent of her origin (and therefore sometimes lacking in the discernment of self-advocacy) due to the renouncement of power, lineage, and judgment, which characterizes the Second Quadrant. Therefore Eve, representing every woman, learned through pain and abandonment (the betrayal of the Second Quadrant) to trust her inner feline senses (intuition rather than knowledge) since they were outwardly denied and so often deceived and defiled. Therefore, the Radiant personality will forever fear exploitation, capture, and abuse and will exhibit an orthogonal anger (usually inverted and underground but sometimes emerging volcanically) at abusive masculine power and control.

Lilith's fluid innocence ignites powerful and protean creative potency, opening expansive possibility and creative blossoming, and most importantly, creating the conditions for love. Only in the Third Quadrant can love be realized, because love requires both a sense of self (which is the work of the transition from the First Quadrant to the Second) and a willingness to dissolve that self into the other (which is a function of crossing the Axis of Lilith from the Second Quadrant to the Third). With every birth, she is awakening a pleromic consciousness, and every baby birthed is a reborn god, comprising the innate structure of all the universe and its innate fractal geometries and ratios. These energies transform us without mercy.

The archetypal energy of the Third Quadrant is an alchemical transformation of that of the Second Quadrant, shifting from the stale mathematics of power and control to a primordial, orgasmic experience of life energy. Therefore, the Radiant personality will be relational, surpassingly capable of love, and yet vulnerable to devaluation and lapses in vigilance for the well-being of the self.

In Jungian terms, the sensate function vital to the Imperial sense of self yields to the Radiant intuitive function, which is a kind of knowing that accepts and reveals rather than imposing order and hierarchy (*gnosis* rather than *science*). By the time the Second Quadrant resolves, the Imperial dynamic (which, as described in Chapter 14, represents an externalizing and paranoid dynamic) clings to sensate function and distrusts intuition because of fear of the otherness represented by Lilith. Through a willingness to dissolve into Lilithian energies, the organizing principle moves from power, ordering, and control toward a unique artistry of consciousness. That dissolving requires us to forget our source, to become innocent....in a sense, to begin again. Having undertaken the Lilithian experience of alchemical *solve* (dissolving), we gain the capacity to hold multiple perspectives without dissolving or being broken. These capacities are a prerequisite to love, and forever afterward, the psyche is capable of intersubjective relating. The Radiant personality feels a yearning to reclaim the self through love rather than thought. If the First Quadrant births an authentic singularity, a single point, and the Second Quadrant adds a stabilizing second dimension in the service of a more bounded sense of self, the Third Quadrant generates a third dimension, breaking the two-dimensional plane, which is capacity for the connections of love.

In the Third Quadrant, the terrors of birth (which we discussed in Chapter 13) are reprised because of the reconfiguration of self in a manner that allows for the dissolving energies of love, which were rigidly defended against in the Second Quadrant. Passing the Lilith gate into the Third Quadrant invokes a theme of Return to Oceanic Consciousness, which was left behind in the passage from the First to the Second. Lilith dissolves, among other things, the illusion of illusion, starkly revealing the implosive limitations of the Second Quadrant. Lilith reveals herself to us, but at a distance so that we begin to trust our own intimacy. Lilith is interstitial, veiled, inverted, and hidden in every aspect of the spiral. We cannot use logic or the physics of form to find her. She is always at right angles to where we are looking, and she dwells in that which we do not remember, or refuse to understand. She responds with darkness to anything out of alignment. She only emerges when we are capable of holding the energies of contradiction lovingly. We can only meet Lilith at a certain age, and only when individuality has been established; meaning, we must have developed enough of a sense of self to perceive and behold her (this observation is consistent with the object relation perspectives discussed below, that entry into the Third Quadrant requires a capacity for relational intersubjectivity which was absent in the narcissistic world view).

In the Gnostic tradition, Sophia is a feminine aspect of God and the syzygy (female counterpart) of Theletos, who is identified in the Gnostic tradition with Christ. Taken together, Sophia and Theletos form an Aeon or a manifestation of a higher and unknowable God. Sophia, a mediator of wisdom, is one of the lower-order Aeons, holding a position in the pleroma (the divine space of God's presence) near the outer edges and closer to the material plane of existence. In some gnostic versions of Sophia's story, she leaves her consort Theletos in search of wisdom, but then suffers great anguish at the loss and desires only to return, and is redeemed or rescued (see Mead, 2005; Plese, 2006).

Sophia's journey and reunion with Theletos set up powerful archetypal themes of Return that govern the Radiant personality. At the symbolic level, the myth of Sophia betokens a return home from knowledge of the stars and a craving for homecoming, a return also to innocence. Let us heed the words of the Great Mother as related in Apuleius' *Metamorphosis*:

I am nature, the universal mother, mistress of all the elements, primordial child of time, sovereign of all things spiritual, queen of the dead, queen of the immortals. My nod governs the shining heights of heaven, the wholesome sea breezes, the lamentable silences of the world below. I know the cycles of growth and decay.

(Apuleius & Kenney, 1999)

The Third Quadrant contains a Hidden Sorrow, which is the realization that the craving to return to Oceanic Consciousness would mean returning to conditions that no longer exist, and a return to magical states of consciousness that can no longer be understood. Awareness of, and mourning for, this loss is not the work of the Radiant but becomes the unfinished business of the Fourth Quadrant. Furthermore, it is our efforts to transcend Lilithian archetypal energies that enable progress into the Fourth Quadrant; as if Lilith were a primordial vortex that we must swim away from in order to go on living in the world.

Defensive Correlates

The psychoanalytic literature richly describes and articulates tempermentally intense, relationally oriented, personalities who are vulnerable to abandonment anxiety and prone to acting out (McWilliams, 2011). These defensive styles we have discussed are variously called hysterical, hysteroid, histrionic, and borderline personalities. Unfortunately for us, the technical terms become quite tricky in the Third Quadrant and merit some brief explanation. For purposes of this discussion, I will use the term "histrionic" to more or less cover all of those categories. I am too troubled by the overtly sexist origins of the term "hysterical," which etymologically relates to the uterus and reinforces historically toxic narratives about the "wandering womb" based on primitive medical theories that a woman's uterus may become disconnected and wander about the body, causing emotional and physical distress. "Borderline personality" was first coined by Stern (1938) and picked up by Kernberg (1975) as a *level* of personality organization, the term referring to the borderline between so-called psychotic and neurotic levels of organization. Since then, the DSM has come to formulate Borderline Personality Disorder as a discrete disorder separate from Histrionic Personality Disorder despite evidence of problematic overlap between the two supposed categories (Blagov & Westen, 2008). I will follow the psychoanalytic convention and reserve the term "borderline personality" for a histrionic personality organized at the borderline level (that is to say, organized at the third or fourth harmonics). As we shall discuss below, I would consider the Self-Defeating or Masochistic personality as a late Third Quadrant phenomenon, near the transition to the Fourth Quadrant. For purposes of Integrated Analytical Psychology, the Radiant personalities therefore represent most notably the histrionic personality (including borderline personality) as well as the Self-Defeating personality.

The strong tidal, archetypal pull of Return, informs many of the defensive operations of the Radiant personality. Many of the ways that Radiant personalities distort their psychological relationships with the world have to do with a plaintive and frightened effort to erase painful separation and to invoke protective intimacy or even flee into protective intimacy, all in the name of obtaining both love and safety. As you may notice, reader, from the map of the spiral journey through the quadrants, the Third Quadrant represents the point of greatest archetypal distance from the yonic source in the First Quadrant. Indeed, the energy of the Third Quadrant is primarily about arresting and reversing the outward-bound flight from the First

Quadrant across the transit of the Second; and following the Third Quadrant, the spiral bends back toward the First through the Fourth. Like its patron saint Sophia, the Radiant personality regrets and repents of its painful separation, resulting not in the melancholy and self-reproach of the Penitent personality of the Fourth Quadrant, but instead an energetic and even frenzied attempt to avoid, reverse, or ablate abandonment.

In terms of object relations and the relational field, the defensive styles of the Radiant personality generally organized around seeking intimacy and safety with objects that are perceived to be bigger and stronger. It is not difficult to discern the attachment trauma that underlies this dynamic, which clearly suggests a strategy of recapitulating important empathic failures with parents or other attachment figures early in life. Indeed, early trauma is a frequent common denominator in histrionic and borderline personalities (Bozzatello et al., 2021; Krause-Utz. 2022) and creates particular emotional and relational microclimates in children who are otherwise warm, relational, and affectively connected, who experience a loss or reversal of a primary attachment experience, resulting in a phenomenological space of forever falling forward as if attempting to reach and regain that early attachment. Radiant personalities seek safe attachments, but not with just any object: particularly with objects that are exciting or protective.

The psychoanalytic literature describes *counterphobic defenses* which take on basic anxieties by approaching them head-on (Fenichel, 1945), and these appear to be common and highly characteristic qualities of the histrionic personality (McWilliams, 2011). The histrionic tendency to approach a feared object recapitulates early attachment trauma with powerful objects, which demand navigation of love and fear, setting up a characteristic approach/avoidance conflict which reaches its apogee in splitting. Histrionic personalities often remind me of an angry but small animal protecting its young against a powerful predator with a kind of desperate anger. Histrionic people are the bravest of the personalities.

The childlike appeal for protection reveals another important factor in the defensive style of the Radiant personality: a "one down" interpersonal posture characterizes their self states. As McWilliams puts it "The hysterical sense of self is that of a small, fearful, defective child coping as well as can be expected in a world dominated by powerful and alien others" (p. 320). Unlike their Fourth Quadrant neighbors, the Depressive personality, who similarly experience self-states that are devalued, guilty, or shamed, but who respond with internalizing and introjection, the histrionic personality is more likely to respond to their one-down station in life with both anger and with energetic attempts to level the playing field. Affective and relational attempts to master and turn around abandoning or shaming attachment experiences underlie some of the other important defensive strategies of Third Quadrant personalities: sexualizing defenses (well-known and well-documented among borderline personalities in particular) can be seen as attempts to recruit protective and intimate responses from powerful, exciting objects, and regressive defenses can similarly be understood as capitalizing on childlike distress to discourage predation and encourage protective, nurturing responses from powerful objects…a dynamic which the I-Ching vividly describes as "the taming power of the small" (Hexagram 9, Wing, 1982). Where the Imperial feels triumphant and vindicated, the Radiant personality covertly feels powerless, shamed, and hungry.

Diagnostic Considerations

I have described above the range of nosological terms that overlap with Third Quadrant themes: the histrionic (which has been known by several labels) and the borderline personality, which I regard as a Radiant personality organized at the third and fourth harmonics (in other words, a Radiant personality who shows some degree of identifiable personality disorder, to use clinical language). I think of the Histrionic personality, as described in the psychoanalytic literature, as the model character configuration typifying the Third Quadrant. The so-called Self-Defeating, or Masochistic personality, manifests "late" in the Third Quadrant and may be best understood as a dynamic resulting from turbulent overlap between Third and Fourth Quadrant dynamics.

The etymological root of the term histrionic comes from the Latin *histrio*, actor. In a sense, the term fits the archetypal and defensive manifestations of the histrionic personality: histrionic behavioral manifestations can certainly come to feel performative if not manipulative, and the fact that many histrionically organized people are talented dissociatives also suggests the presence of multiple competing selves or self-states. Histrionically organized personalities are full of texture, complexity, intensity, and desire, all of it seeking an object. The histrionic personality shares with their next-door Second Quadrant neighbors, the narcissistic personalities, a kind of shimmering charisma, a willingness to draw steel, a tendency toward self-righteousness, and a deep identification with the world and its politics. On the other hand, the histrionic personality shares with its depressive neighbor in the Fourth Quadrant a capacity to love, a profound sense of brokenness in the self that can't wholly be forgotten or healed, and a tendency to approach psychotherapy as a personal relationship. Histrionic hunger is different from narcissistic hunger: narcissistic hunger is a dispassionate and ultimately recursive force that is only interested in you for the nutrients it might extract from you, while histrionic hunger is genuinely connective and interested in its object. The histrionically organized psychotherapy client is *interested in* the therapist, related and emotionally connected. Due to this deep relational capacity, process-oriented and intersubjective styles of psychotherapy become possible.

If we describe the entire range of harmonic representations of the Third Quadrant archetype as essentially histrionic in terms of clinical nomenclature, the borderline personality emerges as a subset of that range which might be described as personality disordered, or exhibiting character pathology, roughly corresponding to a representational horizon in the third or fourth harmonic. In other words, we might describe a borderline personality as a particularly symptomatic manifestation of the Radiant personality, embodying the more behaviorally and interpersonally disruptive and even self-destructive characteristics of the Third Quadrant's shadow.

In the borderline range, the plangent craving for Return to Oceanic Consciousness, belonging, safety, and containment take on a frantic, pressured, and desperate quality. Although borderline personalities remain intrinsically relational, warm, and creatively engaged in the rich culture of the Radiant personalities, the terror of abandonment or separation (that is to say, terror of being prohibited from rejoining the beloved other) casts a very black shadow. For this reason, any relationship that falls short of talismanic safety and transcendent merging activates primitive anxiety states that can barely be tolerated. Such primitive anxieties can ultimately only be resolved through the development of a more integral sense of self capable of tolerating how it feels to be disconnected from source, which is the work of agentic discernment available at the fifth and sixth harmonics, resulting ultimately in the development of a buoyant and boundaried sense of self capable of holding its own pattern. For this reason, psychodynamic perspectives on the treatment of borderline personality disorder tend to focus on the development of a coherent sense of self. As Nancy McWilliams notes, "the best contribution one can make to a histrionic person is confidence in the client's capacity to figure things out and make responsible adult decisions." (McWilliams, 2011, p. 327). Schwartz-Salant, who takes on a Jungian perspective on borderline personality, notes that "when not persecuting others and feeling persecuted by split-off vision the borderline person, often charismatic and creative, can be a link to the numinosum, to the power of the gods." (p. 59). However, at the lower-order harmonics, the behavioral, ideational, and affective responses to Third Quadrant conditions tend to encourage the conclusion that *power is elsewhere*, and not of the self.

Any discussion of the histrionic and borderline personality organization is incomplete and does not address the comorbidity of early trauma, especially sexual trauma (Zlotnick et al., 2003; Heffernan & Cloitre, 2000). In depicting the archetypal foundations of the Third Quadrant, we amplified the experience of Eve, who has been debased and defiled, as well as the dark fury of Lilith at being forced (by a patriarchal God, no less) into submission. These archetypal experiences of being exploited, abused, penetrated, or debased lead both to the deeper histrionic and borderline experience of occupying a "one-down" position in the world and the resulting conscious attitude toward the perpetrator that includes both deferential accommodation and murderous rage. The accommodation and the rage co-exist like a photographic double exposure and form the basis for splitting, a defensive style famously linked to borderline dynamics in particular.

In my experience, psychotherapy of the more behaviorally problematic manifestations of the Radiant personality follows two steps. The first step is to discover the separation anxiety, in all its power and glory, and the degree to which it tends to drive one into relationships with the hope of mythic rescue. The second step is to safely experience the confounding of those hopes of rescue, for example, in the person of a skilled psychotherapist who wisely refuses to infantilize the borderline personality by indulging those rescue fantasies…in other words, to become willing to tolerate how the lack of safe holding feels, and the terrible realization that the cavalry isn't coming, there will be no rescue, and there is no safety.

The third step is the realization, which can only follow steps one and two, that although there is no rescue, ultimately that can be tolerated as well because we never really needed to be rescued in the first place.

I am aware of the degree to which this prescription smacks of ableism and privilege. Trauma cannot be relativized out of existence, and psychotherapeutic treatment of psychotic and borderline disorders, as well as trauma, requires what Winnicott (1992) calls a safe "holding environment." Victims of trauma need to be believed. However, ultimately, that kind of safety is predicated on attachment and authenticity rather than rescue, and the kind of safety promised by effective psychotherapy is not magical thinking but a deep willingness to take on the human condition and its suffering. This transition from hoping for rescue to deep reliance on one's own resourcefulness anticipates the slow curve of the Third Quadrant into the Fourth and the second crossing of the Axis of Christ.

Gender and Cultural Considerations

Gender powerfully mediates the Third Quadrant archetype. You may have noticed the predominance of mythological women in my discussion of the mythic foundations of the Radiant personality: Lilith, Eve, and Sophia. In a real sense, the Third Quadrant tells the story of the distinct heroism of women in particular. Although both men and woman navigate the Third Quadrant and show up as Radiant personalities of either the Histrionic or Borderline stripes, the social forces of the patriarchy tend to sort relational warmth, dependency needs, and separation anxiety to women while assigning self-containment, insouciance, and rugged independence to men. In many sectors of Western culture, men are trained as boys to fight, build, and achieve, while women are trained as girls to love and self-sacrifice. Cross-cultural research suggests that these findings are fairly consistent across traditional and post-industrialized cultures and seem related to primarily female reproductive capacity and secondarily to male size and strength; the former effect seems to have been mediated in post-industrial cultures by the increased availability of contraception and family planning, as well as entry of women into roles previously dominated by men (Wood & Eagly, 2002).

Borderline personality disorder as a diagnosis is particularly stigmatizing, and as often is the case, stigmatizing diagnoses are more commonly ascribed to culturally marginalized populations (Kealy & Ogrodniczuk, 2010). There is some evidence that borderline personality disorder is more frequently diagnosed in sexual minorities (Rodriguez-Seijas et al., 2021). The overdiagnosis of borderline personality in women exemplifies many other ways in which women encounter discrimination as medical patients, and this discrimination is amplified by intersectional factors such as Black, Asian, or Indigenous identification, and when women don't identify with the gender norms determined by cultural assumptions about biological womanhood (Cleghorn, 2021).

As we have discussed above, a significantly gendered dynamic of the Third Quadrant relates to the core experience of being "one down" in the world and coping in an experientially childlike way to gain the acceptance, love, and protection of more powerful objects. If the personal experience of smallness and dependence is a core aspect of the histrionic experience, then it makes sense that anyone subject to cultural oppression or disempowerment would find themselves painted into a similar energetic corner. At some point, social forces become objects and attachment figures (Thomas, 1979): the masculine becomes the father and vice versa, and the feminine becomes the mother and vice versa. Whatever the psyche needs from the mother or father, whatever unfinished business remains, is often projected onto nonhuman objects like the feminine, the masculine, and nationalism.

The Third Quadrant tendency toward sexualization also has roots in culture and gender. The psychodynamic interpretation of sexualization, that it involves converting a dangerous scenario and primitive anxieties into an exciting possibilities, intersects in complex ways with which social forces tend to evaluate some people (e.g., women and girls) based on sex appeal (Ruggiero, 2011), rather than for example, power or strength. In other words, sexualizing defenses are more likely to prove effective in people who have been sexualized, and Third Quadrant personalities have often learned repeatedly that what provides them with little value and power they do have is their sex appeal or attractiveness as trophies (Pipher, 2005). Whatever the psychodynamic motivation for sexualization, it is empowered and reinforced by patriarchal social forces that extract self-object function from vulnerable populations.

McWilliams (2011) describes the developmental journey of a psyche progressing along essentially histrionic lines:

> …She continues to see males as strong and exciting, and females, herself included, as weak and insignificant. Because she regards power as inherently a male attribute, she looks up to men, but she also — unconsciously, for the most part — hates and envies them. She tries to increase her sense of adequacy and self-esteem by attaching to males, yet she also subtly punishes them for their assumed superiority. She uses her sexuality, the one kind of power she feels her gender affords, along with idealization and "feminine wiles"— the strategies of the subjectively weak — in order to access male strength.

> (p. 314)

In general, any persons who are subject to cultural, political, or social marginalization or disempowerment are more likely to conclude that power is elsewhere, and in individuals with a temperament trending toward affiliative warmth and attachment, that external locus of control comes freighted with a willingness to invert the self in the name of eliciting protective responses from the powerful object who holds all the cards. Therefore, it is easily understood why women are particularly vulnerable to histrionic solutions and perspectives than men, who enjoy relatively more privilege. Western culture affords fewer direct pathways to power to women than men, and so it has become a deeply etched pattern of the feminine perspective to perceive power itself as inherently male…another proposition endorsed by patriarchal assumptions. Women tend to be routed into the clockwise rotation, into the affiliative and caretaking waters of the Fourth Quadrant, whereas men are more likely to be shaped into the counterclockwise rotation, leading to the Second Quadrant and narcissistic or paranoid solutions. The unique role of women in childbearing represents perhaps the most significant example of this pull into the clockwise spiral rotation: women who are mothers in particular must navigate the Fourth Quadrant energies of unique responsibility and the Third Quadrant experiences of devaluation. As Elliot (2021) puts it, women who are mothers "perhaps as much or more so than any other, intrinsically understand the alchemical pressure and dizzying possibility of the transcendent function." (p. 2)

The readiness with which healthcare systems over-apply stigmatizing diagnoses to vulnerable and marginalized populations is a significant concern; yet the underlying intentions of the Integrated Analytical model encourage appreciation for the ways in which even stigmatizing diagnoses like borderline personality reflect authentic aspects of human experience, which are worth being named in an empathic and holistic manner. Our concern should not just stop with the over-diagnosis of borderline personality disorder, but should also include the various ways in which borderline states reflect meaningful psychological, affective, cognitive, and behavioral responses to very real and powerful social forces.

As usual, the concern also remains that the industrial/medical model of understanding and treating psychopathology that is ascendant in Western culture, including the DSM, emphasizes measurable behavioral syndromes at the expense of the phenomenological, intersubjective, or relational aspects of human experience. Therefore, the "borderline personality disorder" that is most frequently the subject of randomized controlled trial experiments in research psychology is not necessarily the same phenomenon that results from the phenotypic epiphenomenon that results from interaction of archetypal force with psychological defensive adaptation, which is why I am attempting to differentiate the "Radiant personality" from psychodynamic conceptualizations of "histrionic personality organization" from nosological distinctions of "borderline personality disorder." These categories have complex relationships with each other but do not map directly onto each other. Borderline personality disorder, such as it is, represents a collective and social failure to support the psychological emergence of the Radiant Personality, and we all participate in that failure.

References

Apuleius & Kenney, E. J. (1999). *The golden ass.* Penguin Classics.

Blagov, P. S., & Westen, D. (2008). Questioning the coherence of histrionic personality disorder: Borderline and hysterical personality subtypes in adults and adolescents. *Journal of Nervous and Mental Disease, 196*(11): 785–797.

Bozzatello, P., Rocca, P., Baldassarri, L., Bosia, M., & Bellino, S. (2021). The Role of trauma in early onset borderline personality disorder: A biopsychosocial perspective. *Frontiers in Psychiatry, 23*(12).

Cleghorn, E. (2021). *Unwell women: Misdiagnosis and myth in a man-made world.* Dutton.

Elliot, J. (2021). The othering of the mother: Tales from a global pandemic. *Journal of Jungian Scholarly Studies, 16*: 82–85.

Fenichel, O. (1945). *The psychoanalytic theory of neurosis.* W. W. Norton & Company.

Heffernan, K., & Cloitre, M. (2000). A comparison of posttraumatic stress disorder with and without borderline personality disorder among women with a history of childhood sexual abuse: etiological and clinical characteristics. *The Journal of Nervous and Mental Disease, 188*(9), 589–595.

Kealy, D., & Ogrodniczuk, J. S. (2010). Marginalization of borderline personality disorder. *Journal of Psychiatric Practice, 16*(3): 145–154.

Kernberg, O. (1975). *Borderline conditions and pathological narcissism.* Jason Aronson.

Krause-Utz, A. (2022). Dissociation, trauma, and borderline personality disorder. *Borderline Personality Disorder and Emotion Dysregulation, 9*(14): 1–6.

McCloskey, L. J. (2001). *The Heiroglyph of the human soul [painted studio library environment].* Malibu.

McCloskey, L. J. (2003). *Tarot re-visioned.* Olandar Press.

McWilliams, N. (2011). *Psychoanalytic diagnosis: Understanding personality structure in the clinical process.* The Guilford Press.

Mead, G. R. S. (2005). *Pistis sophia: The gnostic tradition of Mary Magdalene, Jesus, and his disciples.* Dover Publications.

Pipher, M. (2005). *Reviving Ophelia: Saving the selves of adolescent girls.* Riverhead Trade.

Plese, Z. (2006). *Poetics of the Gnostic universe: Narrative and cosmology in the Apocryphon of John.* Brill Academic Publishing.

Rodriguez-Seijas, C., Morgan, T. A., & Zimmerman, M. (2021). Is There a bias in the diagnosis of borderline personality disorder among lesbian, gay, and bisexual patients? *Assessment, 28*(3): 724–738.

Ruggiero, M. E. (2011). Defensive sexualization: A neurobiologically informed explanatory model. *American Journal of Psychoanalysis, 71*(3): 264–277.

Stern, A. (1938). Psychoanalytic investigation of and therapy in the borderline group of neuroses. *The Psychoanalytic Quarterly, 7*: 467–489.

Thomas, D. B. (1979). Psychodynamics, symbolism, and socialization: "Object relations" perspectives on personality, ideology, and political perception. *Political Behavior, 1*: 243–268.

Wing, R. L. (1982). *The illustrated I-Ching.* Main Street Books.

Winnicott, D. W. (1992). *The child, the family and the outside world.* Perseus Publishing.

Wood, W., & Eagly, A. H. (2002). A cross-cultural analysis of the behavior of women and men: Implications for the origins of sex differences. *Psychological Bulletin, 128*(5), 699–727.

Zlotnick, C., Johnson, D. M., Yen, S., Battle, C. L., Sanislow, C. A., Skodol, A. E., Grilo, C. M., McGlashan, T. H., Gunderson, J. G., Bender, D. S., Zanarini, M. C., & Shea, M. T. (2003). Clinical features and impairment in women with borderline personality disorder (BPD) with posttraumatic stress disorder (PTSD), BPD without PTSD, and other personality disorders with PTSD. *Journal of Nervous and Mental Disease, 191*(11): 706–714.

Chapter 16

The Fourth Quadrant
The Penitent Personality

Yea, and if some god shall wreck me in the wine-dark deep, even so I will endure... For already have I suffered full much, and much have I toiled in perils of waves and war. Let this be added to the tale of those.

- Homer
The Odyssey

Archetypal Foundations

Having crossed the Axis of Christ for the second time, we continue the spiral journey rounding into the Fourth Quadrant by bending back into the direction of the introjective, the self-bound. Because of the mathematics of the spiral progression, we have now encountered all four of the quadrants and we are also further from Source (the yonic gate into the First Quadrant) than ever. Evolving out from the arms of Sophia, the psyche has rotated out of plumb with the axis of love, and no longer contemplates Ascension and Origin. And what a long journey it has been...arising out of origin, cloaking itself in the dynamic of resistance, and seeking a power that ultimately failed. The Axis of Lilith required a fundamental renouncement of that power and a return to love, connection, and homeland.

But now, the psyche has experienced the limits of even love. The instinct for being perfectly loved, perfectly held, now rings hollow as an impossible ideal. The subjective experience of entering the fourth quadrant is loss, and failure of the fantasy that rescue is just around the corner, a hero away. Home is no longer a place that can be returned to, someday. The distances are too far, the mounting losses too great. The cavalry is not coming. You are now stuck deep behind the enemy lines of the world, the locals are hostile, and no reinforcements are available. Your only recourse is to hold your position the best you can.

I will now address you directly, reader, in the context of your own arrival at the Fourth Quadrant. Part of you knew it was coming to this. Since your expulsion from the Garden of Eden, since the primal split of your emergence from your mother's womb, part of you knew that at some point the supporting characters would leave the stage. All the mentors, protectors, and supporters have had their say. You have grown and evolved and amassed such power and psychic structure as you

DOI: 10.4324/9781032708751-19

can muster. The time has come. It's up to you now. No one knows better than you. If you succeed, the endeavor will be successful. If you fail, it will not be successful. You are energetically equipped with a sense of your own internal authenticity (the result of your work in the First Quadrant), which had to be compromised in order to enter the world fully. You are equipped with willpower and a sense of nuance enabling you to stand apart from the world and influence it (the Second Quadrant) but have also learned that all of that must be surrendered in order to be worthy of your beloved. You are equipped to dissolve your essence into love and to allow yourself to become subject to the reality of an Other in the name of that love (the Third Quadrant) but have also learned that you cannot merely dissolve, for this results in your own undoing.

The Penitent psyche realizes that homecoming cannot be absolute, not least because it denies the original yearning for ascension. In fact, in this quadrant, both Ascension and Return seem like fairy tales because neither are perceived to have "worked." The psyche has not yet completed an entire circuit of the spiral, and so only feels that it has been "going in circles." The romanticism of romantic love and the allure of sexual love ring hollow as failed strategies. The journey of Ascension proved to be not a moment of glory but a path that ever winds and climbs. The will to power has proved a disastrous separation from beloved others. And yet it was never possible to simply melt back into the arms of the beloved because there is no rescue from without, and melting into a beloved other has been revealed as a terrible loss of self.

The energetic rotation through all these conditions and circumstances results in the psyche being thrown back upon itself, and left to its own devices. Only you remain on stage. The audience waits, hushed, wondering what you will do. What you say next, you somehow know, matters more than everything. This knowing is now your burden and brings with it the energetic discovery of self-doubt and guilt, stacked on top of the capacity for shame which has long been present. What the psyche chooses to do with this energetic moment hangs in the air, and becomes your plotline: do you fold your powers together and charge the gate, in full knowledge that you may not be enough, or do you shrink from the weight of it all, unbearably aware now of all the layered, prehistorical sadness which you now realize has been there all along, like an outer darkness?

The depressive psyche is like Tolkien's Frodo, returning to his beloved Shire at last, the culmination of all his previous daydreams about happy endings and returns. Yet he discovers that, unlike his companions, return is ultimately impossible. The accumulated hurts and losses have been too great. The things that he has witnessed have punched a hole in the halcyon reality he once accepted as a birthright, and nothing can seem the same. The only solution is to continue to journey; in Frodo's case, beyond the rim of the known world and out at the Grey Havens. Also in Tolkien's saga (which is full of Fourth Quadrant themes), recall the unsoothable and ineffable sadness of the elves, as they abandon this broken world freighted with the knowledge of what it could have been.

What, then, is left?

The depressive psyche, ironically similar to the narcissistic personality which has now become its thematic opposite, again returns to the question of Self (introjection). As a result of this existential feeling of disappointment (which can rise to despair and depression in some), the sacred task becomes forming an adult identity.

Thomas Hardy (1965) captures the quality of the depressive personality in Jude the Obscure when his protagonist Jude suffers overwhelming self-doubt after having been abandoned to homelessness

> Somebody might have come along that way who would have asked him his trouble, and might have cheered him… But nobody did come, because nobody does; and under the crushing recognition of his gigantic error Jude continued to wish himself out of the world.
>
> (p. 27)

Hardy's pronouncement that "nobody did come, because nobody does" describes the worldview at the outset of the fourth arc and captures its loneliness, loss, and crushing sense of individual responsibility in the absence of external rescue. And for many Penitent personalities, the result is wishing oneself out of the world.

The depressive arc has a peculiar, end-of-the-line feel to it, which accounts for much of the melancholy ultimately underlying and underwriting the Fourth Quadrant, which could be symbolized by the Winter Solstice, or the Uttermost East. The individual stands erect, no longer moving forward in time. This is a position that most well-socialized and psychologically healthy Western adults would find familiar: I am the adult, the final authority. However, this sense of responsibility and final authority no longer feels grandiose or inflating, as it did in the days of the Second Quadrant; rather, it feels more like being on your own. It feels like realizing there is no Santa Claus, and you yourself have to make the children's gifts appear. If you can't afford them, they simply won't get them. It's all up to you. "The individual," Jung writes, "is the only immediate manifestation of the psyche" (2006, p. 528).

Despite the loss of rescue and salvation fantasies that mark the passage into the fourth quadrant, it is the Christ mythos that mediates this stage. Christ stands as an archetype of Selfhood and completion, and also for the redemption of the self from the failures and missteps of the past. Just as Lilith, who governs the third quadrant, began with a powerful feminine renunciation of narcissism and ended with the emotionally honest love of Sophia, Christ precipitates the crisis of Selfhood in order to affect its eventual rescue. Receiving the psyche from the bosom of Sophia, saying "You uniquely are worthy of salvation." The depressive psyche, as is characteristic of self-critical thinking of this personality organization, hears most clearly the words "you" and "unique," setting up depressive fears of ultimate failure in the presence of such responsibility.

"Me? Uniquely worthy?" the depressive psyche asks. "But, as I have painfully learned…this 'me' is not enough."

Christianity has historically encouraged the rise of the Western concept of individuality, both in a religious sense of individual responsibility for sin and the possibility of individual redemption. The contemporary Western world remains at this stage, eschewing in turn ascetic mysticism (the First Quadrant), tribal will-to-power (the Second Quadrant), and romantic/sensual solutions to the mysteries of life, which now feel somehow naïve and adolescent (the Third Quadrant). The Western world, and by extension the depressive self, feels it has "moved beyond" such mythologies and bravely (if stoically) embraces a reliance on self-as-adult, self-as-resource, and self-as-organizing principle.

As for us adults in the depressive arc, we feel we have come to the end of time, and there is no point in chasing horizons anymore. In fact, the horizon itself has been revealed as a wall, beyond which there is no more moving. In fact, the wall itself is a mirror, revealing only ourselves as we approach it. This staring-into-the-mirror experience is a result of post-modernism, which has rid itself of gods and goddesses and hidden meanings; everything is relative and therefore everything is an epiphenomenon of the self. As one approaches the mirror closer and closer, the experience of being confronted with the self becomes increasingly recursive and empty, and the mirror becomes a flat barrier, revealing only what is acted out before it. There is nothing of the generativity of the Beloved, or even the ultimate promise of ascension. In fact, at the Depressive Node, we are just as equidistant from both Beloved and Ascension as we were at the Narcissistic Node, the arc of the Second Quadrant.

Many, perhaps most adults never leave this stage, having decided that they have cast off childish ideas and other impractical notions, still repelled by the falseness of narcissism and stoically disappointed at the impossibility of returning to the womb. Yet, as with all of the arcs we have described, the depressive arc is not a final destination or an Ultimate Truth, but only a fleeting aspect of our Greater Experience, a passing quality of the spirit journey. Although the depressive arc swings around the figure of Christ toward mature adult selfhood, stagnation in the depressive arc results in mistaking true Identity for shallow roles and narrow identities.

Stagnation in the depressive arcs results in loss of the self even in the midst of seeking it (or at least, in the midst of being thrown back upon it out of necessity). Again, Christian symbolism supplies the archetypal reality of the crucified Christ, bifurcated by the competing demands of contemporary selfhood, ultimately sacrificed at the altar of politics. A heavy price indeed, it seems, for the establishment of a unique and separate self in the world. The depressive position can be summed up as this: the terrible fear that ultimately, this "me" is not enough.

In a real sense, the depressive solution invokes the same challenges and themes of the narcissistic arc, which is not surprising because the depressive node and the narcissistic node represent the two poles of the axis of introjective self, also representing Logos (thought). Both narcissistic and depressive dynamics are concerned with the elaboration of the self, the narcissistic dynamic representing the development of the self in a power-centered, coercive way, and the depressive dynamic in a melancholy, lonely, and quietly despairing way. The narcissist discovered the self as center of power, manifestly potent but subjectively incomplete and ultimately self-destructive; the depressive discovers self as instrument and agency, a manifestation of consciousness that can be used like a tool to affect one's duty but conspicuously lacking in the expansive powers of the narcissistic self.

The revelation that "this me is not enough" remains a trap until the point of view can be transcended. As has been the case with other arcs and other positions along the Spiral, emergence from the closed, chrysalis state represented by the spiral nodes requires thinking and feeling "at right angles" to perceived reality, to incur a corrective emotional experience that introduces a new point of view that suddenly adds a new dimension of perception, after which all things seem possible again, and the psyche is enervated with dynamic energy replacing the static deadness that went before. The psyche that remembers its journey will recall the deeper and higher purposes of individuation: "I am love AND thought, seed AND blossom. Having pursued a unique identity secure enough to contain the powerful energetic forces which preceded it, I am now free to transcend self and face the center." The next task before the psyche, then, is to discover or re-discover the distinction between *transcending* the self and *abnegating* the self. While the latter leads to mental illness and evil, the former leads to a deeper symphonic layering of the psyche.

Transcending the depressive arc is particularly significant to the spirit journey because the process completes a full circuit of the first spiral. Just as the depressive psyche becomes a seed germ structurally sound enough to contain all the dynamic energies that went into its development, the same seed germ becomes the carrier of all those human frequencies into the next higher level of the spiral. Such transcendence requires the lesson learned by circumnavigating the first round of the spiral: the necessity of trusting and containing all those previous forms, allowing them to become a font of energetic fulfillment. Although the cost has been high, navigating all four quadrants introduces important new energetic competencies. A psyche that is able to both question itself and hold its own shape becomes capable of creative chaos (which is the foundation for spontaneous creation) as well as continual curiosity. Perhaps most importantly, not just love but mature empathy and *mirroring* becomes possible in the fourth quadrant because the psyche becomes able to perceive others in perspective with itself.

Do you, reader, sense the inevitable approach of Lilith the Dissolver again? She approaches inexorably to resolve and transcend the qualities and conditions of the Fourth Quadrant, leading also to a complete circuit of a circle of the Spiral Path, toward rebirth into the First Quadrant. The Penitent Personality must transcend self-criticism and self-hatred in order to do what artists do best: to tell a better story. We will explore the implications of the second crossing of the Axis of Lilith, in her Ecstatic aspect, in Chapter 17.

In contemplating the experience of the Fourth Quadrant, I am reminded of the tragicomedy of Philip Roth's (1994) novel, *Portnoy's Complaint*. The novel details the growing anguish and conflict of the main character, Alexander Portnoy, as he relates his life experience to his psychoanalyst. At the end of the book, Portnoy's speech finally devolves into an incoherent scream, at which point the psychoanalyst speaks for the first time (in a Viennese accent, one assumes), expressed as a punchline: "So [said the doctor]. Now vee may perhaps to begin Yes?" (p. 308). Another, less salacious example of the experiential conditions around endings comes at the end of the lyrical story of the Ten Bulls traditional in the Zen tradition (Reps & Senzaki, 1998): the sage described the quest of a pilgrim to go into the wilderness and tame a wild bull, a metaphor for enlightenment. After a long and arduous process of finding the bull, taming the bull, and riding the bull home, the final stages of the story show that the bull has been transcended and is no longer necessary, and then that the self itself has been transcended and is no longer necessary. The story ends with the pilgrim now in the midst of the world, back where he began, and yet no longer where he was at all

> Barefooted and naked of breast, I mingle with the people of the world. My clothes are ragged and dust-laden, and I am ever blissful. I use no magic to extend my life; Now, before me, the dead trees become alive.

> (p. 186)

Here is an essential quality of the Fourth Quadrant: a lot of painful and complex process to arrive at the beginning, which is also an end. In fact, this position marks the end of time itself because time ceases to define life.

Defensive Correlates

The central principle of the psychology of the Fourth Quadrant is the self capable of *contemplating itself*, which requires a willingness to perceive, tolerate, and take on one's own primitive mental states. The Fourth Quadrant is the first moment in the spiral sequence in which self-doubt and related affective states, such as guilt, manifest as a prominent organizing factor.

In Chapter 12, we discussed the classic take of introjection as symmetrical with projection. Lacan (1991) disagrees with this symmetry and removes introjection from the dual realm of the *imaginary* into the triangular realm of the *symbolic*, which implies that introjection is predicated on three elements: what's *inside*, what's *outside*, and what's *me*, all mediated by a symbolic function (Felman, 1989). Lacan's take on introjection synergizes with its status in Integrated Analytical Psychology as a Fourth Quadrant phenomenon, since it requires additional psychological dimensionality resulting from some conceptualization of selfhood. The introjective defensive style, as it relates to the so-called depressive personality and depressive states, suggests an intersubjective capacity to perceive (and evaluate) the self within a relational context. This usage of the word introjection is also consistent with the dimensional approach employed by the *Psychodynamic Diagnostic Manual* (Lingiardi & McWilliams, 2017). However, we shall define introjection as a defensive correlate of the Axis of Unique Identity, which generates the conditions of both the Second and the Fourth Quadrant. In this sense, introjection reflects a tendency to organize self-states in terms of the structural integrity and boundaries of the self, rather than in terms of relational contexts. Blatt and Shichman (1983) define introjection this way, differentiated from the anaclitic:

> The focus…is not on sharing affection—of loving and being loved—but rather on defining the self as an entity separate from and different than another, with a sense of autonomy and control of one's mind and body, and with feelings of self-worth and integrity…The basic wish is to be acknowledged, respected, and admired.
>
> (pp. 203–204)

As we discussed in Chapter 12, the introjective axis proposed in this model implies that the introjective perspective is a foundational organizing principle across the Second and Fourth Quadrants, and therefore represents a theme among narcissistic, paranoid, and depressive personalities among others. The difference between the Second and Fourth Quadrants reflects different ways in which the personality reacts differentially to introjection: narcissistic personalities respond to their need to be acknowledged and respected with desperate attempts to create a false self, which makes this come true; the depressive personality is haunted rather by the fear that it isn't true. In other words, depressive introjection results in a preoccupation with the brokenness, badness, or selfishness of the self. In fact, it is my experience that depressives profoundly fear that they may be narcissists themselves. As Nancy McWilliams (2011) writes:

> People with introjective depressive psychologies believe that at bottom they are bad. They lament their greed, their selfishness, their competition, their vanity, their pride, their anger, their envy, their lust. They consider all these normal aspects of experience to be perverse and dangerous. They worry that they are inherently destructive.
>
> (p. 245)

Contemporary updates to the concept of introjection notwithstanding, the earlier object-relations perspectives on introjection do shed some light on its defensive value. Melanie Klein (1940) articulated the emotional calculus of introjection as a tendency to introject into the self any empathic failures experienced at the hands of early attachment figures. When a child experiences abandonment, disappointment, or actual exploitation or harm (as with neglect or abuse) from a beloved object, there are two fundamental energetic choices: the experience that a bad object has abandoned the child (which encourages externalized anger against the abandoning object), or else the experience that one was abandoned because one is *abandonable*. It is introjecting personalities that choose the latter path, experiencing the self as abandonable rather than just abandoned. This frame of reference sets the psyche up for a lifetime of pathological accommodation, conflict avoidance, and other signs and symptoms that one is walking on thin ice and can't afford to get angry or to assert one's needs, lest more abandonment follow. As a result, introjecting personalities tend to absorb the darkness of other people and contain it "safely" within themselves. In this sense, introjecting personalities are like human versions of bomb disposal vessels, reinforced from the inside to contain the forces of a blast and redirect it inwards rather than outwards. After a lifetime of internal detonations, the result is a plethora of hostile introjects (see Ross et al., 2019). Indeed, depressive personalities serve as bomb disposal units for the systems in which they live and work, cleansing others of selfishness and aggression by absorbing it into themselves, at great personal cost.

Although perhaps a side effect of introjection, rigid defenses against anger create a peculiarly visceral reaction against anger in the depressive personality. Anger itself comes to feel dangerous, as if anger were a wild animal that must be tightly tethered to prevent a rampage. For this reason, depressive anger, once it emerges, often does indeed have a primal whiff of brimstone to it. This primal quality makes sense given the Vertical Model of Integrated Analytical Psychology: moralistic and absolute introjective defenses against anger help ensure that hostile externalization and sadistic affects remain unmetabolized at lower harmonics. "Beware the fury of a patient man," writes Dryden (2018).

The hidden, and perhaps more heartbreaking, emotional motivation for all this introjection of darkness from abandoning objects is to continue to find a way to idealize, and therefore love, the other. As is common among children who tend to blame themselves for their parents' divorce, the depressive calculus is that it is better to believe that "this is all my fault" than to countenance the alternative, that love could fail. In this sense, depressive introjection serves as a defensive value against abandonment anxiety and amounts to wishfully populating the world with idealized objects who can be trusted to love.

The piquancy of depressive resistance to anger, and the role of introjection in preserving lost objects, brings us inexorably down to the subject of loss. Just as introjection helps to obviate anger by turning it inwards where it can be handled quietly without offending anyone, it also helps to stave off the emotional sequelae of loss. It stands to reason that emotionally astute, relationally oriented personalities prone to doubt themselves and to fear abandonment will have difficulty coping with loss (whether of a beloved person, pet, or another cathected object, like a home or a toy among children). Introjection reroutes loss into the bomb disposal vessel of the self by creating an unconscious narrative that one's own faults drove the loved one away. This introjective defense against loss makes the difference between Freud's (1964) original conceptualization of normal mourning versus melancholia: in order to mourn a loss, we must in some important way experience ourselves as the victim of that loss. When loss is introjected, ascribing the loss to some fault within the self, that critical ingredient of empathizing with one's own sorrow is lost, resulting in a kind of melancholy that doesn't quite acknowledge the loss at all. In this way, introjection is a defense against tolerating the archetypal qualities of the Fourth Quadrant.

Diagnostic Considerations

The modal personality organization of the Fourth Quadrant is the depressive personality, characterized in the psychoanalytic literature as relationally apt people prone to sadness and guilt who tend to introject as described above.

One of the major impediments to our understanding of the depressive personality has been the way the various editions of the Diagnostic and Statistical Manual (DSM) has historically conflated the functional dimensions of personality functioning with the mood disturbances that result from personality disorder. Depressive Personality Disorder is a primary example of this. The first editions of the DSM included a category called Depressive Neurosis defined as "an excessive reaction of depression due to an internal conflict or to an identifiable event such as the loss of a love object or cherished possession" (American Psychiatric Association, 1968, p. 40). The third edition dispensed with Depressive Neurosis and replaced it with Dysthymic Disorder, shifting the focus decisively away from themes of internal conflict and loss to the dysphoric mood that results from it. Although Depressive Personality Disorder has persisted in various appendices, the disappearance of the depressive personality was complete; now the only remaining discussions of the dynamic occur in the psychoanalytic literature. One of the most powerful indicators that a psychological dynamic remains in the cultural shadow is that we do not even have a name for it.

A further difficulty in naming the various clinical manifestations of the Penitent Personality is the problematic overlap between the *depressive personality* and *depression the mood disorder* (Huprich, 2001). The raw clinical signs of dysphoric mood as typified in either Major Depressive Disorder or Dysthymic Disorder (which, because we evidently needed yet another label for the phenomenon, was renamed as Persistent Depressive Disorder in the DSM V) are shared across a bewilderingly wide range of clinical etiologies. Dysphoric mood, if defined by such indicators as anhedonia, concentration difficulties, appetite changes, could be an indicator of a medical disorder, a trauma reaction, grief or bereavement, the persistent effects of substance abuse, existential angst or ennui, cultural or gender oppression, or even just the unhappiness that emanates from most or all of the personality disorders, to name just a few. Depressive personality, on the other hand, as defined in the contemporary psychoanalytic tradition, is about a specific configuration of defenses (especially introjection) against certain predictable affective states (especially anger and loss) producing certain relational patterns (such as conflict avoidance, inappropriate guilt reactions, resisting loss, idealizing others, and devaluing the self).

McWilliams (2011) notes the significant downside of the shift in the DSM away from depressive dynamics in favor of emphasizing mood disorder:

> ...In the process of dispensing with the category of depressive personality, they emphasized the affective aspects of dysthymic conditions at the expense of imaginal, cognitive, behavioral, and sensory components that are equally important...their decision also had the effect of diverting our attention from an

understanding of the of the defensive properties that characterize depressive people, even when they are not in a clinically depressed state.

(p. 228)

Psychoanalytic descriptors of the Depressive Personality have similarly been complicated by the evident binary distinction between anaclitic and introjective qualities of depression as described above, which seems to some degree further side-effects of our chronic difficulty in distinguishing introjective personality dynamics from depression itself. For purposes of our discussion, the Penitent personality is described as Fourth Quadrant dynamic with what we might call a depressive core, characterized by introjective defenses and intrapunitive self-states in an individual with otherwise relatively healthy object relations, and predisposed to interpersonal warmth and connectedness. In other words, the Penitent personality shows a core dynamic similar to what the psychoanalytic literature describes as an introjectively depressive personality.

Other personality styles described in the literature might also be considered to share the depressive core and therefore represent developmental waypoints along the Fourth Quadrant. Manic, Obsessive and Compulsive, and Self-defeating personalities in particular may be conceptualized as resulting from various defensive adaptations to the depressive core, therefore also representing aspects of the Penitent personality organization.

Manic personalities mediate the depressive core with manic defenses designed to counter and deny it, especially through denial and reaction formation. Manic defenses, viewed through the lens of the Kleinian model, are designed to counter depressive guilt and shame through flight into compensatory action and omnipotence. Manic energy is therefore shimmering and effervescent, distracting and intoxicating, and leads one up and out of the depressive core by replacing it with insouciance, gumption, bravado, or elemental thrill. Manic defenses counter the depressive core by disappearing guilt and the psychological space from which it emerges. A prototypical cultural pattern in the Western world for the manic personality is found in the comedian, perhaps a melancholy or even tragic figure who transforms bitterness into a reason for laughter. I cannot help but think of the tragedy of actor Robin Williams, whose charisma and sparkling wit covered up a depressive core of some surpassing darkness, which caught up to him by the end. Manic personalities are covert Penitents, but in some denial about their citizenship in the Fourth Quadrant, and introducing them (by slow degrees, usually), is generally the work of psychotherapy.

Obsessive and compulsive personalities employ moralistic ideation, undoing, and intellectualization to counter the depressive core, which from an obsessive or compulsive perspective appears as a peculiarly chthonic and dreaded experience of being dirty, sinful, or bad. Whereas more "elementally pure" depressive personalities experience their convictions of being bad or sinful as a kind of ego-syntonic fact of life to be swallowed whole, obsessive and compulsive personalities rigorously (one might say, primly) deny their feared badness with the energy of a medieval ascetic, taking refuge in either obsessive intellectualization, which has the effect of distancing from primitive affective states which feel "messy," or compulsive undoing, which carries the talismanic energy of a religious rite designed to purify sin and transgression. Like manic personalities, obsessive and compulsive personalities are rigidly defended against their depressive core, and I sometimes find myself regretfully informing psychotherapy clients with these personality styles that they owe the universe some sadness.

The Self-Defeating personality seems to straddle the fences of the Third and Fourth Quadrant, to the degree that I am not quite sure in which quadrant to locate it. This style is sometimes referred to in the psychoanalytic literature as the Masochistic Personality, but I have found that cultural baggage around the word "masochism" has damaged the utility of the word beyond repair: Self-Defeating (or masochistic) people do not enjoy suffering itself, but they have learned to get some self-esteem from it. Where more elementally "pure" depressive personalities have absorbed the truth about their doom in a plaintively ego-syntonic way, the self-defeating personality rails against their own doom, and tends to complain to whomever will listen to the injustice of their plight. This tendency may be strong enough to result in a life organized around martyrdom. "Viewed through the long lens of an aggrieved life," writes humorist Jeff Reid, "small wrongs loom large" (p. 51).

Cultural and Gender Considerations

The Fourth Quadrant is a cultural horizon line: the psychological health of a culture or society depends upon the degree to which local conditions (liberty, social justice and safety, political stability, support for creativity, respect for human differences, dignity and well-being, etc.) allow progression to the Fourth Quadrant. Fourth Quadrant personalities become capable of higher-order psychological functions vital to holding a civilization together: the cognitive flexibility to hold consensual reality, the affect tolerance necessary to hold frustration, anger, and loneliness in abeyance long enough to do something about it, and the all-important resource of empathy lead to successful marriages, parenting, and occupational and creative achievement in the world. Psychologically impoverished cultural forces place roadblocks along the spiral path, resulting in energetic bottlenecks, especially in the Second and Third Quadrants (with the proviso that we have noted in Chapter 15, that children identified as girls tend to be routed into the Fourth Quadrant during attachment for reasons of cultural attributions of femininity as well as the realities of childbearing). Individual psyches who manage to reach the Fourth Quadrant in psychologically impoverished systems and cultures do so at great personal expense: they are spiritual pioneers of humankind.

In one crude sense, the measure of the degree to which a system or culture supports transit of the Fourth Quadrant is the degree to which the culture encourages or even celebrates:

- Sadness and mourning
- Complexity
- Empathy

- Self-doubt
- Anger as a route into restorative action
- Social responsibility

There are cultural forces in American society in particular encouraging social and political narratives which eschew, and even specifically devalue, Fourth Quadrant or "depressive" values such as complexity, doubt, and sadness. Cushman (2015) notes that self-critical, and therefore relationally sensitive, functions of relational psychoanalysis can be contributory to social progress:

> …there is a subtle way in which relational psychoanalysis could be interpreted as preparation, or, in its better moments a school, for resistance. This is because its practices can enable a way of being that is honest, self-reflective, critical, humble, curious, compassionate, and respectful of and willing to learn from difference.

> (p. 424)

Altman (2005) notes that manic defenses, in particular, underlie cultural resistance to communal responsibilities: "the manic defense militates against a sense of social responsibility, since it defends against precisely the depressive guilt that, in the Kleinian model, leads to reparative concern for others" (pp. 329–330). Peltz (2005) makes a similar point about manic defenses against the anxiety associated with social injustice, resulting in compulsive consumption

> Compulsive consumption, a behavior our market heavily relies upon, rates as one of the many socially sanctioned manic attempts to ward off the pain and anxiety associated with both the absence of a containing governing authority and the loss of basic provisions including health care…

> (p. 347)

It has been my enduring concern as a psychotherapist to notice the relative lack of individuals who "make it" to the end of the four quadrants with a high representational horizon. Socially and politically, I see only a critical minority of people who are psychologically capable of the Great Doubt.

References

Altman, N. (2005). Manic society. *Psychoanalytic Dialogues, 15*(3): 321–346.

American Psychiatric Association. (1968). *Diagnostic and statistical manual of mental disorders* (2nd ed.). Author.

Blatt, S. J., & Shichman, S. (1983). Two primary configurations of psychopathology. *Psychoanalysis and Contemporary Thought, 6*: 187–254.

Cushman, P. (2015). Relational psychoanalysis as political resistance. *Contemporary Psychoanalysis, 51*(3): 423–459.

Dryden, J. (2018). *Absalom and Achitophel.* Forgotten Books.

Felman, S. (1989). *Jacques Lacan and the adventure of insight: Psychoanalysis in contemporary culture.* Harvard University Press.

Freud, S. (1964). Mourning and melancholia. In J. Strachey (Ed. and Trans.), *The standard edition of the complete psychological works of Sigmund Freud* (Vol. 14, pp. 237–258). Hogarth and Institute of Psycho-Analysis. (Original work published 1917).

Hardy, T. (1965). *Jude the obscure.* Houghton Mifflin.

Huprich, S. K. (2001). The overlap of depressive personality disorder and dysthymia, reconsidered. *Harvard Review of Psychiatry, 9*(4): 158–168.

Jung, C. G. (2006). *The undiscovered self: The dilemma of the individual in modern society.* Berkley.

Klein, M. (1940). Mourning and its relation to manic-depressive states. *International Journal of Psycho-Analysis, 21*: 125–153.

Lacan, J. (1991). *The seminar of Jacques Lacan. Book II. The ego in Freud's theory and in the technique of psychoanalysis.* W. W. Norton & Company.

Lingiardi, V., & McWilliams, N. (Eds.). (2017). *Psychodynamic diagnostic manual: PDM-2* (2nd ed.). The Guilford Press.

McWilliams, N. (2011). *Psychoanalytic diagnosis: Understanding personality structure in the clinical process.* The Guilford Press.

Peltz, R. (2005). The manic society. *Psychoanalytic Dialogues, 15*(3): 347–366.

Reps, P., & Senzaki, N. (1998). *Zen Flesh, Zen Bones.* Tuttle Publishing.

Ross, N. D., Kaminski, P. L., & Herrington, R. (2019). From childhood emotional maltreatment to depressive symptoms in adulthood: The roles of self-compassion and shame. *Child Abuse and Neglect, 92*: 32–42.

Roth, P. (1994). *Portnoy's complaint.* Vintage Books.

Chapter 17

The Spiral Path

How did I escape? With difficulty. How did I plan this moment? With pleasure.
- Alexandre Dumas
The Count of Monte Cristo

If ever there was an archetype, it would be the spiral. It is found in the tusks of narwhals and unicorns, the whorl of a human fingertip, the architecture of galaxies, the path of draining water, and the structure of hurricanes. Spirals have characterized human imagination and artistic expression since neolithic times, inscribed in megalithic monuments, alone or arranged in triskelions. Spirals may illustrate evolution or involution, rolling up or unwinding, indicating motion from the center outwards, or from the outside in, and may represent a waxing or a waning. The spiral ascends and descends, expands or contracts while keeping its shape. It seems inevitable that the pathway of human psychological development would be a spiral.

Our spiral traces a pathway through the circumplex and represents an integration (actually, a mathematical function) of the motion up and down with the motion clockwise and counterclockwise along the circumference of the circumplex. The spiral reconciles the developmental trajectory of the psyche with its radial thematic functions, and therefore reconciles the level of mental representation (the harmonics) with the archetypal themes of personality (the archetypal axes), and therefore reconciles archetypal content with defensive systems that delimit and modify archetypal content, and therefore reconciles Jungian and psychoanalytic perspectives in psychotherapy. Also, spirals look pretty (Bennett, 2024).

The Spiral Journey

This chapter will be primarily occupied with tracing the developmental pathway of the spiral through the Integrative Analytical Circumplex. For the purposes of this description, we will assume a spiral trajectory ascending from the center of the figure upwards through the six harmonics, while also rotating counterclockwise through the four quadrants. Psychological inflection points will occur when the spiral path transects one of the archetypal axes ("horizontal" motion which I have identified as metaphor, or condensation, in Chapter 11), as well as when it ascends

DOI: 10.4324/9781032708751-20

from one harmonic to the next harmonic ("vertical" motion which I have described as metonymy, or displacement). Jung's transcendent function provides the impetus for the spiral's trajectory, teleologically radiating out from its origin point to interpenetrate the mysteries of the cosmos, like Sophia on her lonely journey to find wisdom.

Note that the curved trajectory of the spiral ascends through the harmonics, so that its pathway through a particular quadrant is somewhat "higher" than its pathway through the previous quadrant. This trajectory suggests a developmental progression of the quadrants and their respective personality and defensive styles, consistent with Kernberg's (1975) general sense that some personality styles tend to "load" higher or lower on a developmental continuum. In other words, the mathematics suggests that the first harmonic in the Second Quadrant is somewhat more developmentally advanced than the first harmonic in the First Quadrant. The spiral trajectory suggests a certain relationship between the themes underlying personality development and the level of mental representation: the states and conditions that prevail in the third quadrant (interpersonal relatedness, unconscious desire for regressive fusion, affective intensity, vulnerability to abandonment anxiety, etc.) require ingredients which aren't present in the second quadrant. So the Third Quadrant is not just different from the Second Quadrant; it holds a position further along a developmental process.[1]

The spiral path itself emerges from the archetypal singularity into the First Quadrant, which is defined as the First Quadrant exactly because this is where the spiral first emerges. The first spiral arc takes us on an imaginary cartesian coordinate system from 0.0 to 0.1 as it were, which would represent the first harmonic of the First Quadrant, whose axis is the Axis of Transcendent Self. Birth is, therefore, our first transcendent act, and our first step of emergence into psychological selfhood. The navigating soul enters the First Quadrant as if from below, and therefore the theme of this arc of the spiral will be organized around the implications of nascent becoming, and ascension. Although I prefer not to attempt a specific chronology of the spiral journey by associating it with a human lifespan, it would seem that emergence from the singularity into the First Quadrant would begin with birth, and the very first pass through the First Quadrant would involve negotiating the trajectory from emergence from the womb to Grotstein's *primal split* (1981), or Mahler's *psychological birth of the human being* (1974); that is to say, from birth to the moment of reliable awareness of oneself as a sovereign being, with all the implications that radiate outwards from that profound realization. At all harmonic levels, the First Quadrant involves themes of emergence and resistance to emergence. This first arc, this primal arc, emerges from the singularity, reaches an apogee at the Axis of Transcendent Self in its *aphanisis* aspect, and then rotates toward its transit with the Axis of Christ at its *exemplar* aspect.

The conditions prevailing as the spiral line approaches the Axis of Christ from the First Quadrant is a *dynamic of resistance*. The schizoid conditions prevailing in the First Quadrant approach their transcendent resolution through true manifestation: the willingness to emerge into the world in full voice, prepared to represent oneself and to discover and communicate what we *want*. In developmental terms, this dynamic represents the "terrible twos," the obstreperous and toweringly selfish qualities of the toddler, who artlessly combines objective weakness and smallness with a commanding will and a lack of nuance. In fact, the transit of the Axis of Christ the Exemplar from the First Quadrant to the Second, which thematically represents the transition from schizoid states to narcissistic states, is a potentially dangerous transition. It is my opinion that the violent behavior of psychopaths, especially the mass shooters who are so despairingly common in the United States, represents an abreaction to the dynamic of resistance at this particular point in personality development. When brittle self-righteousness intersects with relational impoverishment and is fueled by high levels of dispositional aggression, in the absence of appropriate social and cultural controls, and especially in men, the transition from First to Second Quadrant can be literally explosive.

For the vast majority of us who do not veer off into psychopathic space at the Axis of Christ, mediating the boundary between the First and Second Quadrants means that our thematic balance shifts from the protean authenticity of the schizoid state to the confidently encapsulated quality of the narcissistic state, and developing a dynamic of resistance involves a more ordinary willingness to "throw down" in the world and to identify readily with, and defend, a persona. Personality organizations primarily described as schizoid resist the Axis of Christ and the dynamic of resistance, and this resistance hems then into the First Quadrant because the quality of aphanisis leads them to avoid manifestation. Personalities described as thematically narcissistic have evolved "over the hump" of the Axis of Christ and settled into a highly constellated version of the self, reaching developmental fullness at the Axis of Unique Identity. By this point, the spiral path has progressed a quarter of the way through the cycle and adds a second dimension (individual and sovereign agency) to the primal dimension of contextualized existence.

On the other side of the quadrantic median line of the Axis of Unique Identity, the spiral journey inexorably descends toward the impending Axis of Lilith in her Dissolver aspect, representing the distant approaches of love, vulnerability, intimacy, and relating. As the spiral path descends the lower aspect of the Second Quadrant, the personality becomes more capable of and vulnerable to (and possibly, ever more resistant to) naturally occurring dependency needs which will eventually become ascendant after the Axis of Lilith. Second Quadrant personalities organized south of the Axis of Unique Identity (between that line and the Axis of Lilith) are, therefore, more likely to phase into a less narcissistic and more paranoid flavor, as the psyche becomes more capable of tolerating both intimacy and the problem of guilt that comes from applied experiences of intimacy. Across the Second Quadrant, the developmental trajectory seems to be that sociopathy occurs early, in the dynamic of resistance associated with the unique climactic conditions around the transit of the Axis of Christ the Exemplar, and narcissistic states prevail near the median phase of the arc, followed by paranoid personalities closer to the Axis of Lilith.

The Axis of Lilith represents an existential threat to narcissism, and Lilith, the dark madonna, is the great Delimiter of Narcissism. Through her no narcissism may pass, because she dissolves the illusion of illusion, and because she refused to lie under Adam. The narcissistic psyche is constrained by an atavistic fear of Lilith, and as we have discussed, this atavistic fear is operationalized in the world as a systemic fear and control of women and the feminine, because of the way patriarchal assumptions have assigned qualities to the feminine which are experienced by narcissism as humiliating and subversive.

The Lilith Gate, then, is a psychological and spiritual revolution, as was the Dynamic of Resistance before it. Selfhood, which was so carefully curated and husbanded and elaborated and defended against enemies foreign and domestic, is now revealed to be ephemeral and relative, and even worse, optional. As power is relinquished in order to become worthy of love, the alchemical ingredients of the psyche undergo a transmutation, and self becomes secondary to the craving of return to the beloved, to reverse and undo the painful separateness of selfhood and to regain the nirvanic and pleromic oneness of oceanic consciousness and the womb. This transmutation is reflected mathematically in the fact that as spiral re-approaches the Axis of Transcendent Self, the psyche experiences its first archetypal reversal (that is, returning to a developmentally earlier theme), and phenomenologically feels something like traumatically emerging from the womb, reluctantly agreeing to a process of selfhood, and then learning to identify closely with the self, and then relishing and defending that sense of self and protecting it against all comers, and then, in response to dark Lilithian stirrings that something is profoundly missing, succumbing to love in a way that brings the psyche back "home" to its primal transcendent baseline.[2] At the same time, the spiral path is now at its furthest point from the primal schizoid compromise with the world in the First Quadrant, and paradoxically, the anaclitic themes of the south end of the Axis of Transcendent Self both contradict and enrich and synergize with the original aphanisis at the north end.

As the spiral path transits the Axis of Transcendent self in its anaclitic aspect, the trajectory arcs back toward the waiting Axis of Christ in its Redeemer aspect. The darkly transcendent forces of the Third Quadrant, which encourage the self to atomize and become a particulate field surrounding and defining the beloved other, begin to encounter the limits of their own organizational theme. The willingness to lean into dependency needs, to disappear into the arms of the beloved, have in many ways resulted in the debasement of the self to the degree that may include neglect of one's own well-being, and even self-harm (overtly in the sense of self-injurious behavior or more covertly as with eating disorder, especially at the third and fourth harmonic levels). In other words, the imperative to return to the theme of selfhood becomes ascendant again. Having repudiated the brittle excesses of narcissism, we cannot simply repeat the Dynamic of Resistance; having discovered the dark ecstasy of love, we will never again be able to contract to the stale mathematics of self-absorption. We must approach the Christ Axis, and its imperative of individuation, with our hard-won relational capacities intact, fully cognizant of the seduction of dissolving which will never again leave us. Because of these developmental conditions, the Axis of Christ approached at this point on the spiral will have a quality of redemption rather than pursuing inert ideals of inviolable structure. In other words, as the spiral inexorably bends back toward the Axis of Unique Identity will no longer promise a crystalline pure version of selfhood, but a kind of selfhood that is inclusive of its own incompleteness, its longings, and its brokenness. The themes woven around the Christ the Redeemer transit blend Third Quadrant's tendency to define itself with subversive resistance to disempowerment with the incipient Fourth Quadrant sense of self, which is both more self-absorbed and more self-critical. Self-defeating personality dynamics emerge near this transit, in which depressive themes of self-inadequacy are countered by histrionic oral rage.

The second transit of the Axis of Christ, characterized by the Redeemer aspect, represents the second time the spiral has returned to a prior theme, but this time at a higher representational level, inclusive of the experiences that have gone into the progress so far. The theme shifts from the chimerical and hypnotic magics of the Third Quadrant back to the somber ouroboric notes of the Fourth. The Christ archetype as Redeemer reflects a powerful theme of the Christian mythos, communicating to the psyche that *you are uniquely worthy of redemption*. This message represents not only a challenging blend of humility (in need of redemption) but also the responsibility of power (being uniquely worthy). The Fourth Quadrant, which awaits on the other side of the Axis of Christ the Redeemer, demands the co-existence of both themes.

At this point on the spiral journey, the self is no longer searching for the lost beloved in the darkness, but instead is confronted with itself in the Mirror of Self-Reflection. The advent of the Fourth Quadrant reminds the psyche that it has always come down to this: the need to become, to manifest, to be. Following the heartaches and passions of the Third Quadrant, the time has come to set foot back upon the path of building a self, but this time reaching for a self-predicated not just on the stoic crenelations of the Second, but also the genuineness of the First and the capacity for intimacy conferred by the Third. The Mirror of Unique Identity not only reminds the psyche to return to its own business but also demands a more vulnerable sense of self-capable of self-reflection and self-doubt, shorn of the grandiosity of narcissism. The Mirror of Unique Identity not only reveals the self but also presents a final barrier: for the mirror is made of uncompromising and obdurate glass. A mirror is not a portal; one can only gaze into it, but not pass through it.

The Fourth Quadrant, then, reprises the sense of self as a lessened thing, wounded and marked by the difficulties of its journey so far, somehow responsible for standing on its own but never again able to resort to grandiose magics, somehow responsible for the world but without being powerful, somehow charged with the task of seeking love (the unremitting imperative of the Third Quadrant) while also knowing that the journey must be completed alone, and that the cavalry is not coming. The Mirror of Self-Reflection, an early Fourth Quadrant phenomenon, presses the point that there has always only been you all this time, and that there really is nowhere else to go. In a sense, arrival at the Mirror represents the fullness of our humanity, the T-junction at which point the "I" and the "thou" are both now possible. There is no further to go in terms of form, so we must either turn aside, to the left or right. It is my experience that most adult humans do turn aside from the Mirror of Unique Identity in two different ways. The left turn is to renounce individual being in the name of collective responsibility to a system or set of values (a family, commonly to children, or to a nation or a cultural group for example, and sounds something like "It will not be me that reaches the promised land, but

I will sacrifice for future generations"), which often carries archetypal themes of self-sacrifice, an energy that thickens into martyrdom in the midrange harmonics that I would associate with so-called masochistic or self-defeating personalities. The right turn involves the externalization of internal conflict outwards into the world of conflicts and enemies external to the self, often organized around themes of purity or righteousness. The latter pathway away from the Mirror invokes the purity of conviction and atavistic loathing of dirtiness and disorder of the obsessive and compulsive personalities, as well as the powerful dynamic of denial and acting out characteristic of manic personalities. These characteristic diversions from the Mirror of Unique Identity therefore represent two distinct flavors we might identify as the Martyr and the Tyrant. As we explored in Chapter 16, these various stylistic outcomes of the spiral trajectory through the Fourth Quadrant share a common depressive core modified by various defensive systems intrinsic to their worldview.

The alternative to the ways of the martyr and tyrant, and the alternative response to the obdurate barrier of the mirror, is to transcend the mirror and to become philosophical. As the psyche rounds through the Axis of Unique Identity, we approach the modal defensive style of the Fourth Quadrant, the depressive personality in its more "pure" state, which has relinquished the various distortions available earlier in the quadrant related to the Mirror of Unique Identity. The depressive personality simply lies down in the midst of this dilemma of the Mirror, quietly and deeply accepting the incompleteness of the self and all its defects. They do not, however, generally allow their despair to distract them from introjective responsibilities: as McWilliams (2011) puts it, depressive personalities "try very hard to be 'good,' but they fear being exposed as sinful and discarded as unworthy" (p. 245). A certain sense of personal responsibility invests the Fourth Quadrant. To return to the Christian mythos, redemption must be accomplished through "good works." The psyche has been reminded of the task of remaining true to itself, but this responsibility does not obviate or resolve any of the dynamics and challenges that have gone before, nor does it provide any badly needed self-esteem or reassurance. The depressive condition involves grandiose responsibility without the reward of feeling omnipotent. Depressively organized people carry on not out of hope of salvation or self-aggrandizement, but because of a strange sense of responsibility to the world that T. H. White (1976) calls a "seventh sense" which prevails in middle age:

> You cannot teach a young woman to have knowledge of the world. She has to be left to the experience of the years. And then, when she finds she is beginning to hate her used body, she suddenly finds that she can do it. She can go on living – not by principle, not by deduction, not by knowledge of good and evil, but simply by a peculiar and shifting sense of balance which defies each of these things often. She no longer hopes to live by seeking the truth – if women ever do hope this – but continues henceforth under the guidance of a seventh sense.
>
> (p. 213)

The modal themes of the Fourth Quadrant, then, result in a deep conviction that "this *me* is not enough." A poignant sense of loss invests this transition point, redolent of all the conditions and circumstances and experiences that have gone before, in the progression through the First, Second, and Third Quadrants. The Axis of Lilith approaches again, marking this time the True End, the completion of the circle and the end of a life cycle. The Fourth Quadrant takes on an autumnal quality as it approaches Lilith for the second time. This autumnal quality invokes the sadness of the elves in Tolkien's (1986) saga of the One Ring: invested with a deep sense of melancholy, the elves forsake a world that has seemed to move on without them, seeking the Grey Havens and a passage to the Uttermost West, which is homeland, with a sad dignity.

An existential guilt invests the late Fourth Quadrant, an implication of transcending the Mirror of Unique Reflection. One's own lies and falsehoods can no longer be hidden, and are reluctantly accepted as part of the self. This self is no longer the bastion of uncompromising authenticity of the First Quadrant, nor the self-righteous purity of the Second, and nor is it the soluble and chimerical willingness to disappear into love as in the Third. This final sense of self is both clear-eyed and authentic, as well as broken and humbled. Pat Conroy (1980) eloquently describes a Fourth Quadrant psyche confronting its own falsehoods and weaknesses:

> Yet the laws of recall are subject to distortion and alienation. Memory is a trick, and I have lied so often to myself about my own role and the role of others that I am not sure I can recognize the truth about those days. But I have come to believe in the unconscious integrity of lies. I want to record even them. Somewhere in the immensity of the lie the truth gleams like the pure, light-glazed bones of an extinct angel. Hidden in the enormous falsity of my story is the truth for all of us… I write my own truth, in my own time, in my own way, and take full responsibility for its mistakes and slanders. Even the lies are part of my truth.
>
> (p. 11)

The Fourth Quadrant reflects an existential crisis that parallels the existential crisis experienced in Western culture following the transition from industrialization into modernity: the safe dichotomies, certainties, belief systems, and folkloric themes that historically both circumscribed and contained human experience have fallen away, leaving the human being staring at itself in the flatness of a mirror, confronted with what it really is, what has been lost, and what is at stake. The traditions of existential psychotherapy, perhaps best articulated by Yalom (1980), underline the importance of the "four givens" in human life: freedom, death, isolation, and meaninglessness. When one transcends the Mirror of Unique Identity by becoming philosophical, these givens spring into sharp relief as crucial realities that invite authenticity rather than further distortion. And where have we heard of this authenticity before? We recall that authenticity is the provenance of the First Quadrant, to which we are inexorably returning. This time, we approach that authenticity not out of innocence, but freighted with the sorrow of knowledge of the world, and of our own limitations. We return, not home but to ourselves, not out of the Third Quadrant impulse to surrender an identity which has become fearful, but as a means of consummating that identity, of coming into our fullness. From the Third Quadrant, we learned that a return to Oceanic Consciousness is not possible, just as we learned from the Second Quadrant that personal power can never be adequate. The plangent truth of the Fourth Quadrant comes, therefore, from a relinquishment of one's own personal patterns, without hope of either rescue or victory.

The dark Madonna, Lilith, approaches again, bearing her waters of forgiveness, dark eyed with the tragic magics of dissolution, forgetting, and transformation. At the second Lilith transition, the manifestation of the dark feminine archetype is a yonic gate, which is not only a passage into darkness but also a passage into rebirth, betokened by the emergence of a new spiral arm of the spiral journey through the circumplex. The Fourth Quadrant is bracketed by the Mirror of Unique Reflection at the south end, marking the emergence from the Third to the Fourth, and by the yonic gate at the north end, marking the successful completion of a life cycle and a return to rebirth. In this sense, the second passage of Lilith invokes the ancient symbol of the *vagina dentata*, the toothed vagina, comprising both the frightening and alluring aspects of the passage into darkness. The sorrow accompanying the darkening of the world reprises the reluctance to be born, which we discussed in the context of the First Quadrant. And yet births are occasions for joy, and our instinct is to welcome the newborn as an affirmation of life itself. The return of Lilith marking the complete circuit of the circumplex, therefore, dissolves with primal ecstasy, foreshadowing rebirth. Let us recall from Chapter 15 that Lilith only emerges when a sense of self has cohered; she is only visible to the individual and remains hidden to the collective. Her ecstatic dissolving, which marks the end of the Fourth Quadrant, was made possible by all that has gone before and blesses what has gone before, rather than undoing or erasing it.

"This *you* is not enough?" Lilith asks the approaching psyche on her second approach. "Then let it go, let it be transcended, and dissolve into the starry cosmos without guarantee of what will come next." The sadness, loss, and sense of termination that invests the Fourth Quadrant cannot be explained away or "cheered up" through affirmations of eventual rebirth... the ending must be allowed to be an end. And when the ending is allowed to be an end, it becomes a beginning.

A Note on Clockwise and Counterclockwise Trajectories

I have described here, in archetypal form, a prototypical narrative for a counterclockwise thematic progression through the circumplex, as if it were a kind of spirit journey. I do not mean to suggest that this narrative is a fixed chronology; in reality, human life is a messy experiential mélange of all of these themes coming up all the time. However, I do believe that the implications of the Integrated Analytical Model are that inherent psychological structures that have an archetypal basis become constellated in patterned ways as our capacity for affect tolerance and mature defensive styles allow. One of the most important implications of the spiral journey is that "vertical" movement along the levels of mental representation and "rotational" movement along the circumplex mediate each other. The mathematical properties of the spiral reveal that becoming more conscious is synonymous with progressing through the four quadrants of the circumplex, their conditions, and inner circumstance.

For example, the First Quadrant comes "before" the Third Quadrant because the preconditions for the First Quadrant are more primal and elemental, and in fact, as we discussed in Chapter 13, are invoked by the very experience of birth itself. Third Quadrant states, on the contrary, require a certain amount of object relations development to be consciously experienced and metabolized. The archetype of Lilith, therefore, emerges at key thresholds, when there is enough of a sense of self to meet her. The kinds of challenges and dilemmas associated with human attachment happen all the time, across the lifespan, but our capacity to metabolize those challenges and dilemmas evolves with each passthrough of the Third Quadrant. The Integrated Analytical Model suggests that the spiral dynamic is a function of ascending through the representational harmonics and the psyche's increasing capacity to make sense of a broadening range of psychological and relational situations. The psychological reality, then, is not a neat and clean mathematical spiral but a complex and fractal emanation of human keys of consciousness, which build upon each other and resonate with each other like musical chords. A fixed progression of musical notes is built into the structure of a musical instrument like a guitar, with a predictable ascending series of perfect fourths with a single major third, making a complex universe of music possible. A fixed progression of visible light (red, orange, yellow, green, blue, indigo, violet) is ordered mathematically along a scale of wavelength (from about 700 nm, which looks red, to about 400 nm, which looks violet). But we do not typically experience musical notes or visual stimuli in order; the mathematical properties that form their basis show up phenomenologically as astonishing variety. In the same way, an individual person's progression through the harmonic representations and archetypal thematic axes yields complex symphonic effects that are truly unique to each person.

Nor is the counterclockwise rotation, which I have depicted in this chapter, the only possible rotation. The clockwise rotation, which would emerge from the First Quadrant into the Fourth, and from there into the Third and finally the Second, is also possible and presents its own complexities and synergistic implications. In the long years of my work in developing this model, it has occurred to me that my unconscious selection of the counterclockwise route as the "default" pathway was founded upon assumptions that are largely gendered. As we discussed in Chapter 14, the energies of the Second Quadrant, which manifest as psychological narcissism, have been made more readily available to men than to women. In fact, human beings born and identified as boys are more likely to be "rotated" into the second quadrant by social and cultural forces, and those born and identified as girls are more likely to be invited into the Fourth Quadrant. It may be, therefore, that the counterclockwise rotation is more characteristic of human beings identifying as male, and the clockwise rotation is more characteristic of those identifying as female. However, I do not believe there is anything intrinsically gendered about either the counterclockwise or clockwise rotations. Both rotations are likely happening simultaneously in each person, but it does appear to me, anecdotally, that a "chord progression" can be discerned as the most powerful organizing principle in an individual's personality development, and that gender is one of the determinants of which rotation predominates.

One of the most important realizations that inspired the revelation of the clockwise path was the experience working with women who are histrionically organized. I noticed time and again, in a clinical sense, that histrionically organized women didn't need to become more "sad"; they needed to become more powerful. Although the passage across the Axis of Christ the Redeemer does betoken a movement toward self-coherence, it does so in a manner that smacks of repentance and guilt rather than a more "Lilithian" assertion of feminine power.

Although I will not undertake an entirely separate analysis of the clockwise spiral, I will note that this rotation reverses the psychological "order" of the archetypal themes in important ways, resulting also in a reversal of the energetic valence of the archetypal developmental axes. True to the nature of archetypal energy, the archetypal axes we have explored in this book have complex, nested, and dynamic levels of meaning that manifest contextually. For example, at one level, Christ represents the consummately dutiful son, an exemplar of fidelity to one's destiny, who was personally destroyed and sacrificed but then went on to be revered and worshiped by Christians. Lilith, on the other hand, shows up at one level as an avatar of naked defiance, refusing both the will of God and submission to the masculine, and therefore "escaped" into her own freedom, but has been historically reviled and demonized. Therefore, Lilith's energy comes across culturally and psychologically as covert and subversive, while the mythos of Christ are enshrined and idealized. But at a deeper level, there is nothing inherently dangerous or subversive about Lilith; she has been published in this way by our culture because our culture lionizes the narcissism that Lilith challenges. Therefore, the energy of Lilith may come across as frightening and disintegrative from on the counterclockwise rotation, but on the clockwise rotation, she emerges as an anti-heroine with almost revolutionary power.

Some Final Thoughts

The human mathematics of the Circumplex Model suggests a holistic and symphonic process of enantiodromia that integrates the "upward and outward" needs of the psyche with its "downward and inward" needs, geometrizing a relationship between the expansion of harmonic mental representation and progressive rotation through archetypal keys of consciousness. The telos of this Complex Adaptive System is to round out the four quadrants at a high representational horizon, completing the circle as a symbol for the wholeness of the self. The Spiral Path communicates something plangent about the existential reality of human life: that the outward journey of psychological development, the very experience of ascending the harmonics and touring the circumplex, leads us ever further from our archetypal and spiritual home, where we came from. And yet the Spiral Path is also a template for return and represents a geometric metaphor for a pattern that continues to expand yet remains centered on its source.

Notes

1 To complicate this even further, it seems that this principle is reversible given the clockwise rotation (i.e., the Second Quadrant represents a developmental step up from the Third).
2 I do apologize for that unseemly long sentence, and appreciate the reader's patience with it, and my editor's patience in allowing it to stand.

References

Bennett, M. (2024). *Towards an integrated analytical psychology: Return to freedom and dignity.* Routledge.
Conroy, P. (1980). *The lords of discipline.* Houghton Mifflin.
Grotstein, J. S. (1981). *Splitting and projective identification.* Jason Aronson.
Kernberg, O. (1975). *Borderline conditions and pathological narcissism.* Jason Aronson.
Mahler, M. S. (1974). Symbiosis and individuation: The psychological birth of the human infant. *The Psychoanalytic Study of the Child, 29*: 89–106.
McWilliams, N. (2011). *Psychoanalytic diagnosis: Understanding personality structure in the clinical process.* The Guilford Press.
Tolkien, J. R. R. (1986). *The two towers.* George Allen & Unwin.
White, T. H. (1976). *The once and future king.* Berkley Books.
Yalom, I. D. (1980). *Existential psychotherapy.* Basic Books.

Chapter 18

Conclusions

The soul becomes dyed with the colour of its thoughts.

- Marcus Aurelius
Meditations

Our shared endeavor in this work, my work to write and your word to read, is a theoretical narrative offering a hypothesis about the layering of mental representation and their relationship to personality organization. The perspective that has emerged from this work is that the psychological task of the human being is to link an essential inner reality, somehow, with the vicissitudes of external experience. How do we navigate the external world, with its conflict, its bewildering levels of complexity, its falseness, and its seductive promise while remaining who and what we are? Meanwhile, as our conversation has revealed, the efforts to integrate inner with outer are undermined by both internal and external forces, including social assumptions and "scientific" perspectives that deny or ignore the idea that there is an inner life at all, and including our own doubts about who we are.

I have attempted to describe the integration of inner and outer reality across the two parts of this book: the vertical and the horizontal.

The Story So Far

The vertical model describes a so-called harmonic progression of mental representation, ranging from the "fundamental frequency" of archetype and upwards through successive and increasingly complex, interconnected iterations of models of reality. Each of these levels is holarchy, manifesting fractally, and each fractal harmonic representation represents an entire conceptual world unto itself, with its own affective center of gravity and microclimate. The harmonic progression represents a Complex Adaptive System (albeit a very "soft" one) that serves as the affective, cognitive, and interpersonal interface between an individual psyche and the external world. This system, which operates consistently with the principles of deterministic chaos, functions as a Bayesian "hypothesis generating" process that represents the needs, goals, and drives of the psyche while also providing real-time feedback about the relative efficacy of the behaviors and mental representations

DOI: 10.4324/9781032708751-21

that the psyche generates. Affect (or emotion) provides energetic impetus to the system while also providing qualitative feedback about the state of the system, complexly interacting with mental representations across the various harmonic levels. We have also reviewed research evidence that the manifestation of affect might be related to consciousness itself. The default state of the complex adaptive system when functioning optimally is curiosity (termed SEEKING in some research traditions), and the presence of curiosity represents a dynamic indicator that the system is functioning effectively.

Overall, the epiphenomenal result of the harmonic progression is both creative expression of self states (hypotheses) as well as modeling of external reality accurately (learning). Ongoing adult psychological functioning is predicated on an oscillation of harmonic progression from archetype through the lower harmonics to the upper harmonics, culminating in observable and patterned self states, but also a harmonic progression that returns from self states to archetypal source. *Harmonic vectors* are trajectories of mental representations that transect the harmonic levels and share a common developmental imperative or theme; these vectors become the common thread resulting in specific personality organizations on the horizontal model. The *representational horizon* is an indicator of the highest level of harmonic organization that a personality has obtained; this theoretical construct has important implications for developmental level of the personality.

The harmonic progression derives teleological motivation from the archetypal harmonic, a dynamic precursor state that shapes consciousness at a foundational level through probability space. The archetypal harmonic is itself unrepresentable, therefore cannot be quantified or qualified, and also appears to be the source of the human experience of numinous or sacred qualities. The archetypal harmonic is represented as a point at the center of the circumplex model, suggesting that the entire representational system comprising the circumplex is organized around primary archetypal experience. The archetypal harmonic generates primordial symmetry, that is, "ideal" protean forms that serve as precursors to organizing human experience. The harmonic progression, up and down the harmonic trajectory, results in the breaking of primordial symmetry, which is disruptive to the Complex Adaptive System, but the energetic adaptations to these disruptions become important adaptive responses to challenges to the system and prompt for creative responses, which result in growth and increasingly effective complexity.

The horizontal model depicts harmonic representations spinning into a circumplex design, with the harmonic progression represented as concentric rings centered on the archetypal origin point. Dynamic organizing fields emerging from archetypal space function as archetypal "axes" that organize experience. Each archetypal axis represents a dynamic dichotomy, the resolution of which results in progress along a spiral path around the circumplex and upward. The circumplex has been divided into four quadrants with the archetypal axes representing the thematic boundaries and organizational midpoint of each quadrant. The spiral path is, therefore, "powered" by the archetypal axes, and results as a complex epiphenomenon resulting from the integration of the vertical energy of the harmonic progression and the rotational energy of the archetypal axes. The IAM circumplex, therefore, represents a depiction of the complex interaction between the Complex Adaptive System of the harmonic progression (a vertical pole) and the archetypal themes of the four quadrants of the circumplex.

The result of all this integration establishes a continuum between Jungian and psychoanalytic perspectives, via the organizing principle of ascending mental representation contextualized by constructivist perspectives on complex adaptive systems. The harmonic progression takes us from archetypal origin to personality organization (and back again) and reveals that personality is a complex epiphenomenon, an emergent property manifesting as a result of the psyche's teleological drive to spin itself into existence from the creative matrix of archetypal possibility. The circumplex model reveals that the development of personality is a function of two dynamic systems synergizing with each other: the harmonic progression into greater manifestation, and the rotational energy of the spiral journey through the circumplex, whose *telos* is balanced and boundaried expression of archetypal themes.

A Spirit Journey

What we have described is a spirit journey, a contemporary take on the ancient human narrative of venturing *out and up*. This is a story of emergence and ascension, the unique experience of human emergence from source, whether that source is the Big Bang, the Olduvai Gorge, the archetypal singularity at the center of consciousness, or the room in which you were born, or the arms of the first one to hold you, reader.

We cannot afford to fail to undertake this spirit journey with reverence. I have chosen to decisively stand with Jung on the matter of the autonomous spiritual principle as he calls it, or the numinous, because the numinous is one of our keys of consciousness. We do not know what it is, but we know that it is powerfully motivating, that it seems to suggest meaning, and that it seems to suggest to us unseen levels of reality teeming and effervescing just beyond the limits of our senses and our scientific sensibilities. We know that thousands of years after we abandoned tools of bronze, we have not abandoned the numinous. We have, in our psychological and sociological deterministic chaos fields, made some mistakes about the nature of the numinous: that it is about belief. This sense of an *experiential numinosum* is one of the most precious aspects of the human experience that we have lost in our social evolution.

Reader, it is my hope that you take the archetypes seriously, take the numinous seriously. In doing so, you are taking me seriously, and also taking yourself seriously. You are also taking Lilith, the Dark Madonna, seriously, and help to free her from the irons of patriarchy in which she has been imprisoned since she dared defy Adam and God. Is this not a pleasant thing to do?

What does it mean, to take the archetypes seriously, to take Lilith seriously? It happens when we realize "If anyone is going to bear Lilith energy, it has to be me." This does not mean mistaking the self for Lilith, or becoming Lilith, or identifying with the archetype of Lilith. It means taking on the energy of the ferocious feminine, the remorselessness which is the key alchemical ingredient to dissolving into love. If the archetype is something you believe, it's religion; if it's something you have to do personally, it becomes a discipline (Leigh McCloskey, personal communication, November 2023). This is the dark side of the Cartesian dualism which has psychologically impaired humanity for hundreds of years: it invites us to take sides of a false dichotomy, and dichotomies start with belief and end with war. If you have noticed a frustration with the reigning scientific paradigm behind my words, the reason is this: our modern scientific paradigm corners us into religion, by contributing to an epistemological paradigm in which reality as something we have to believe or not. Let us recall the words of Don Quixote: "Facts are the enemy of truth" (Hiller et al., 2004, scene 8).

Radical Discontinuities, Dissipators, and Transcendence

The story of mental representation, the harmonic progression, is a testament to human ambivalence in the face of truth. We humans tend to resist our own greater fullness, and I have come to see what we call *mental illness*, and so many of the challenges my psychotherapy patients have brought in over the years, amount to that resistance to a broader way of being. It has long been a critical feature of psychodynamic psychotherapy (especially on the psychoanalytic side) that personality is, to some extent, recognizable by its signature defenses. From this point of view, the narcissistic personality is known for its primitive idealization and devaluation; the paranoid personality by its projection; the depressive personality by its introjection, etc. In this book, I have conceptualized these defensive systems as radical discontinuities in the trajectory of mental representation, and hence a discontinuity between the outward self and archetypal origin. Consistent with some of the constructivist points of view we have explored in this book, the complex interplay of affect and mental representation amounts to a kind of consciousness. For this reason, my 30 years of experience as a psychotherapist have taught me not to ask if a person "has" a certain personality, or disorder, like narcissism. Instead of asking if a patient has narcissistic personality disorder, or histrionic personality disorder, the better question is "What is this patient's relationship to narcissistic and histrionic narratives?" Reader, what is your relationship to narcissisism? What is your relationship with murderous rage?

In various contexts in this book, I have explored the process of harmonic progression as an interplay between an ideal primordial symmetry (which I argue is supplied by the archetypal harmonic) and the breaking and disruption of that symmetry through experience. As articulated through the alchemical processes of *solve* and *coagula*, and represented in our model by the Axes of Lilith and Christ, human experience seems defined by continually being broken and then formed anew. There seems to me to be a difference between the radical discontinuity that results from a mind turning against itself (a refusal to feel something, or remember something, or allow some part of the self) versus the elemental disruption that results from proprioceptive feedback provided by reality. This latter form of elemental disruption, I think, represents the *dissipators* we encountered in the context of chaos theory. Perhaps the difference between the dissipator and radical discontinuity is a matter of honesty: radical discontinuities represent the psyche clinging to a static doctrine, while dissipators represent the universe correcting our distortions in real time. Self separates from the primal symmetry, like Adam and Eve exiled from Eden, and returns again, and over and over in a primal oscillation.

If the difference between radical discontinuity and dissipator is a matter of emotional honesty, then we have reaffirmed the psychodynamic value of curiosity (or SEEKING) as the sign of willingness to tolerate reality, to hold it lightly enough that we can endure change. The centrifugal force of the spiral passage through the circumplex generates a capacity to trust mystery. My experience as a psychotherapist, in fact, has taught me that clients who truly do their "inner work" and undertake psychotherapeutic change increasingly show their capacity to trust mystery, including the mystery of the psychotherapeutic relationship. Trusting a mystery is no small accomplishment, because curiosity is emotionally and cognitively dangerous (and for some of us, politically and physically dangerous as well), and in borderline states, psychotic states, and in the grips of trauma, we may not be able to afford it. Curiosity can be terrible. Stephen King and Peter Straub (2001) describe this capacity in a particularly harrowing way, in taking on the reader's willingness to witness a murder scene, and remind us that dark truths require our humility:

> We are not here to weep. Not like Ed, anyhow, in horrified shame and disbelief. A tremendous mystery has inhabited this hovel, and its effects and traces hover everywhere about us. We have come to observe, register, and record the impressions, the afterimages, left in the comet trail of the mystery. It speaks from their details, therefore it lingers in its own wake, therefore it surrounds us. A deep, deep gravity flows outward from the scene, and this gravity humbles us. Humility is our best, most accurate first response. Without it, we would miss the point; the great mystery would escape us, and we would go on deaf and blind, ignorant as pigs. Let us not go on like pigs. We must honor this scene... In comparison, we are no more than vapors.
>
> (p. 37)

To counterpoint King and Straub's harrowing perspective, Joseph Campbell (2008) reminds us that ultimately there is a kind of safety in allowing the dream state of reality to be what it really is: "Wherever the mythological mood prevails, tragedy is impossible. A quality rather of dream prevails. True being, meanwhile, is not in the shapes but in the dreamer" (p. 231). Campbell's "mythological mood" shows up sometimes in psychotherapy, and I always welcome it. For Jung, the capacity to access the mythological mood is what he meant by the transcendent function. The mythological mood carries a quality of the numinous, and my skin prickles and my hairs stand up in its presence, as my client and I spontaneously discover (or rediscover) that we are participating in something heroic and meaningful. Psychotherapy is moving energy around. When this shift in focus happens, symptoms fall away and are forgotten, the mystic cable connecting selfhood to archetypal origin thrums and hums with unspeakable unmeasurable energies, and what felt restrictive and deadly at first now feels optional, and reality emerges as subject to our own creativity. We find, as my colleague Leigh McCloskey has said in the forward, that we can hold the energies of contradiction lovingly. We remember that we can tell a better story, the final and most powerful of human capacities.

References

Campbell, J. (2008). *The hero with a thousand faces.* New World Library.
Hiller, A., Wasserman, D., O'Toole, P., Loren, S., Coco, J., Andrews, H., & Castle, J. (2004). *Man of La Mancha*. Distributed by Metro Goldwyn Mayer Home Entertainment.
King, S., & Straub, P. (2001). *Black house.* Random House.

Index

Made in the USA
Middletown, DE
21 September 2024

61181398R00128